21世纪旅游英语系列教材

英语导游听说教程

Listening and Speaking for Tour Guides

（第三版）

朱 华 编著

北京大学出版社
PEKING UNIVERSIYT PRESS

图书在版编目(CIP)数据

英语导游听说教程/朱华编著.—3版.—北京:北京大学出版社,2014.5
(21世纪旅游英语系列教材)
ISBN 978-7-301-24139-4

Ⅰ.英… Ⅱ.朱… Ⅲ.导游–英语–听说教学–高等职业教育–教材 Ⅳ.H319.9

中国版本图书馆CIP数据核字(2014)第072481号

书 名:	英语导游听说教程(第三版)
著作责任者:	朱 华 编著
责 任 编 辑:	刘 爽
标 准 书 号:	ISBN 978-7-301-24139-4/H·3508
出 版 发 行:	北京大学出版社
地 址:	北京市海淀区成府路205号 100871
网 址:	http://www.pup.cn 新浪官方微博:@北京大学出版社
电子信箱:	nkliushuang@hotmail.com
电 话:	邮购部 62752015 发行部 62750672 编辑部 62759634 出版部 62754962
印 刷 者:	北京大学印刷厂
经 销 者:	新华书店
	787毫米×1092毫米 16开本 12印张 350千字
	2006年8月第1版 2008年3月第2版
	2014年5月第3版 2019年5月第3次印刷
定 价:	38.00元(配有光盘)

未经许可,不得以任何方式复制或抄袭本书之部分或全部内容。
版权所有,侵权必究
举报电话:010-62752024 电子信箱:fd@pup.pku.edu.cn

前　言

《英语导游听说教程》自出版以来，深受广大师生欢迎。第三版采用视听说互动教学模块设计，通过科学的编写结构和练习设计，把传统的单一、独立的视频课、听力课、口语课教学形成系统的视、听、说相结合的三位一体的导游英语教学课程。

第三版注重职业教育与职业培训相结合。教材模拟导游服务全过程，将导游专业知识、导游服务规范和专业英语能力提升相结合，在一定程度上突破了我国专业英语教材普遍存在的"语言学习"和"专业学习"相割裂的"二元结构"，较好地解决了英语语言学习与导游专业知识学习二者之间的关系。

第三版包括七个教学模块：1. 导游案例；2. 导游听力训练；3. 导游情景对话；4. 旅游视频；5. 景点讲解；6. 景点阅读；7. 景点翻译。附MP3光盘一张，送电子课件和样题一套。需要电子课件的老师，可致函ernestzhu@126.com，或在北京大学出版社官方网站www.pup.cn下载。

中国正在从世界旅游大国向世界旅游强国迈进。目前，我国已经成为世界第一大客源国和世界第一出境旅游消费国，接待外国旅游者人数仅次于西班牙和美国，世界排名第三。根据世界旅游组织预测，到2020年，我国将超越西班牙和美国，成为世界第一大旅游目的地国。北京大学出版社《英语导游听说教程》第三版的出版正值我国旅游产业转型升级的关键时期，相信教材的出版将为我国旅游院校提供更好的教学资源，为我国培养更多的高素质旅游人才。

朱　华
2014年1月15日

教材使用建议

由于各个学校学生英语水平存在差异,因此应当根据不同的教学对象合理使用教材和教学资源包,以提高导游英语的教学质量。为了更好地学习《英语导游听说教程》第三版,建议如下:

一、如果学生听力较困难,可参照教材后的听力文本,将听力部分改为旅游阅读教学,以增强学生对导游实务、导游案例和旅游景点知识的理解。

二、视频教学是教学难点,可让学生预习生词、短语和专用名词,并逐句跟读,分段讲解;在了解景区、景点基本内容的基础上,再进行模拟英语导游的教学。

三、教程采用了模块化教学设计,任课教师可以根据教学内容的难易程度进行取舍或整合,开展针对性的教学。

根据各个学校教学实践、导游实训以及导游培训的反馈,结合教程第三版的编写体例和教学内容,建议课时分配如下:

教学内容	课时分配		
	专科	本科	培训
	72	54	60
第1单元 北京游	6	4	4
第2单元 上海游	6	4	4
第3单元 江苏游	6	4	4
第4单元 四川游	6	4	4
第5单元 安徽游	6	4	4
第6单元 山东游	4	4	4
第7单元 河南游	4	4	4
第8单元 湖南游	4	3	4
第9单元 陕西游	4	3	4
第10单元 重庆游	4	3	4
第11单元 浙江游	4	3	4

第12单元 云南游	4	3	4
第13单元 贵州游	4	3	4
第14单元 广西游	4	3	3
第15单元 广东游	4	3	3
总复习	2	2	2

  《英语导游听说教程》第三版是我国多年来英语导游教学和实践的新成果,凝结了我国旅游教育工作者和一线导游人员的智慧和心血。教程附MP3一张,有听力文本和参考答案,为任课教师提供电子课件。与本书配套的课件、视频等教学资料包可在北京大学出版社官方网站www.pup.cn下载,或致函ernestzhu@126.com索取。

朱 华

2014年1月15日

Contents 目 录

Unit 1   Touring Beijing ··· 1
Focus on Learning 学习要点
    导游案例　　Preparations for Meeting Tour Group 接团准备
    导游听力　　1. Beijing City 北京市
    　　　　　　2. Beijing Opera 京剧
    欢 迎 词　　A Welcome Speech 欢迎词
    情景对话　　Summer Palace 颐和园
    旅游视频　　Forbidden City 紫禁城
    导 游 词　　The Great Wall 长城
    导游阅读　　Imperial Palace Museum 故宫博物馆
    导游翻译　　Tian'anmen Square 天安门广场

Unit 2   Touring Shanghai ··· 13
Focus on Learning 学习要点
    导游案例　　Meeting Tourists at the Airport 机场迎客
    导游听力　　1. Shanghai City 上海市
    　　　　　　2. Huangpu River Cruise 黄浦江巡游
    情景对话　　The Nanjing Road 南京路
    旅游视频　　Shanghai Oriental Pearl TV Tower 上海东方明珠塔
    导 游 词　　The Bund 外滩
    欢 送 词　　A Farewell Speech 欢送词
    导游阅读　　Yuyuan Garden 豫园
    导游翻译　　Huangpu River 黄浦江

Unit 3   Touring Jiangsu ·· 24
Focus on Learning 学习要点
    导游案例　　Taking Tourists by Mistake 错接游客
    导游听力　　1. Nanjing City 南京市
    　　　　　　2. Yangzhou City 扬州市
    旅游线路　　China Discovery 中国发现之旅
    情景对话　　Zhuozheng Garden 拙政园
    旅游视频　　Zhouzhuang 周庄

　　　　　　导　游　词　　Tongli 同里
　　　　　　导游阅读　　Zhongshan Mountain 钟山
　　　　　　导游翻译　　Zhouzhuang 周庄

Unit 4　　Touring Sichuan ……………………………………………………… 36
Focus on Learning 学习要点
　　　　　　导游案例　　The Luggage Lost 丢失行李
　　　　　　导游听力　　1. Chengdu City 成都市
　　　　　　　　　　　　2. Tourism Resources in Sichuan 四川旅游资源
　　　　　　途中讲解　　Chengdu—Ya'an 成都——雅安
　　　　　　情景对话　　Wuhou Temple 武侯祠
　　　　　　旅游视频　　Dujiangyan Irrigation Project 都江堰水利工程
　　　　　　导　游　词　　Mugecuo 木格错
　　　　　　导游阅读　　Du Fu's Thatched Cottage 杜甫草堂
　　　　　　导游翻译　　Mt. Qingcheng 青城山

Unit 5　　Touring Anhui ………………………………………………………… 49
Focus on Learning 学习要点
　　　　　　导游案例　　Checking in the Hotel 入住酒店
　　　　　　导游听力　　1. Hefei City 合肥市
　　　　　　　　　　　　2. Lord Bao's Memorial Temple 包公祠
　　　　　　途中讲解　　Mt. Jiuhua 九华山
　　　　　　旅游视频　　Hongcun Village 宏村
　　　　　　导　游　词　　Mt. Huangshan 黄山
　　　　　　导游阅读　　Tangyue Memorial Archways 棠樾牌坊群
　　　　　　导游翻译　　Ancient Street of Tunxi 屯溪老街

Unit 6　　Touring Shandong …………………………………………………… 59
Focus on Learning 学习要点
　　　　　　导游案例　　Rooms below the Contract Standard 客房低于合同标准
　　　　　　导游听力　　1. Jinan City 济南市
　　　　　　　　　　　　2. Dacheng Hall 大成殿
　　　　　　情景对话　　Mt. Taishan 泰山
　　　　　　旅游视频　　Qufu 曲阜
　　　　　　导　游　词　　The Confucius Temple 孔庙
　　　　　　导游阅读　　Qingdao City 青岛市
　　　　　　导游翻译　　Mt. Taishan 泰山

Unit 7   Touring Henan ·· 68
Focus on Learning 学习要点
    导游案例 Food and Dietary Change 饮食变化
    导游听力 1. Zhengzhou City 郑州市
         2. Yellow River Scenic Area 黄河景区
    情景对话 Longmen Grottoes 龙门石窟
    旅游视频 Shaolin Temple 少林寺
    导 游 词 Shaolin Temple 少林寺
    导游阅读 Yin Ruins 殷墟
    导游翻译 White Horse Temple 白马寺

Unit 8   Touring Hunan ·· 78
Focus on Learning 学习要点
    导游案例 Shopping 旅游购物
    导游听力 1. Changsha City 长沙市
         2. Tourist Sites in Hunan 湖南旅游景点
    情景对话 A Splendid Tour of Hunan 锦绣湖南游
    旅游视频 Zhangjiajie 张家界
    导 游 词 Dongting Lake 洞庭湖
    导游阅读 Phoenix Town 凤凰城
    导游翻译 Yueyang Tower 岳阳楼

Unit 9   Touring Shaanxi ··· 89
Focus on Learning 学习要点
    导游案例 Passports Lost 丢失护照
    导游听力 1. Xi'an City 西安市
         2. Xi'an City Wall 西安城墙
    情景对话 Mt. Huashan 华山
    旅游视频 Huaqing Palace 华清宫
    导 游 词 The Terra Cotta Warriors and Horses 兵马俑
    导游阅读 Shaanxi History Museum 陕西省历史博物馆
    导游翻译 Daci'en Temple 大慈恩寺

Unit 10   Touring Chongqing ··· 99
Focus on Learning 学习要点
    导游案例 The First Aid 急救
    导游听力 1. Chongqing City 重庆市
         2. Ciqikou 磁器口

情景对话　　Dazu Rock Carvings 大足石刻
旅游视频　　The Yangtze River Cruise 长江巡游
导　游　词　The Three Gorges 三峡
导游阅读　　Northern Hot Spring Park 北泉公园
导游翻译　　Baidi City 白帝城

Unit 11　Touring Zhejiang ·· 110
Focus on Learning 学习要点
导游案例　　Hotel on Fire 酒店着火
导游听力　　1. Hangzhou City 杭州市
　　　　　　2. Leifeng Pagoda 雷锋塔
情景对话　　Lingyin Temple 灵隐寺
旅游视频　　Wuzhen 乌镇
导　游　词　West Lake 西湖
导游阅读　　Three Pools Mirroring the Moon Island 三潭印月岛
导游翻译　　Melting Snow at Broken Bridge 断桥残雪

Unit 12　Touring Yunnan ··· 119
Focus on Learning 学习要点
导游案例　　A Breach of Security 治安事故
导游听力　　1. Kunming City 昆明市
　　　　　　2. Dianchi Lake 滇池
情景对话　　Stone Forest 石林
旅游视频　　Colorful Yunnan 七彩云南
导　游　词　Lijiang Ancient Town 丽江古城
导游阅读　　Dali 大理
导游翻译　　Yunnan Ethnic Village 云南民族村

Unit 13　Touring Guizhou ·· 129
Focus on Learning 学习要点
导游案例　　Traffic Accident 交通事故
导游听力　　1. Guiyang City 贵阳市
　　　　　　2. Zhijin Cave 织金洞
情景对话　　Mt. Fanjing 梵净山
旅游视频　　The Forest of Ten Thousand Peaks 万峰林
导　游　词　Huangguoshu Waterfall 黄果树瀑布
导游阅读　　Qingyan Ancient Town 青岩古镇
导游翻译　　Xijiang —No.1 Village of Miao Ethnic Group 西江——苗族第一寨

Unit 14   Touring Guangxi ·· **140**
Focus on Learning 学习要点
    导游案例 Policies and Religions 政策与宗教
    导游听力 1. Nanning City 南宁市
          2. Elephant Trunk Hill 象鼻山
    情景对话 West Street 西街
    旅游视频 Yangshuo 阳朔
    导 游 词 Lijiang River 丽江
    导游阅读 Seven-Star Park 七星岩
    导游翻译 Mt. Fubo (Wave-Subduing Hill) 伏波山

Unit 15   Touring Guangdong ··· **150**
Focus on Learning 学习要点
    导游案例 Sending off the Tourists 离站送客
    导游听力 1. Guangzhou City 广州市
          2. The Five-Ram Sculpture 五羊雕塑
    情景对话 Yuexiu Park 越秀公园
    旅游视频 Danxia Mountain 丹霞山
    导 游 词 The Sun Yat-sen Memorial Hall 孙中山纪念堂
    导游阅读 Splendid China Miniature Tourist Site 锦绣中华微缩景区
    导游翻译 Window of the World 世界之窗

Listening Scripts 听力文本 ·· **160**
Bibliography 参考文献 ··· **179**

Unit 1

Touring Beijing

Focus on Learning 学习要点

导游案例	Preparations for Meeting the Tour Group 接团准备
导游听力	1. Beijing City 北京市
	2. Beijing Opera 京剧
欢 迎 词	Welcome Speech by the Local Guide 地陪致欢迎词
情景对话	Summer Palace 颐和园
旅游视频	Forbidden City 紫禁城
导 游 词	The Great Wall 长城
导游阅读	Imperial Palace Museum 故宫博物馆
导游翻译	Tian'anmen Square 天安门广场

 Part I Tips for Tour Guides

Case 1

Preparations for Meeting Tour Group

Mr. Wang will meet a tour group from Nanjing. He is sorting out the documents before he goes to the airport. Listen to the passage and remind him of the documents he must take with him. Fill in the blanks with the missing information.

(1) Mr. Wang must wear his _____ and take with him a copy of the certificate, as well as the operation schedule of the tour group.

(2) He should accomplish _____ if he works for a travel agency other than his own travel agency.

(3) He is required to take with him _____ if he takes a group of more than 10 members.

(4) He should take with him copies of the insurance policies, various vouchers, _____ and a loudspeaker.

Words and Expressions

tour guide certificate 导游证	insurance policy 保险单
operation schedule 运营证	voucher 票据
tour group 旅游团队	travel schedule 旅行日程表
tour guide banner 导游旗	loudspeaker 喇叭, 扩音器

Exercise ➡ ➡ ➡

Directions: Act as the local guide of the travel service and discuss with your colleagues the documents you should take with before you receive the tour group.

 Part II Listening Activities

Listening 1

Beijing City

Words and Expressions

venerate ['venəreɪt] v. 崇敬	strew [stru:] vt. 点缀; 撒满
epitome [ɪ'pɪtəmi] n. 摘要; 典型	monastery ['mɒnəstri] n. 修道院, 寺庙
palatial [pə'leɪʃl] adj. 富丽堂皇的	complex ['kɒmpleks] n. 建筑群
emblem ['embləm] n. 象征; 徽章	paragon ['pærəgən] n. 模范
immense [ɪ'mens] adj. 极广大的, 无边的	artifact ['ɑːtəˌfækt] n. 人造物品
Catholic ['kæθlɪk] adj. 天主教的	

Proper Nouns

Great Wall 长城	Temple of Heaven 天坛
Summer Palace 颐和园	Peking Man 北京人
UNESCO 联合国教科文组织	Taoist temple 道观
Yonghegong Lamasery 雍和宫	Big Bell Temple 大钟寺
Forbidden City 紫禁城	

Exercise ➡ ➡

Directions: Listen to the passage and decide whether the statements are true or false. If it is true, put "T" in the space provided and "F" if it is false.

1. _____ The ruins of Peking Man at Zhoukoudian is one of the UNESCO-endorsed world cultural heritage sites.
2. _____ There are 130 museums worth seeing, including Museum of Chinese History and China Art Gallery.
3. _____ The Tian'anmen Square in the center of Beijing is the world's largest city square.
4. _____ The Forbidden City is the second largest royal palatial complex in China.
5. _____ The Summer Palace in the northwestern suburb of Beijing was built in 1715 and a paragon of Chinese gardens.

Listening 2

Words and Expressions

limitation [ˌlɪmɪˈteɪʃn] n. 限制
essential [ɪˈsenʃl] adj. 实质的,精华的
stylized [ˈstaɪlaɪzd] 程式化的
signify [ˈsɪɡnɪfaɪ] vt. 表示,意味
whip [(h)wɪp] n. 鞭子;车夫
flank [flæŋk] vt. 在……的侧面
spotlight [ˈspɒtlaɪt] n. 聚光灯
oar [ɔː(r)] n. 桨,橹
simulate [ˈsɪmjʊleɪt] vt. 模拟,模仿

symbolism [ˈsɪmbəlɪzəm] n. 象征
reproduce [ˌriːprəˈdjuːs] v. 再生,复制
manner [ˈmænə(r)] n. 方式,样式
wade [weɪd] vi. 跋涉,费力行走
attendant [əˈtendənt] n. 服务员
somersault [ˈsʌməsɔːlt] n. 翻筋斗
grope [ɡrəʊp] v. 摸索
paddle [ˈpædl] n. 短桨,划桨
demonstrate [ˈdemənstreɪt] vt. 示范,证明

Proper Nouns

Beijing Opera 京剧

Beijing Opera

Acting in Beijing Opera is not subjected to the limitations of time and (1)_____; here symbolism is essential. Since some activities in everyday life cannot possibly be (2)_____ on the stage, Beijing Opera gives expression to them in a stylized, (3)_____. Thus, particular (4)_____ signify opening a door, entering or leaving a room, going upstairs or down, climbing a mountain or wading across (5)_____. Circling the stage, whip in hand, suggests riding a horse; riding in a carriage is represented by an attendant holding (6)_____ with a wheel design on either side of (7)_____; walking in a circle indicates a long journey; four soldiers and four generals flanking both sides of the stage (8)_____ an army several thousand strong; two men somersaulting under (9)_____ shows the audience how they are groping and (10)_____ in the dark; and on a stage bare of scenery, a performer holding an oar or paddle and doing knee-bends to simulate a heavy swell, demonstrating traveling on a boat.

Exercise

Directions: Listen to the passage and fill in the words or phrases you have heard.

Part III Welcome Speech

A Welcome Speech

Ladies and Gentlemen! Welcome to Beijing!

Please sit back and relax. Your luggage will be sent to the hotel by another coach, so you don't have to worry about it.

Let me introduce my Chinese colleagues to you. This is Mr. Li, our driver. He is an experienced driver and has a driving experience of more than 10 years. Miss Liu, a trainee tour guide who just graduated from Beijing Tourism Vocational School. My name is Yang Yun. My English name is Jane. You can just call me Jane or Xiao Yang. We're from the China International Travel Service. On behalf of the travel service and my colleagues, I'd like to extend a warm welcome to all of you.

During your stay in Beijing, I will be your local guide. We will try our best to smooth your visit, making it a pleasant and rewarding experience. If you have any problems or special requests, please don't hesitate to tell us. As a Chinese old saying goes, "Isn't it delightful to have friends from afar?" And we highly appreciate your understanding and cooperation.

Beijing is one of the largest metropolises in China. It is among the first group of famous historical and cultural cities ratified by the State Council. The well-known scenic spots are the Great Wall, Imperial Palace Museum, Temple of Heaven, Summer Palace, the Tian'anmen Square and the ruins of Peking Man at Zhoukoudian, just to name a few. Now I'd like to explain the itinerary to you. I hope you would enjoy it.

At 8:30, we'll go sightseeing in Beijing. The first scenic spot we'll visit is the Tian'anmen Square, the largest square in the world. Then, we shall visit the Imperial Palace Museum—the most well-preserved royal palace in China. At 18:00, we'll have the Bejing roasted duck and later watch Beijing Opera at the theater.

Tonight you're going to check in Beijing Hotel, a luxurious, five-star hotel. As you're tourists and you're not familiar with Beijing, you need to remember the number of the coach.

The number is Jing A-56738. Let me repeat it: Jing A-56738. My mobile telephone number is 13096312598. I would have it on for 24 hours. Don't hesitate to contact me whenever you are in need.

I sincerely wish you a pleasant and comfortable stay and a fantastic holiday here. I shall do all I can to make everything easy for you. It will take us about fifty minutes to get to the hotel. So you may have a short rest on the coach or just look at the splendid city of Beijing through the windows. I'll let you know when the coach arrives at the hotel.

Thank you for your attention!

Words and Expressions

colleague [ˈkɒli:g] n. 同事,同僚
rewarding [rɪˈwɔ:dɪŋ] adj. 有益的,值得的
delightful [dɪˈlaɪtfl] adj. 令人愉快的
metropolis [məˈtrɒpəlɪs] n. 首都,大城市
itinerary [aɪˈtɪnərəri] n. 线路

trainee [ˌtreɪˈni:] n. 实习生,新兵
hesitate [ˈhezɪteɪt] v. 犹豫,踌躇
luxurious [lʌɡˈʒʊəriəs] adj. 奢侈的,豪华的
ratify [ˈrætɪfaɪ] vt. 批准,认可

Proper Nouns

Beijing Tourism Vocational School 北京旅游职业学校
China International Travel Service 中国国际旅行社
Imperial Palace Museum 故宫
Tian'anmen Square 天安门广场
Temple of Heaven 天坛
Zhoukoudian 周口店

Exercise ➡ ➡ ➡

1. On behalf of China International Travel Service, make a welcome speech to tourists from the United Kingdom.
2. Make a short welcome speech on behalf of your travel service when you receive a tour group from Denmark.

Part IV Situational Dialogue

Summer Palace

(A=Miss Yang Yun, a local guide; B=Abraham)

A: Today it is fine. We're going to visit the Summer Palace. It is situated in the western outskirts of Haidian District, only 15 kilometers from central Beijing.

B: That's fine. I've been to the gardens of the south Yangtze River. Is there anything different in the style of the gardens in north and south China?

A: Yes, the Summer Palace is the largest royal park in China while most of the gardens in south China are private. The Summer Palace is one of the most famous and classical gardens in the world. In 1998, it was listed as one of the World Heritage Sites by UNESCO.

B: Who built this beautiful palace?

A: It was constructed in the Jin Dynasty. Later it was expanded during the succeeding reign of emperors. Originally it was called "Qingyi Garden" (Garden of Clear Ripples), known as one of the famous "three hills and five gardens." Empress Dowager Cixi embezzled navy funds to reconstruct it for her own benefit. She changed its name to the Summer Palace.

B: I think she lived a very happy life here in such a beautiful garden.

A: Not exactly. Like most of the gardens of Beijing, it was destroyed by the Anglo-French Allied Force. Empress Dowager Cixi had it reconstructed in 1888, but it was captured and ransacked by the Eight-Power Allied Force in 1900.

B: So the Summer Palace suffered a lot of hardship like the Chinese in the modern history.

A: Right. Empress Dowager Cixi and Emperor Guangxu met officials, conducted state affairs and rested here. The Hall of Benevolence and Longevity served as the office of the Emperor, the Hall of Jade Ripples is the place where Guangxu lived, and the Hall of Joyful Longevity is Cixi's residence. China gradually became a semi-feudal and semi-colonial state under their reign.

B: I'm sorry to hear that.

A: After the success of the 1911 Revolution, it was opened to the public.

B: Miss Yang, what can we see in the Summer Palace?

A: The Summer Palace occupies an area of 294 hectares. It is mainly composed of the Longevity Hill and the Kunming Lake. Three quarters of the palace is water. The Summer Palace can be divided into four parts: the court area, the front-hill area, the front-lake area, as well as the rear-hill and back-lake area. Here you can see the fantastic pavilions, towers, bridges, corridors, gardens, temples and the charming lake.

B: It is a great palace. We may not have enough time to go sightseeing in the palace this afternoon.

A: Right. I'm afraid we've no time to lose. I'll tell you more about the Summer Palace while we're sightseeing.

B: OK, let's go!

Words and Expressions

outskirts ['aʊtskɜːts] *n.* 边界，市郊
heritage ['herɪtɪdʒ] *n.* 遗产，继承权
succeeding [səkˈsiːdɪŋ] *adj.* 随后的
navy ['neɪvi] *n.* 海军

royal ['rɔɪəl] *adj.* 王室的，皇家的
expand [ɪkˈspænd] *vt.* 使膨胀，扩张
embezzle [ɪmˈbezl] *vt.* 盗用，挪用
benefit ['benɪfɪt] *n.* 利益，好处

ransack [ˈrænsæk] vt. 掠夺,洗劫
longevity [lɒnˈdʒevətɪ] n. 长命,寿命
hectare [ˈhekteə(r)] n. 公顷
corridor [ˈkɒrɪdɔː(r)] n. 走廊
sightseeing [ˈsaɪtsiːɪŋ] n. 观光

hardship [ˈhɑːdʃɪp] n. 艰难,辛苦
semi-feudal [ˈsemɪˈfjuːdl] adj. 半封建的
pavilion [pəˈvɪlɪən] n. 亭,阁
charming [ˈtʃɑːmɪŋ] adj. 迷人的,娇媚的

Proper Nouns

Haidian District 海淀区
Jin Dynasty 晋朝
Empress Dowager Cixi 慈禧太后
Eight-Power Allied Force 八国联军
Jade Ripples 玉澜堂
Kunming Lake 昆明湖
Hall of Benevolence and Longevity 仁寿殿

Yangtze River 长江
"Qingyi Garden" (Garden of Clear Ripples) 清漪园
Anglo-French Allied Force 英法联军
Emperor Guangxu 光绪皇帝
Longevity Hill 万寿山

Exercise ➡ ➡ ➡

Directions: Listen to the dialogue. Imagine that you are the local guide and your classmates are tourists. Do the dialogue again with additional information that the teacher may offer.

Part V   Video for Tourism
旅游视频

Forbidden City

Words and Expressions

grand [grænd] adj. 宏伟的;豪华的
axis [ˈæksɪs] n. 中轴线
concubine [ˈkɒŋkjubaɪn] n. 嫔妃
convert [kənˈvɜːt] v. 转变
abdication [ˌæbdɪˈkeɪʃn] n. 退位

approximately [əˈprɒksɪmətli] adv. 大约
supreme [suːˈpriːm] adj. 最高的,至高的
royal [ˈrɔɪəl] adj. 皇家的
cease [siːs] v. 停止

Proper Nouns

Forbidden City 紫禁城
Hall of Supreme Harmony 太和殿
Hall of Preserving Harmony 保和殿
Palace of Union and Peace 交泰殿
Puyi 溥仪

Emperor Yongle 永乐皇帝
Hall of Centre Harmony 中和殿
Palace of Heavenly Peace 乾清宫
Palace of Terrestrial Tranquility 坤宁宫
UNESCO 联合国教科文组织

The Forbidden City, situated in the very heart of Beijing, was home to 24 emperors of the Ming and Qing Dynasties. The construction of the grand palace started in 1406, in the 4th year of Emperor Yongle of the Ming Dynasty and ended in 1420. The Forbidden City covers an area of about 72 hectares of the total floor space of approximately 150,000 square meters. It consists of 90 palaces and courtyards, 980 buildings and 8,704 rooms. To represent the supreme power of the emperor given from God and the place where he lived in the center of the world, all the gates, palaces and other structures of the Forbidden City were arranged about the south, north, and central axis of Beijing.

The Forbidden City is divided into two parts. The outer court was where the emperor exercised his supreme power of the nation. It is made up of three main buildings: the Hall of Supreme Harmony, the Hall of Centre Harmony, and the Hall of Preserving Harmony. These halls were where the emperor attended the grant ceremonies and conduct his state affairs.

The inner court was where he lived with his royal family. It is composed of three main structures at the rear of the Forbidden City, mainly the Palace of Heavenly Peace, the Palace of Union and Peace and the Palace of Terrestrial Tranquility. Besides the three main buildings, there are six eastern palaces and six western palaces where the emperor used to handle everyday affairs and was the living courters for the emperor, empresses and concubines. Those places have been converted into exhibition halls where its spectacular set of imperial collections is displayed.

After being the home of 24 emperors, 14 of Ming Dynasty and 10 of Qing Dynasty, the Forbidden City ceased being the political centers of China in 1912 with abdication of Puyi, the last emperor of China. Since 1925, the Forbidden City has been under the charge of the palace museum. In 1987, the Forbidden City was declared the world heritage site and listed by UNESCO as the largest collection of preserved ancient wooden structure of the world.

Step 1: Watch the video and write down the key words or phrases in the video. You may use the key words or phrases as the reminders when you watch it the second time.

_____
_____
_____
_____

Step 2: Watch the video again and decide whether the statements are True or False.

1. _____ The Forbidden City, situated in the heart of Beijing, was former residence of 24 emperors of the Ming and Qing dynasties.
2. _____ The Forbidden City consists of 90 palaces and courtyards, 980 buildings and 8704 rooms. All the gates, palaces and other structures were arranged about the along east and west axis of Beijing.
3. _____ There are six eastern palaces and six western palaces in the ourter court where the emperor used to live with his empresses and concubines.
4. _____ The Forbidden City is a world heritage site listed by UNESCO as the largest collection of preserved ancient wooden structure of the world.

Part VI   Tour Commentary

The Great Wall

Good morning, ladies and gentlemen! Today I feel very happy to visit this great site with friends from the United States. And I hope all of you'll enjoy yourselves there. As we know, the Great Wall of China is one of the greatest wonders of the world. It has a history of more than 2,000 years; some of the sections are now in ruins or even entirely disappeared. However, it is still one of the most appealing attractions all around the world because of its architectural grandeur and historical significance. The construction of Great Wall demonstrates the wisdom and tenacity of the Chinese people.

Who constructed the Wall? Why did they construct the Wall here? Anybody knows? Well, I'd like to take this chance to have a brief introduction of the history of the Great Wall.

The Great Wall was originally built in the Spring and Autumn Period and Warring States Period as a defensive fortification by the three states: Yan, Zhao and Qin. Later, it became an entire one after the unity of China in the Qin Dynasty. Emperor Qin Shihuang had the walls joined together to fend off the invasions from the Huns. Since then, the Great Wall has served as a monument of the Chinese nation throughout history. From the Qin Dynasty onwards, Huns, an ancient tribe that lived in North China, frequently harassed the northern border of the country. During the Han Dynasty, in order to maintain the safety of the Hexi Corridor, Emperor Wu Di, ordered the extension of the Great Wall westward into the Hexi Corridor and Xinjiang region.

Ladies and Gentlemen! The present Great Wall in Beijing is mainly remains from the Ming Dynasty. During this period, bricks and granite were used when the workers laid the foundation of the wall and skillful designs and passes were built in the places of strategic importance. The Ming Wall starts from Yalujiang River, through today's Liaoning, Hebei, Inner Mongolia, Shanxi, Shaanxi, Ningxia provinces to Gansu. The total length reaches 12,700 li (over 5,000 kilometers), and the Shanhaiguan Pass and the Jiayuguan Pass are two well preserved passes at either end.

Well, we've reached the top of the Juyongguan Pass. It was praised as the No.1 Pass under the heaven. Look far! The Great Wall, just like a gigantic dragon, winds up and down across mountains and stretches from east to west of China. A magnificent view, isn't it? The Great Wall does not only have a beautiful landscape but also have many moving legends. Among those legends, Meng Jiangnü's story is the most famous one and it has widely spread all over China. Now, just have a short rest here, and I'll tell you her touching story.

During the Qin Dynasty, Meng Jiangnü's husband Fan Qiliang was caught by officials and sent to build the Great Wall. Meng Jiangnü heard nothing from him after her husband left, so she set out to look for him. Unfortunately, by the time she reached the Great Wall, she found that her husband had already died. She cried bitterly and her weeping caused the collapse of a part of the Great Wall. Stories and legends about the Great Wall keep alive Chinese history and culture. In each dynasty after the building of the Great Wall, many more stories were created.

Now, it's time for free sightseeing. Remember our coach number: Jing A-56738. I repeat it! Jing A-56738. We'll meet at the parking lot at 11 o'clock. Have a good time!

Words and Expressions

wonder ['wʌndə(r)] n. 奇迹；惊奇
architectural [ˌɑːkɪ'tektʃərəl] adj. 建筑学的
significance [sɪɡ'nɪfɪkəns] n. 意义，重要性
fortification [ˌfɔːtɪfɪ'keɪʃn] n. 防御工事，要塞
Hun n. 匈奴
tribe [traɪb] n. 部落，部族
maintain [meɪn'teɪn] vt. 维持，维修
granite ['ɡrænɪt] n. 花岗岩
stretch [stretʃ] v. 伸展，伸长
collapse [kə'læps] n. 倒塌，崩溃

appealing [ə'piːlɪŋ] adj. 吸引人的
grandeur ['ɡrændʒə(r)] n. 庄严，伟大
tenacity [tə'næsəti] n. 坚韧
invasion [ɪn'veɪʒn] n. 入侵
monument ['mɒnjʊmənt] n. 纪念碑
harass ['hærəs] v. 打扰，骚扰
remains [rɪ'meɪnz] n. 遗迹
gigantic [dʒaɪ'ɡæntɪk] adj. 巨大的
magnificent [mæɡ'nɪfɪsnt] adj. 华丽的，宏伟的
indicate ['ɪndɪkeɪt] vt. 显示，象征

Proper Nouns

Yan 燕国
Qin 秦国
Han Dynasty 汉朝
Emperor Wu Di 汉武帝
Ming Dynasty 明朝
Liaoning 辽宁

Zhao 赵国
Emperor Qin Shihuang 秦始皇
Hexi Corridor 河西走廊
Xinjiang 新疆
Yalujiang River 雅鲁江
Hebei 河北

Inner Mongolia 内蒙古	Shaanxi 陕西
Shanxi 山西	Ningxia 宁夏
Gansu 甘肃	Shanhaiguan Pass 山海关
Jiayuguan Pass 嘉峪关	Juyongguan Pass 居庸关
Meng Jiangnü 孟姜女	Fan Xiliang 范喜良

Exercise ➡ ➡ ➡

Directions: Act as the local guide and show the tourists around the Great Wall. Try to make your introduction more situational and attractive using the proper body language.

Part VII   Readings

Directions: Read the following passage and fill in the blanks with the words or phrases given below.

layout	yellow	precious	imperial	ranks
throne	symbol	well-preserved	beautification	

Imperial Palace Museum

　　The Forbidden City in Beijing was the (1)_____ palace of the Ming and the Qing dynasties. In 1925 it was changed to the Imperial Palace Museum. It is the largest and most (2)_____ complex of palaces in China, as well as the largest group of palaces in the world. As the representative of the Chinese architecture, the exquisite (3)_____ fully shows the etiquette of the ancient times that "court is in the front and living quarters are at the rear." The Imperial Palace has the (4)_____ in the front court and the "three palaces and six yards" in the back.

　　The colors used to apply on the palatial buildings in the Imperial Palace, except for the outside (5)_____ , attributed much more to the feudalistic implications in politics. The purple-red walls in combination with the (6)_____ roofs form a strong and eye-catching contrast, showing the absolute "authority," "supremacy" and "richness" of feudal emperors. The difference in the number of animals on the ledges of the palace buildings suggested the different (7)_____ and positions the inhabitants held in the Imperial Palace.

　　With its perfect architectural art, large quantity of historic relics and embodiment of rich culture, the Imperial Palace has become the (8)_____ of ancient Chinese civilization. The Imperial Palace Museum holds a great number of historical and cultural relic as well as (9)_____ works of art. Therefore, it is the largest museum of culture and art in China.

Words and Expressions

etiquette [ˈetɪket] n. 礼节
ledge [ledʒ] n. 壁架，屋脊

feudalistic [ˌfjuːdəˈlɪstɪk] adj. 封建制度的
embodiment [ɪmˈbɒdɪmənt] n. 体现，化身

Proper Nouns

Forbidden City 紫禁城
Imperial Palace Museum 故宫博物馆
"court in the front and living quarters at the rear" "前朝后寝"
"three palaces and six yards" "三宫六院"
historic relic 历史遗迹

Part VIII   Translation

Tian'anmen Square

1. Located on the central axis (中轴线) of Beijing, Tian'anmen Square begins from the northern red wall, reaches Zhengyangmen Gate Tower (正阳门楼), or Front Gate, in the south and the Great Hall of the People (人民大会堂) in the west, and includes the Museum of Chinese History (中国革命博物馆) and the Museum of Chinese Revolution (中国历史博物馆) in the east.

2. It is 880 meters from north to south, and 500 meters from east to west, and has a total area of 440,000 square meters. As many as one million people can gather here at one time.

3. First named Chengtianmen Gate (承天门), meaning by the Grace of God ("承天启"), Tian'anmen Gate was regarded as an important place for the emperor to worship God.

4. 天安门初建时只是辨认六柱五门(six pillars and five doors)的木牌坊(wooden arch)，后被火烧毁重建，成为一座面阔九间、进深五间的门楼(a gate tower with nine-room wide and five-room deep)，以体现帝王的"九五之尊"(The number nine and five embodies the supremacy of the emperor)。

5. 天安门广场，就像莫斯科的红场(Red Square)、巴黎的凯旋门(Arc de Triomphe)、华盛顿的纪念碑(Washington Monument)一样，是中国首都北京的标志性建筑物(symbolic architecture)。

6. 它以其悠久和历史和雄伟的身姿，每年吸引着数以百万计的游客观光游览，成为向国内外游客展示北京风采(Beijing's charm)的象征。

Unit 2

Touring Shanghai

Focus on Learning 学习要点

导游案例	Meeting Tourist at the Airport 机场迎客
导游听力	1. Shanghai City 上海市
	2. Huangpu River Cruise 黄浦江巡游
情景对话	The Nanjing Road 南京路
旅游视频	Shanghai Oriental Pearl TV Tower 上海东方明珠塔
导 游 词	The Bund 外滩
欢 迎 词	Farewell Speech 地陪致欢送词
导游阅读	Yuyuan Garden 豫园
导游翻译	Huangpu River 黄浦江

 Part I Tips for Tour Guides

Case 2

Meeting Tourists at the Airport

Mr. He Yan is a trainee tour guide from the Shanghai Oriental Travel Service. He has taken with him all the papers necessary for meeting the tour group. What else could you advise him to meet the tourists at the airport? Situation 1: prior to his arrival at the airport; Situation 2: upon the arrival of the tour group. Listen to the passage and write down your advice in the blanks.

(1) Prior to arrival:

   A. Confirm _____;

   B. Arrive at the airport _____ prior to expected arrival time and confirm the exact parking place of the coach in parking lot;

   C. Reconfirm _____;

   D. Contact the porter and inform him of _____;

   E. Stand at a highly visible location in the lobby, in full view of the arriving tourists with an identifying _____.

(2) Upon the arrival of tour group:

   A. Meet the tour group and check _____ , group code, number of _____ and name of the tour leader;

   B. Make sure that all luggage has been claimed and collected by _____ to transfer to coach;

   C. Lead the tour group to the coach and assist them in boarding. The guide should _____ to politely greet tourists and confirm the number of the group.

> **Words and Expressions**
>
> arrival time 抵达时间
> luggage claim 提取行李
> group code 团号
> porter 行李员
>
> parking lot 停车场
> cardboard sign 接站牌
> tour leader 领队

Exercise ➡ ➡ ➡

Directions: Act as a local guide of the Shanghai Oriental Travel Service and demonstrate to your classmates how to receive the tourists at the airport.

 Part II   Listening Activities

Listening 1

Shanghai City

> **Words and Expressions**
>
> delta [ˈdeltə] n. 三角州
> jurisdiction [ˌdʒʊərɪsˈdɪkʃn] n. 权限
> intrigue [ɪnˈtriːg] vt. 激起……的兴趣
>
> municipality [mjuːˌnɪsɪˈpæləti] n. 市政当局,自治市
> assemblage [əˈsemblɪdʒ] n. 集合,集会
> thrive [θraɪv] v. 兴旺,繁荣,旺盛

Proper Nouns

the Bund 外滩
Huangpu River 黄浦江
Chongming Island 崇明岛
Shenshuigang Area 深水港区
Nanjing Road 南京路
Xujiahui Shopping Center 徐家汇购物中心
Jiali Sleepless City 嘉里不夜城

the People's Square 人民广场
Mt. Sheshan 蛇山
Dingshan Lake 淀山湖
"Oriental Paris" "东方巴黎"
Huaihai Road 淮海路
Yuyuan Shopping City 豫园商城

Exercise

Directions: Listen to the passage and decide whether the statements are true or false. If it is true, put "T" in the space provided and "F" if it is false.

1. _____ Shanghai, also named "Hu" or "Shen" in short, is a gate to the Yangtze River delta.
2. _____ Shanghai has made an effort to develop the city tourism mainly featuring "city scenery," "city culture," and "city festival."
3. _____ Modern Shanghai has three key areas of interest to the visitor. These comprise sightseeing, business and shopping centered upon the People's Square and along the Huaihai Road.
4. _____ Known as "the Oriental Paris," Shanghai is a shopper's paradise.

Listening 2

Words and Expressions

cruise [kru:z] n. 巡游,巡航
quintessence [kwɪnˈtesns] n. 精萃,精华
brilliant [ˈbrɪliənt] adj. 灿烂的,闪耀的

significant [sɪgˈnɪfɪkənt] adj. 有意义的
prospect [ˈprɒspekt] n. 前景,前途

Proper Nouns

Nanpu Bridge 南浦大桥
Wusongkou 吴淞口
"two dragons playing with a pearl" "二龙戏珠"

Yangpu Bridge 杨浦大桥
Oriental Pearl TV Tower 东方明珠电视塔

Huangpu River Cruise

Huangpu River cruise is a traditional (1)_____ in Shanghai's tours. It is significant not only because Huangpu River is Shanghai's (2)_____ but also of the collection of the quintessences of Shanghai scenes. Here, one can find the expression of Shanghai's past, present and (3)_____ for a brilliant future. The cruise begins at (4)_____ towards south against the current up to the Nanpu Bridge and turns back towards (5)_____, passing the Yangpu Bridge to reach Wusongkou and then back to the Bund. During the cruise, one can see both the Nanpu Bridge and the Yangpu Bridge and the (6)_____ Oriental Pearl TV Tower. The two bridges are like two (7)_____ sprawling on the Huangpu River while the Oriental Pearl TV Tower in between like "two dragons playing with a pearl." On the west bank of the river, (8)____ of magnificent tall buildings of different foreign architectural styles are in contrast with the modern high-risers on (9)_____, presenting an attractive view to visitors.

Exercise ➡ ➡ ➡

Directions: Listen to the passage and fill in the words or phrases you have heard.

Part III   Situational Dialogue

The Nanjing Road

(A=Miss Chen Lu; B=Adam)

A: It's fine today. I'd like to guide you along the Nanjing Road.

B: There are so many roads in Shanghai. Why should we travel on the Nanjing Road?

A: If you were traveling in Paris, I bet you would travel on Champs Elysees Avenue. Today Nanjing Road is a must-see metropolitan destination and attracts thousands of tourists from all over the world.

B: I see. Shall we go?

A: Yes, please! Now, we're at the Jing'an Temple. Walk down the street, we'll reach the Bund, the most famous tourist site in Shanghai.

B: I've heard of the Bund. It used to be the paradise of the adventurers from the world.

A: Yes, it is. After the Opium War, Shanghai became a treaty port. Nanjing Road was first the British Concession, then the International Settlement. It was the earliest shopping street in Shanghai.

B: Well, this famous road must attract a lot of foreign businesses. I see a lot of foreign products in the showcases.

A: Exactly. Today over 600 businesses on Nanjing Road offer countless famous brands, superior quality and new fashions. You can almost buy whatever you like.

B: I want to buy some fashions for my girlfriend. Can I get it?

A: Of course. Big traditional stores no longer dominate the market since modern shopping malls, specialty stores, theatres, and international hotels have mushroomed on both sides of the street. If you want to go shopping, Nanjing Road is your first choice.

B: I'm very happy that you guide me here. It is really a shopping paradise.

A: Yes, it is.

B: Miss Chen, it is getting hot. Can we find somewhere to have a rest?

A: All right. For shopping convenience, the eastern end of Nanjing Road has an all-weather pedestrian arcade. We can get there to have a rest.

B: But I'm a bit hungry, too. I want to have something to eat first. May I take the Kentucky fried chicken?

A: No problem. Besides Chinese restaurants, there are KFC, McDonald's, Pizza Hut, and other world-famous restaurants on the Nanjing Road.

B: Really? I cannot expect there are so many choices of western food here.

A: After dinner, we can take the trackless sightseeing train to the Bund. You can have a night cruise on the Huangpu River.

B: Very good! I'll pay for you today.

A: No, I'm your guide. I must pay myself.

B: Then, we'll go to the Dutch.

A: A good idea!

Words and Expressions

metropolitan [ˌmetrəˈpɒlɪtən] *adj.* 首都的, 大城市的
opium [ˈəʊpiəm] *n.* 鸦片
dominate [ˈdɒmɪneɪt] *v.* 支配, 占优势
convenience [kənˈviːniəns] *n.* 便利, 方便
arcade [ɑːˈkeɪd] *n.* [建]拱廊

adventurer [ədˈventʃə(r)] *n.* 冒险家
showcase [ˈʃəʊkeɪs] *n.* 陈列橱
mushroom [ˈmʌʃrʊm] *vi.* 迅速增加
pedestrian [pəˈdestriən] *n.* 步行者
trackless [ˈtræklɪs] *adj.* 无轨的

Proper Nouns

Champs Elysees Avenue 香榭丽舍大街
British Concession 英租界
Kentucky 肯塔基州
McDonald's 麦当劳

Jing'an Temple 静安寺
International Settlement 国际租界
KFC 肯德基
Pizza Hut 必胜客

Exercise ➡ ➡ ➡

Directions: Listen to the dialogue. Imagine that you are the local guide and your classmates are tourists. Do the dialogue again with additional information that the teacher may offer.

Part IV　Video for Tourism
旅游视频

Shanghai Oriental Pearl TV Tower

Words and Expressions

metropolis [mə'trɒpəlɪs] n. 大都市
navigate ['nævɪgeɪt] v. 驾驶,行走
mediocre [ˌmiːdiˈəʊkə(r)] adj. 平凡的
fledgling ['fledʒlɪŋ] n. 初出茅庐者
state-of-the-art adj. 最新式的;顶尖水准的

meteoric [ˌmiːtiˈɒrɪk] adj. 迅速的
potential [pə'tenʃl] n. 潜能
epitomize [ɪ'pɪtəmaɪz] v. 概括
nightmare ['naɪtmeə(r)] n. 噩梦
hustle and bustle 熙熙攘攘

Proper Nouns

Shanghai Oriental Pearl TV Tower 上海东方明珠电视塔
Shanghai Stock and Goods Exchange 上海证券商品交易所
Jinmao Tower 金茂大厦
Shanghai World Financial Center 上海国际金融中心

What a difference a day makes! Look at it, it's bright and sunny, so I've chosen to come on my own. Now you can still get really rainy during spring time in Shanghai. As you can see, we're in luck. Now, this is Oriental Pearl TV Tower, open from 8:30 a.m. to 9:30 p.m., so you can get both day and night shots.

The History Museum at the Oriental Pearl TV Tower takes you through the development of Shanghai's transport from its early day right up to today. It's a well worth that 35RMB to track the city's cultural progress through the exhibits.

This is the place to visit for a complete introduction to Pudong's meteoric rise as an international metropolis. Here you will learn Pudong has attracted over US 25 billion dollars in overseas investment. Known today as the growth engine for China's economy, Shanghai was the focus of western interest some hundred years ago. At the History Museum, you'll find state-of-the-art audio-visual devices in English and other languages to help you to navigate around the exhibits.

Shanghai's stock market has also risen to the challenge of building a well-off society. At the end of the Qing Dynasty, Shanghai's guild began to imitate the western style of the goods exchange, and the earliest association formed by Chinese merchants was in the 1920s. It was called the "Shanghai Stock and Goods Exchange." There's a lot of hustle and bustle going on right now. This job is definitely not for the faint-hearted. "Sorry, yeah, give me a five, five..."

The world's leading companies could not help but sit up and take notice of Pudong. As far as its development was concerned, Pudong may have been a fledgling, but its potential as a foothold into China's mass consumer market was quite plain to see.

I'm standing on 259 meters above the ground right now, the view is just spectacular. You can see just right across is the Jinmao Tower and Shanghai World Financial Center. Now, the Oriental Pearl TV Tower was one of the first of those been built in the 90s. And it just epitomizes the height of success that Shanghai hopes to achieve, but if you look down, you might face your biggest nightmare.

Step 1: Watch the video and write down the key words or phrases in the video. You may use the key words or phrases as the reminders when you watch it the second time.

_____
_____
_____
_____

Step 2: Watch the video again and decide whether the statements are True or False.
1. _____ Shanghai is known as the growth engine for China's economy, and it captured the western attention one hundred years ago.
2. _____ The History Museum at the Oriental Pearl TV Tower will provide you the audio-visual devices in English and other languages to help you to understand the development of Shanghai.
3. _____ Shanghai began to set up the first association of the goods exchange at the end of the Qin Dynasty which was called the "Shanghai Stock and Goods Exchange."
4. _____ The Oriental Pearl TV Tower was one of the landmarks, which epitomizes the height of success that Shanghai hopes to achieve.

Part V   Tour Commentary

The Bund

Ladies and Gentlemen! Good afternoon!

Welcome to the Bund! Welcome to Shanghai! Now we are at the Bund of the Huangpu River. I sincerely hope every one of you'll have a good time here. Today, we'll have a cruise on the Huangpu River and see the past and present of Shanghai. Cruising on the river can also give you a better chance to see the different views of both sides of the river—Pudong and Puxi.

Attention please! On your left-hand is the wide Zhongshan Road where the marvelous buildings with European style tower majestically. You can watch "the World Architecture Show." On your right-hand side are the glistening Huangpu River and Lujiazui Finance Trade Area in Pudong. You may watch "the Oriental Pearl TV Tower," a landmark of the New Shanghai.

Look across the river! What a magnificent building complex with the western style! In front of us is the Dongfeng Hotel. This is a building in classical British style. In the past it was the British General Assembly. The six-storey building is topped with two pavilions in the north and south. The interior of the building is decorated luxuriously. There used to be a 110.7 inch-long bar counter on the first floor, the longest one in Asia at that time.

Look at the building with a circular roof in Greek style! It is the famous building of former Shanghai & Hong Kong Bank. The building with five storeys was built in 1923. Plus its dome top, it altogether has 7 storeys. It has reception rooms of the American, British, French, Russian and Japanese styles. The British was proud of it and regarded it as the best building in the area from the Suez Canal to the Far East. Not long ago it was the office building of Shanghai Municipality.

Ladies and Gentlemen! Did you see the building next to the former Shanghai & Hong Kong Bank? On the top of it, there is a big clock. It is the Shanghai Customs Building built in 1927. The clock strikes every 15 minutes, and gives out a short piece of music. You can check your time accordingly because it gives you the standard Beijing time. The former Shanghai & Hong Kong Bank and the Customs Building were designed by a famous British designer. People in Shanghai called them "Sister Buildings." At present, they remain an important landmark of Shanghai.

Please look at the other side of the river! A tower is piercing straight to the clouds and sky. It is the Oriental Pearl TV Tower, the new landmark of Shanghai. The 468-meter Orient Pearl TV Tower used to be the tallest building in Asia and the third tallest TV tower in the world. Our travel boat is leaving the Oriental Pearl TV Tower. And more scenic sites are waiting for us ahead! If you miss the chance to take pictures, don't worry! And you can take photos when we come back. Tonight we'll have our dinner in the rotating restaurant of the Tower. You can have a bird's view of the night of Shanghai on the sightseeing floor.

Have fun!

Words and Expressions

sincerely [sɪnˈsɪəli] adv. 真诚地
commercial [kəˈmɜːʃəl] adj. 商业的，贸易的
miniature [ˈmɪnətʃə(r)] n. 缩图，缩影
landmark [ˈlændmɑːk] n. 标志性建筑
colonialist [kəˈləʊnɪəlɪst] n. 殖民主义者

> **Proper Nouns**
>
> Pudong 浦东
> Zhongshan Road 中山路
> Dongfeng Hotel 东风饭店
> Shanghai Customs Building 上海海关大楼
>
> Puxi 浦西
> "World Architecture Show" "万国建筑博览"
> British General Assembly 英国总领馆

Exercise ➡ ➡ ➡

Directions: Act as the local guide and show the tourists around the Bund. Try to make your introduction more situational and attractive using the proper body language.

Part VI Farewell Speech

A Farewell Speech

Good afternoon, ladies and gentlemen!

Time goes so quickly and your visit to Shanghai is drawing to a close. Tomorrow morning you will be leaving Shanghai for Guangzhou by plane. When you arrive at the Pudong International Airport, I shall be very busy with handling the boarding pass and taking care of your luggage. So I could hardly have time to say good-bye to everyone. So, let me to take this opportunity to say something about our wonderful trip.

First of all, I wish to thank you all for the understanding and cooperation you have given us in the past two and a half days. You have been very punctual on all occasions, which made things a lot easier for our work. You have been very attentive when we had something to tell you. Also, you have been kind enough to offer us suggestions on how to better our guiding service. I'd like to add that you are the best group we've ever been with.

During your stay in Shanghai, you have visited the major scenic spots in Shanghai. Some of you are impressed by the "Oriental Pearl TV Tower," the landmark of Shanghai; some appreciate the European-styled architectures which you may no longer find in Europe; some are fascinated by the night of Shanghai when you cruised on the Huangpu River while others enjoy shopping on the Nanjing Road.

Two days ago, we met as strangers; today, we bid farewell to each other as friends. A Chinese saying goes, "A good friend from afar brings a distant land closer." I hope you'll take back happy memories of your visit to Shanghai.

By the way, please do me a small favor. Would you please leave your comments with us, as well as your friendship? Just fill the evaluation forms with postage-paid, and drop them in the mailbox before you board the plane.

Parting is such sweet sorrow. It is happy to meet, sorry to depart, and happy to meet again. As you have probably observed, Shanghai is developing very quickly. When and if you come back in the future, the city may have changed beyond recognition. I hope to see you again in the future and to be your guide again.

Once again, thank you for your cooperation and support.

Bon voyage!

Words and Expressions

boarding pass 登机牌
punctual [ˈpʌŋktʃuəl] adj. 准时的
evaluation [ɪˌvæljuˈeɪʃn] n. 估价, 评价
sorrow [ˈsɒrəʊ] n. 悲哀, 悲痛
opportunity [ˌɒpəˈtjuːnəti] n. 机会, 时机
comment [ˈkɒment] n. 评论, 意见
postage paid 邮资已付
recognition [ˌrekəɡˈnɪʃn] n. 赞誉; 公认

Exercise ➡ ➡ ➡

1. On behalf of Shanghai Overseas Travel Service, make a farewell speech to tourists who will fly back to England.
2. On behalf of China International Travel Service, Shanghai Branch, make a farewell speech to tourists who will leave for the next tourist resort in China.

Part VII   Readings

Directions: Read the following passage and fill in the blanks with the words or phrases given below.

citizens	outer	private	alone
posts	uprising	skillful	

Yuyuan Garden

Yuyuan Garden is in the northeast of the Old Town of Shanghai. A high official had it designed in the Suzhou style as a (1)_____ garden and built from 1559—1577. Later, it was restored several times. In spite of its relatively small area of two hectares, it seems considerable larger due to the (2)_____ arrangement of 30 different landscape scenes.

The garden consists of an inner and an outer section. The inner garden, Neiyuan, is in the southern part and substantially smaller than the (3)_____ one; but then, it is also more impressive and romantic, if it is possible to visit it in the early morning hours in order to enjoy it (4)_____. The outer part is in the north and contains numerous halls, pavilions and lakes. In 1853, the Pavilion of Spring in the northeast was the seat of the Xiao-dao Hui, the Society of Little Swords, who led an (5)_____ against Qing rule and occupied Shanghai for 17 months.

A man-made, 11-meter-high hill bounds the garden in the northwest. Huxinting teahouse is a favorite with the (6)_____ of Shanghai. It is in the southwest, outside the garden grounds, a two-storey building resting on (7)_____ in the middle of a pond and connected to the shore by a zigzag bridge.

Words and Expressions

substantially [səbˈstænʃəli] *adv.* 充分地
Neiyuan 内园
Xiao-dao Hui (Society of Little Swords) 小刀会
zigzag [ˈzɪɡzæɡ] *adj.* 曲折的, Z字形的
Pavilion of Spring 点春堂

Proper Nouns

Yuyuan Garden 豫园
Huxinting 湖心亭
Suzhou style 苏州园林风格

Part VIII   Translation

Huangpu River

1. Huangpu River (黄浦江) cruise is a traditional tourist item in Shanghai's tours. It is significant not only because Huangpu River is Shanghai's mother river but also of the collection of the quintessences (精华) of Shanghai scenes.
2. Here, one can find the expression of Shanghai's past, present and prospects for a brilliant future.
3. The cruise begins at the Bund (外滩)towards south against the current up to the Nanpu Bridge (南浦大桥) and turns back towards the north, passing the Yangpu Bridge (杨浦大桥) to reach Wusong Mouth (吴淞口) and then back to the Bund.
4. 在乘船游览途中可以看到南浦大桥、杨浦大桥和东方明珠广播电视塔(Oriental Pearl TV Tower)。
5. 两座大桥像两条巨龙横卧(sprawl)于江上，中间是东方明珠电视塔，恰好构成了一幅"二龙戏珠"("two dragons playing with a pearl")的美妙画卷。
6. 浦江西岸一幢幢风格迥异、充满异域风情(different foreign architectural styles)的建筑与黄浦江东岸一座座拔地而起、耸入云间的现代高楼(modern high-risers)相互辉映，令人叹为观止。

Unit 3

Touring Jiangsu

Focus on Learning 学习要点

导游案例	Taking Tourists by Mistake 错接游客
导游听力	1. Nanjing City 南京市
	2. Yangzhou City 扬州市
旅游线路	China Discovery 中国发现之旅
情景对话	Zhuozheng Garden 拙政园
旅游视频	Zhouzhuang 周庄
导游词	Tongli 同里
导游阅读	Zhongshan Mountain 钟山
导游翻译	Zhouzhuang 周庄

Part I Tips for Tour Guides

Case 3

Taking Tourists by Mistake

Mr. Liu Zhenghong was assigned to receive a tour group from the United States this morning. He arrived at the Nanjing International Airport on time. After all the tourists disembarked the plane, he did not expect the arrival of his tour group. He met the tourists other than his own. Later he was told that his tourists have been picked up by another guide. What happened to him? How could he avoid such an incident in the future? Listen to the passage and write down in the blanks the reasons why he failed to meet his tour group and what lessons he should learn from.

I think Mr. Liu is held responsible for such a serious mistake. He should have followed the basic procedures, such as checking the name of the organizing travel agency, the group code, the number of tourists and the name of the tour leader, etc. Mr. Liu should learn from this lesson and take the proper measures under circumstance such as:

(1) If he _____ the tour group of another travel agency _____, he should first report to his own agency and hand it over to the other travel agency. Meanwhile he should _____ to the tourists.

(2) If his own tour group remains _____ , he should meet them immediately and accomplish the formalities concerned.

(3) If the tour group he receives belongs to the same agency that he works for, but he is not supposed to be their guide, he may make the best of the mistake _____ .

Words and Expressions

be held responsible for 对……负责
accomplish the formalities 完成手续
do an apology 道歉
make the best of 充分利用

Exercise

Directions: Act as the local guide and the manager of the travel agency. Discuss the reasons why the guide failed to pick up the tourists at the airport and how he could avoid the same mistakes. Make a presentation according to your discussions.

Part II Listening Activities

Listening 1

Nanjing City

Words and Expressions

strategically [strəˈtiːdʒɪklɪ] adv. 战略上
terrain [təˈreɪn] n. 地形
majesty [ˈmædʒəstɪ] n. 雄伟
regime [reɪˈʒiːm] n. 政体,政权
cluster [ˈklʌstə(r)] vi. 丛生,成群
mausoleum [ˌmɔːsəˈliːəm] n. 陵墓
beam [biːm] n. 梁,桁条,横梁

moist [mɔɪst] adj. 潮湿的
render [ˈrendə(r)] vt. 给予,着色
drive [draɪv] n. 动力,努力
trunk [trʌŋk] adj. 树干的,干线的
worship [ˈwɜːʃɪp] vt. 崇拜,尊敬
pillar [ˈpɪlə(r)] n. [建] 柱子,栋梁

Proper Nouns

Jinling 金陵
Confucian Temple 孔庙
Qinhuai River 秦淮河
Sun Yat-sen 孙中山

Linggu Temple 灵谷寺
Ming Xiaoling Mausoleum 明孝陵
Wuliang (Beamless) Hall 无梁殿
Zhu Yuanzhang 朱元璋

Exercise ➡ ➡ ➡

Directions: Listen to the passage and decide whether the statements are true or false. If it is true, put "T" in the space provided and "F" if it is false.

1. _____ Nanjing today looks new due to the ongoing modernization drive.
2. _____ As one of the nation's six ancient capitals, it was the capital city for ten feudal dynasties or regimes.
3. _____ The Qinhuai River is a trunk waterway as well as a famed scenic belt in Nanjing.
4. _____ The entire layout of Sun Yat-sen Mausoleum, takes the shape of a giant ball.
5. _____ The Linggu Temple is known for its 22-metre-high Wuliang Hall (Beamless Hall), which was constructed with wood, pillar or beam.

Listening 2

Words and Expressions

juncture [ˈdʒʌŋktʃə(r)] n. 接合点
artificial [ˌɑːtɪˈfɪʃl] adj. 人造的，假的
succession [səkˈseʃn] n. 继承，连续性
elegant [ˈelɪɡənt] adj. 端庄的，雅致的
rockwork [ˈrɒkwɜːk] n. 假山
prompt [prɒmpt] vt. 鼓动，促使

Proper Nouns

Yangzhou 扬州
Lean West Lake 瘦西湖
Lesser Pangu Garden 小盘谷
Emperor Qianlong 乾隆皇帝
Tianning Temple Museum 天宁寺
Monk Jianzhen Memorial Hall 鉴真纪念堂
Memorial Hall of Eight Yangzhou Eccentrics 扬州八怪纪念馆
Grand Canal 大运河
Geyuan Garden 个园
Emperor Kangxi 康熙皇帝
"Emperor Qianlong Cruise" "乾隆巡游"
Daming Temple 大明寺

Yangzhou City

Yangzhou, situated at (1)_____ of the Yangtze River and the Grand Canal, has made a name for itself with a wealth of sites of (2)_____ and elegant gardens. These include (3)_____ (actually a natural waterway feeding mountain runoffs into the Grand Canal), Geyuan Garden (whose forte is artificial rockwork), and Lesser Pangu Garden. During their repeated visits to Yangzhou, emperors Kangxi and Qianlong (4)_____ a succession of historical sites on the land of Yangzhou. This has prompted (5)_____ to invent the "Emperor Qianlong Cruise," which transports visitors to a string of (6)_____ . Cruise on the ancient Grand Canal is another (7)_____ tourist program. Other places worth seeing are: Tianning Temple (8)_____, Daming Temple, Monk Jianzhen (9)_____, and Memorial Hall of (10)_____ Yangzhou Eccentrics.

Exercise ➡ ➡ ➡

Directions: Listen to the passage and fill in the words or phrases you have heard.

Part III Tour Itineraries

China Discovery

Cities to visit: Nanjing, Wuxi, Suzhou, Shanghai

Quotation: US $1200/p.p.

Departure time: November, 2013.

Tour Description: The 5-day tour will present you highlights of tourist sites in China, including the old capital city of Nanjing, Jiangsu Province to enjoy the local culture; the water city of Wuxi known for the Taihu Lake; the garden city of Suzhou known for the classic garden landscape and the modern city of Shanghai for the future of China. So the 5-day tour will acquaint you with essence of the Chinese history, culture, nature and people.

Itinerary

Day 01

Arrive in Nanjing by Air China at 5 o'clock in the afternoon (Beijing Time), meet your guide and transfer to Nanjing Hotel. Welcome dinner in the evening, a cruise on the Qinhuai River and the night fair at the Confucian Temple. (D)

Day 02

American buffet breakfast between 07:00—08:30, and take a bus ride to Wuxi. Take a cruise on the Taihu Lake and drive to Zhouzhuang, the first water town in China for sightseeing. (BLD)

Day 03

Leave your luggage out of your room before 07:30, and check out of the hotel before 08:30. Move to Suzhou by coach to visit the Zhuozheng Garden, the Li Garden and the Hanshan

Temple. Free in the evening. (BL)

Day 04

Breakfast between 07:30—8:30, then take a bus ride to Shanghai. Wander along the Nanjing Road and the Bund, and a cruise on the Huangpu River in the evening. (BLD)

Day 05

Get ready with luggage and carry-on before 8:00. Enjoy the last minute excitement along the Bund and set off to the Shanghai Huangpu International Airport for home. (B)

Notes : B=breakfast; L=lunch; D=dinner

Words and Expressions

highlight [ˈhaɪlaɪt] n. 精彩部分　　acquaint [əˈkweɪnt] vt. 使熟知,通知
buffet [ˈbʊfeɪ] n. 自助餐

Proper Nouns

Qinhuai River 秦淮河　　Zhouzhuang 周庄
Hanshan Temple 寒山寺

Exercise

1. Arrange a 3-day itinerary for a group, and discuss it with the manager of the travel service.
2. Plan a 5-day itinerary for a group from UK who will travel in your hometown.

Part IV　Situational Dialogue

Zhuozheng Garden

(A=Miss Dai Jingxing; B=Alexander)

A: Now, we're in front of Zhuozheng Garden. You can see on the horizontal board in the upper part of the brick wall the three carved and gilded characters: "Zhuo Zheng Yuan," which means "Humble Administrator's Garden."

B: It sounds a bit strange. Who was the humble administrator? Why did he build a garden here?

A: The garden was built in the 4th year of the reign of Emperor Zhengde of the Ming Dynasty. A retired official Wang Xianchen went back to his hometown Suzhou because of the setback in his official career. He built a garden based on Dahong Temple and set up pavilions, bridges and planted trees in it.

B: Do you think he was a humble official? How could a humble official offer to build such a grand garden?

A: Wang Xianchen was not humble, but an ambitious official. When he was young, he became one of the successful candidates in the highest imperial exams. Later he was appointed as minister-level official. However, he was taken into custody by Dong Chang and put into prison.

B: Did he become bankrupt?

A: No. Although he was put in jail, he was a millionaire. After he went back, he decided to build a garden where he could plant trees and vegetables, water them as his daily work. He derided himself by saying "That is the office work of a humble administrator."

B: I see. In fact, he lived in seclusion like other disappointed officials, far away from the hustle and bustle of the world.

A: Right. The garden he built is one of the four-well-known gardens in China. It was put under state protection in March 4th, 1961.

B: I've been to the Summer Palace in Beijing and the Chengde Mountain Resort in Hebei. Is there anything special about the Zhuozheng Garden?

A: The Summer Palace and the Chengde Mountain Resort are in north China and represent the Chinese royal gardens; Zhuozheng Garden, together with the Liuyuan Garden, is the masterpiece of the private gardens in south China.

B: What are the architectural features of Zhuozheng Garden?

A: As an excellent example of Suzhou gardens, the Zhuozheng Garden is typical of fantastic and creative artificial landscape and well designed water space. Besides, it is full of tender family aura as well. The whole garden is the embodiment of what the ancient people have been pursuing all the time as the "Earthly Heaven" because it represents the traditional Chinese philosophical concepts of showing high ideals by simple living.

B: I know it is one of the famous gardens in south China. But why is it the most outstanding garden in south China?

A: The Zhuozheng Garden is the treasure of the culture legacy of our nation, an excellent work of classical garden south of the Yangtze River. It was called the Mother of All Gardens for its architecture, paintings, sculptures and gardening, etc.

B: I see. The Garden is not only the garden of landscape, but also a garden of historical interest.

A: That's right. Let's get in! And I'll tell you more about the Garden while we're sightseeing.

B: All right. Thank you very much!

Words and Expressions

humble ['hʌmbl] adj. 卑下的，谦逊的
setback ['setbæk] n. 顿挫，挫折
appoint [ə'pɔɪnt] vt. 任命，委任
bankrupt ['bæŋkrʌpt] adj. 破产的
administrator [əd'mɪnɪstreɪtə(r)] n. 管理者，行政官
ambitious [æm'bɪʃəs] adj. 有雄心的，野心勃勃的
minister ['mɪnɪstə(r)] n. 部长，大臣
millionaire [ˌmɪljə'neə(r)] n. 百万富翁

deride [dɪˈraɪd] vt. 嘲弄，嘲笑
disappoint [ˌdɪsəˈpɔɪnt] vt. 使失望
masterpiece [ˈmɑːstəpiːs] n. 杰作，名著
aura [ˈɔːrə] n. 气氛，气味

seclusion [sɪˈkluːʒn] n. 隔离，隐居
represent [ˌreprɪˈzent] vt. 表现，描绘
creative [krɪˈeɪtɪv] adj. 创造性的
embodiment [ɪmˈbɒdɪmənt] n. 体现，化身

Proper Nouns

Zhuozheng Garden 拙政园
Wang Xianchen 王献臣
Dong Chang 东厂（明朝时期的太监特务机构）
Chengde Mountain Resort 承德避暑山庄

Emperor Zhengde 正德皇帝
Dahong Temple 大弘寺

Exercise ➡ ➡ ➡

Directions: Listen to the dialogue. Imagine that you are the local guide and your classmates are tourists. Do the dialogue again with additional information that the teacher may offer.

Part V   Video for Tourism
旅游视频

Zhouzhuang

Words and Expressions

distinctive [dɪˈstɪŋktɪv] adj. 与众不同的
dwelling [ˈdwelɪŋ] n. 住处，寓所
quarter [ˈkwɔːtə(r)] n. 住处
merchant [ˈmɜːtʃənt] n. 商人
tycoon [taɪˈkuːn] n. 企业巨头

exhibit [ɪɡˈzɪbɪt] v. 陈列
household [ˈhaʊshəʊld] n. 家庭
illustrate [ˈɪləstreɪt] v. 说明
mansion [ˈmænʃn] n. 宅邸
showcase [ˈʃəʊkeɪs] v. 使展现

Proper Nouns

Kunshan 昆山
Chen Yifei 陈逸飞
Armand Hammer 阿曼德·哈默
Yangtzi River 长江

Double Bridge 双桥
Memories of Hometown《故乡的回忆》
Shen's Residence 沈厅

Zhouzhuang is an ancient town of Kunshan City, Jiangsu Province. It lies between Shanghai and Suzhou. It takes a 1.5 hours' drive from Shanghai to Zhouzhuang and 40 minutes away from Suzhou.

Zhouzhuang has many rivers and lakes, and it was considered as the most beautiful water town in China. 13 stone bridges cross the rivers, showing distinctive views of water town.

Double Bridge is the most famous one. In 1984, Chen Yifei, a young artist residing in the United States painted a picture of Double Bridge and named it Memories of Hometown. The painting with Chen Yifei's 37 art works were exhibited and bought by Dr Armand Hammer, an American oil tycoon, and later presented to the late Chinese leader Deng Xiaoping.

Zhouzhuang has about 1000 households, who are living in the old dwelling quarters 600 years ago. Among the many old houses, the hall of Shen's Residence is the most famous. Built during the Ming Dynasty, six hundred years ago, as the private residence of a wealthy merchant family, the huge mansion clearly illustrates the lifestyle of the rich at that time. Zhouzhuang is also famous for its folk arts and craftsmanship. That's becoming a window for showcasing the traditional culture of the regions in the south of the Yangzi River.

Step 1: Watch the video and write down the key words or phrases in the video. You may use the key words or phrases as the reminders when you watch it the second time.

_____
_____
_____
_____

Step 2: Watch the video again and decide whether the statements are True or False.
1. _____ Zhouzhuang is an ancient town of Kunshan City, Jiangsu Province, which lies between Shanghai and Suzhou.
2. _____ It is reputed as the most beautiful water town in China which has distinctive features of the rivers, lakes, folk houses and small hills.
3. _____ In 1984, Chen Yifei painted a picture of Double Bridge and named it Memories of Hometown. Zhouzhuang became famous overnight.
4. _____ The hall of Shen's Residence built during the Ming Dynasty is a private residence which clearly illustrates the lifestyle of the rich at that time.

Part VI Tour Commentary

Tongli

Ladies and Gentlemen! Tongli was originally named Futu. It is a well preserved water town with a history of more than 1,000 years. The town is located on the eastern shore of Taihu Lake, just 18 kilometers from Suzhou City. Tongli is a small town, only 63 square kilometers in area and has a population of over 33 thousand. It is small, but it is popular for its waterscape. True to its reputation, Tongli is a really wonderful destination where you can enjoy a marvelous holiday or experience traditional Chinese culture.

Before we start our journey, I have something to say about the safety. Tongli is a water town with numerous streams, lakes and bridges. Like a water maze, the water system is very complicated. You must be very careful when you walk across small bridges, because the guardrails of the bridges are low. When you go boating, you should sit still. Don't splash water or catch fish in the water! You'll have enough fish when you have your lunch today. Always take care of your children! If you get lost, don't hesitate to call me!

Now, we're walking across the Taiping Bridge (Bridge of Peace and Tranquility). It is small, but very exquisite. The bridge was built during the reign of Emperor Jiaqing of the Qing Dynasty. In Tongli, you'll see a lot of bridges in a variety of styles. These bridges are the important links between the different parts of town. Forty-nine stone bridges join the seven islands which are created by fifteen rivers and five lakes. Each bridge has a name and gives you an idea of the poetic nature of the inhabitants.

Ladies and Gentlemen! We're standing in front of the Jili Bridge. It is an arch bridge. Look at the old-aged couplets inscribed on the bridge! They vividly describe the beautiful painting-like views at either end. Tongli is not only popular for its waterscape, but also for its culture. From ancient times, it has been teeming with poets, painters, Confucian scholars and government officials. Dozens of stone tablets from different periods are preserved in Tongli and many of the streets are named after their official titles. When you walk through the alleys of this water town, you cannot fail to appreciate its pristine and intoxicating atmosphere.

Here we are at the Tuisi Garden (Retreat and Reflection Garden). It is the most spectacular in Tongli. The ingenious design for the Tuisi Garden conforms to the local landforms and covers about 700 square meters. Compact and harmonious, the garden is in two parts. The residential area to the west consists of an outer house and inner house including the sedan hall, the tea hall, a main reception hall and two buildings forming the actual dwelling. The garden in the east has ponds, marble boats, waterside pavilions, halls, kiosks, verandas, rockeries and bridges. Together with flourishing trees and colorful flowers the garden greets visitors with its beauty and charm whatever the season.

Ladies and Gentlemen! Have a short rest here! And we'll go boating in the lake after thirty minutes. Thank you for your attention.

Words and Expressions

waterscape [ˈwɔːtəskeɪp] n. 水景；水景画
guardrail [ˈɡɑːdreɪl] n. 栏杆
exquisite [ɪkˈskwɪzɪt] adj. 优美的，高雅的
couplet [ˈkʌplət] n. 对句，对联
alley [ˈælɪ] n. 小路，巷
compact [ˈkɒmpækt] adj. 紧凑的，紧密的
harmonious [hɑːˈməʊnɪəs] adj. 和谐的；悦耳的
maze [meɪz] n. 曲径，迷宫
tranquility [trænˈkwɪlɪtɪ] n. 宁静
inhabitant [ɪnˈhæbɪtənt] n. 居民，居住者
inscribe [ɪnˈskraɪb] v. 刻，写，雕
spectacular [spekˈtækjələ(r)] adj. 引人入胜的，壮观的

Proper Nouns

Tongli Town 同里古镇
Taihu Lake 太湖
Emperor Jiaqing 嘉庆皇帝
Futu 富土
Taiping Bridge 太平桥
Jili Bridge 吉利桥

Exercise ➡ ➡ ➡

Directions: Act as the local guide and show the tourists around the Tongli Town. Try to make your introduction more situational and attractive using the proper body language.

Part VII Readings

Directions: Read the following passage and fill in the blanks with the words or phrases given below.

| fragrant | mirror-like | present | resorts |
| dragon | over | magnificent | elevation |

Zhongshan Mountain

Zhongshan Mountain was called Jinlin Mountain in ancient times, and it got the (1)_____ name in the Qin Dynasty. It is also called Purple Mountain in the Eastern Jin Dynasty because purple clouds were often found hovering (2)_____ its peaks. The glorious mountain winds like a (3)_____ in the east of Nanjing City. It covers an area of 31 square kilometers and has the highest peak at the (4)_____ of 448m. Zhongshan Mountain boasts rich historic sites and scenic spots of Nanjing, such as the stately Mausoleum of Dr. Sun Yat-sen, the (5)_____ Mingxiaoling Tomb, the vividly-shaped sculptures along the Sacred Avenue, the (6)_____ Plum Blossom Hill, the serene Linggu Temple, the (7)_____ Zixia Lake and the recently-completed Baima Stone Sculpture Park. The natural scenery of Zhongshan Mountain looks more attractive. It has become one of the famous tourist (8)_____ both in China and in the world.

Words and Expressions

hover ['hɒvə(r)] v. 盘旋
boast [bəʊst] v. 自夸
glorious ['glɔːriəs] adj. 光荣的, 显赫的
embellish [ɪm'belɪʃ] v. 修饰

Proper Nouns

Zhongshan Mountain 钟山
Purple Mountain 紫金山
Mingxiaoling Tomb 明孝陵
Plum Blossom Hill 梅花山
Zixia Lake 紫霞湖

Jinlin Mountain 金陵山
Eastern Jin Dynasty 东晋
Sacred Avenue 神道
Linggu Temple 灵谷寺
Baima Stone Sculpture Park 白马石刻公园

Part VIII Translation

Zhouzhuang

1. Zhouzhuang Town (周庄镇) is located 38 kilometers southeast of Suzhou City, 33 kilometers southwest of Kunshan City (昆山市). With a history of more than 900 years, it is just like a pearl set near the bank of Dianshan Lake (淀山湖).

2. The river course of the town takes the shape of Chinese Character "#"(呈井字型). Houses were all built along the river. Over sixty percent of dwelling-houses out of almost one thousand were built in the Ming or Qing dynasties.

3. Over the river are 14 bridges built in the Yuan, Ming and Qing dynasties, among which is a unique bridge in China—Fu'an Bridge (富安桥) as well as the world famous Double Bridge (双桥).

4. 徐逵后裔(descendants)建有张厅(The Zhang's Residence)。民间所说"轿从前门进, 船从家中过"("The sedans enter the front door while boats pass through the house")生动形象地描绘了其建筑特色。

5. 沈万山(Shen Wansan)后裔建有七进五门楼的沈厅(The Shen's Residence), 这里还有叶楚伧

故居(Ye Chucang's Former Residence)等。
6. 黄山集中国山川之美,周庄集中国水乡之美。周庄被誉为"中国第一水乡"("first water town in China"),名不虚传。

Unit 4

Touring Sichuan

Focus on Learning 学习要点

导游案例　　The Luggage Lost 丢失行李
导游听力　　1. Chengdu City 成都市
　　　　　　2. Tourism Resources in Sichuan 四川旅游资源
途中讲解　　Chengdu—Ya'an 成都——雅安
情景对话　　Wuhou Temple 武侯祠
旅游视频　　Dujiangyan Irrigation Project 都江堰水利工程
导　游　词　　Yerenhai (Mugecuo) 野人海（木格错）
导游阅读　　Du Fu's Thatched Cottage 杜甫草堂
导游翻译　　Mt. Qingcheng 青城山

 Part I　Tips for Tour Guides

Case 4

The Luggage Lost

Mr. Tian Qiang is picking up the tourists in the Chengdu Shuangliu International Airport. All luggage had been claimed, but Mr. Qiao's baggage is not found. Mr. Qiao is so worried that he is reluctant to leave the airport while other tourists are waiting impatiently in the coach. Any suggestions you can put forward to Mr. Tian? Listen to the passage and write down your suggestion in the blanks.

(1) Mr. Tian should try his best to look for the luggage and _____ for the tourist though he is not responsible for the loss.
(2) He could take Mr. Qiao to register the lost property _____. With his ticket and luggage tag in hand, Mr. Qiao can specify the number of pieces, the exterior characteristics of _____, and leave a phone number for further contact.
(3) Mr. Tian should write down the address and _____ of the airline office and the lost-and-found office at the airport. In this way, he can keep contact with the people concerned for any further information during the travel. Mr. Qiao could buy _____ and

submit receipts for reimbursement later.
(4) If Mr. Qiao still cannot find the luggage before he leaves, Mr. Tian should help the tourist to lodge a claim against _____, meanwhile inform the administrative staff of the next stop about the address and phone number of the airline company so that they could continue to _____.

Words and Expressions

register the loss 登记遗失物品　　　　lost-and-found office 失物招领处
luggage tag 行李标签　　　　　　　　daily necessities 日常生活用品
airline company 航空公司

Exercise

Directions: Act as Mr. Tian Qiang, the local guide and Mr. Qiao, the tourist. Make a dialogue to demonstrate the scene that both of you try to search for the lost luggage.

Part II Listening Activities

Listening 1

Chengdu City

Words and Expressions

birthplace ['bɜːθpleɪs] n. 诞生地　　　　Taoism ['daʊɪzəm] n. 道教
relic ['relɪk] n. 遗物, 遗迹

Proper Nouns

Mt. Qingcheng 青城山　　　　　　　　Dujiangyan Irrigation Project 都江堰水利工程
Du Fu's Thatched Cottage 杜甫草堂　　Wuhou Temple 武侯祠
Wangjian's Tomb 王建墓　　　　　　　Yangsheng-an Temple 杨升庵
Mausoleum of Prince Xiwang of the Ming Dynasty 明僖王陵
Jin Sha Ruins 金沙遗址　　　　　　　Snow-capped Xiling Mountain 西岭雪山

Longchi Forest Park 龙池森林公园
Chaoyanghu Lake 朝阳湖
Mt. Jiufeng 九峰山
the "Land of Abundance" "天府之国"
Mt. Tiantai 天台山
Yunding Stone City 云顶石城

Exercise ➡ ➡ ➡

Directions: Listen to the passage and decide whether the statements are true or false. If it is true, put "T" in the space provided and "F" if it is false.

1. _____ Mt. Qingcheng is one of the birthplaces of Taoism in China and put on the list of World Natural Heritage.
2. _____ In the downtown areas of Chengdu, there are a number of historic sites, such as Du Fu's Thatched Cottage, Wuhou Temple, Wangjian's Tomb and Dujiangyan Irrigation Project.
3. _____ The Snow-capped Xiling Mountain is a national key tourist resort.
4. _____ Longchi Forest Park is the place where people in Chengdu and tourists from other southern provinces can appreciate winter snow.
5. _____ Chengdu has been known as the "Land of Abundance."

Listening 2

Words and Expressions

fairyland [ˈfeərilænd] *n.* 仙境,乐园,奇境
mundane [mʌnˈdeɪn] *adj.* 世俗的,平凡的
Buddhism [ˈbʊdɪzəm] *n.* 佛教
promising [ˈprɒmɪsɪŋ] *adj.* 有希望的
jasper [ˈdʒæspə] *n.* 碧玉
sacred [ˈseɪkrɪd] *adj.* 宗教的,神圣的
geological [ˌdʒiːəˈlɒdʒɪkl] *adj.* 地质学的

Proper Nouns

Jiuzhaigou Valley 九寨沟
Mt. E'mei 峨眉山
Sanxingdui Ruins 三星堆遗址
Qiang Stockaded Village of Taoping 桃坪羌寨
Wolong 卧龙
Yading 亚丁
Ganzi 甘孜
Huanglong (Yellow Dragon) 黄龙
Leshan Giant Buddha 乐山大佛
Guanghan 广汉
Aba 阿坝
Giant Panda Nature Reserve 大熊猫自然保护区
Shangri-la 香格里拉
Daocheng 稻城

Tourism Resources in Sichuan

Sichuan is a province well known for its rich tourism resources of (1)_____ landscapes, historical relics and ethnic customs. As the old saying goes, "Mountains and waters in Shu are best under the heaven." Speaking of tourism resources, Sichuan has: 1) two sites included in the List of (2)_____ : Jiuzhaigou Valley, the "fairyland" on the earth; and Huanglong (Yellow Dragon), the "jasper lake in the mundane world"; 2) one site included in the World Cultural and Natural Heritages: Mt. E'mei with the Leshan Giant Buddha, (3)_____ of Buddhism; 3) one site included in the List of World Cultural Heritages: Dujiangyan Irrigation Project & Mt. Qingcheng; 4) (4)_____ State 4A-level or 3A-level Scenic Zones; 5) (5)_____ National Key Scenery Resorts; 6) 67 Provincial Scenic Zones; 7) (6)_____ National Nature Reserves; 8) 45 Provincial Nature Reserves; 9) (7)_____ National Forest Parks; 10) 51 Provincial Forest Parks; and 11) (8)_____ National Geological Parks. Among them, the following are promising (9)_____ for the "List of World Heritages": the Sanxingdui Ruins of Guanghan, the Jinsha Ruins of Chengdu, the Qiang Stockaded Village of Taoping in Aba, the Giant Panda Nature Reserve of Wolong, and the (10)_____ of Yading-Daocheng of Ganzi.

Exercise ➡ ➡ ➡
Directions: Listen to the passage and fill in the words or phrases you have heard.

Part III On-the-Way Introduction

Chengdu—Ya'an

Good morning, dear friends! All of you look energetic today. That's very nice. Today we will visit Ya'an. Ya'an is rich in tourism resources. It has unique landscapes as well as rich historical and cultural heritages. Ya'an is a "rain city" for plenty of rainfall, "stone base" for abundant natural granite and marble, "hydropower kingdom" for rich water resources, the real "hometown of pandas" since the first panda specimen was found there in 1868, and also the birthplace of tea culture.

Ya'an is about 130 kilometers from Chengdu. It will take us about one hour and twenty minutes to get there. Along the road, we'll pass quite a few scenic spots: the Chaoyang Lake, the Lake of Stone Elephant and Mt. Mengding. However, we'll travel directly to Ya'an. First, we'll go sightseeing in the old town Shangli, then, we'll hike in the Bifengxia Valley. In the evening we'll check in Yudu Hotel and have a Ya'an fish. It's a nice dish. Remember to take the fish bone as a souvenir.

Now, we are approaching Ya'an. The first scenic spot we come across is the Chaoyang Lake. In fact, it is a reservoir. We'll not go boating there because we'll cruise on the Qingyijiang

River of Ya'an. It is a very beautiful river. And you could view the landscape along the bank and also the towering peaks encircling the city.

Well, look on your right side! It is a football ground. If you love football, you may know Chengdu is a football kingdom. A lot of football fans used to throng the streets in the downtown areas to hail their team. It was very hard to get a ticket sometimes, so they came here to watch the training. This playground was the Quanxing Football Training Base, but now nobody comes here because the fraud of the football game hurts the fans.

We'll arrive at Ya'an in twenty minutes. Would you please look out of the window on your right side? Have you seen a mountain shrouded with surging fog? It is one of the most famous mountains in Sichuan—Mt. Mengding. Mt. Mengding has five towering peaks, taking the shape of a lotus. The fresh rain, surging cloud, bright rainbow, magic light, sunrise and sunset, all of these give amazing touches to the scenery here. Tourists are especially fascinated by the wonderful performance of tea-making skills. The annual sacrificial ceremony of imperial tea is even more spectacular. Hundreds of articles and poems have been written in praise of the tea produced there. As the saying goes, "The Yangtze River tops the waters, while the Mengshan tea is the best of its kind." Mt. Mengding is famous for its scenic beauty and tea culture. Time is pressing, and we shall not climb the mountain today.

Everybody! We're passing the Jinjiguan Pass (Golden Cock Pass) and entering the downtown area of Ya'an. Did you see the statue of Nvwa near the Qingyijiang River? In ancient times, the Fire Spirit and the Water Spirit had a fierce fight for domination of the world in Ya'an. The Water Spirit was defeated. He was so angry that he knocked down one of the pillars supporting the heaven. As a result, it began to rain heavily and constantly as if the sky was leaking. Since that time Ya'an has been called "Xishu Loutian." It rains so often in west Sichuan, and Ya'an gets its nickname the "rain city." In order to save man from the flood, Nüwa refined colorful stones and patched the broken sky, but she died of exhaustion at last.

Now, we're moving close to the statue of Nüwa. The statue of Nüwa was constructed here to commemorate her feasts to help the local people although the unfinished seam of the sky is still leaking water. In Ya'an more than 60 sights are related to Nüwa, especially in the Bifengxia Valley. There are three wonders in Ya'an: Ya'an rain, Ya'an fish and Ya'an maidens.

Ladies and Gentlemen! We're passing the Bifengxia Valley, but we'll visit the old town Shangli first according to the travel schedule. Shangli is just 20 minutes' drive... Here we are. Get off the coach one by one. We'll begin our wonderful trip in Ya'an.

Thank you for your attention.

Words and Expressions

landscape ['lændskeɪp] n. 风景, 山水画
hydropower ['haɪdrəʊˌpaʊə] n. 水电
approach [ə'prəʊtʃ] vt. 接近

marble ['mɑːbl] n. 大理石
specimen ['spesɪmən] n. 样品, 样本
surge [sɜːdʒ] vi. 汹涌, 澎湃

domination [ˌdɒmɪˈneɪʃn] *n.* 统治，支配　　constantly [ˈkɒnstəntli] *adv.* 经常地
nickname [ˈnɪkneɪm] *n.* 诨号，绰号，昵称　　exhaustion [ɪɡˈzɔːstʃən] *n.* 精疲力竭

Proper Nouns

Ya'an 雅安
Chaoyang Lake 朝阳湖
Mt. Mengding 蒙顶山
Bifengxia Valley 碧峰峡
Qingyijiang River 青衣江
Mengshan tea 蒙山茶
Nvwa 女娲

"rain city" "雨城"
Lake of Stone Elephant 石象湖
Shangli 上里
Yudu Hotel 雨都饭店
Quanxing Football Training Base 全兴足球训练基地
Jinjiguan Pass (Golden Cock Pass) 金鸡关
"Xishu Loutian" "西蜀漏天"

Exercise ➡ ➡ ➡

Directions: Make an on-the-way introduction to a package tour in the city where you are living.

Part IV Situational Dialogue

Wuhou Temple

(A=Miss Lei Shenyuan, a local guide; B=Albert)

A: Now we are standing at the axis line of the Wuhou Temple. Look at this magnificent hall! Need not to say, the owner of this hall must have the highest identity in the feudal hierarchy.

B: Let me guess. It must be the Liu Bei's Hall.

A: Bingo! Let's enter the hall. Take care of the high threshold. You may stumble over it. The threshold of the emperor's hall is much higher than that of his ministers and generals.

A: Look at the statue! As an emperor, Liu Bei sits majestically.

B: Who is the one standing by his side?

A: That's his grandson.

B: Then why is his grandson standing by his side, not his son?

A: A good question! After Liu Bei died, his son Liu Chan succeeded his throne. Liu Chan was a playboy, and was sent to Wei Kingdom as a prisoner after his kingdom was captured. In Luoyang he still indulged in drinking and flirting with the beauties. People believed he was not qualified to have a statue here.

B: Very good! People should not respect those who betray their motherland.

A: Turn left please! In the east chamber of the Liu Bei's Hall you can view the statues of Guan Yu and his son Guan Ping and Guan Xing, as well as officers under his command. Look! The statue of Guan Yu is 2 meters high. It is said that Guan Yu was a very handsome man. He had a beautiful beard. I don't know if he is handsome according to your views.

B: I think he is handsome.

A: By the way, have you noticed that Guan Yu was dressed like an emperor?

B: Yeah, but why? I can't understand it.

A: Guan Yu was always loyal to his master and devoted all his life to the goal of China's reunification. He was chosen as an exemplar of dedication and obedience by the emperors of following dynasties. On him was conferred the title of king in the Northern Song Dynasty and the title of Emperor Guansheng in the Ming Dynasty. He is also worshiped as god in Taoism from the Qing Dynasty. That is why he was addressed like an emperor.

B: I see. Well, what about General Zhang Fei. I hear he is also an interesting figure. Where is he enshrined?

A: Now, follow me to the west chamber. Zhang Fei and his descendants are enshrined here. Like Guan Yu, he is also a brave general. But he often got angry and whipped his officers and soldiers when he was drunk. He died tragically because he drank too much.

B: What happened to him? Did he die of alcoholism?

A: Not exactly. It is said that Zhang Fei' eyes were open wide when he was asleep. His two officers Fan Qiang and Zhang Da wanted to murder him when he was sleeping. When Fan Qiang put his sword around Zhang Fei's neck, Zhang Fei thought that it was a mosquito, so he slapped his neck. Ironically, he cut off his head with his own hand when he was asleep.

B: What an unbelievable story!

A: More tragically, Fan Qiang and Zhang Da meant to present his head to the king of Wu Kingdom for money. But when they heard that the Shu and Wu had reached a compromise and the war had ended, they threw Zhang's head into the Yangtze River. A fisherman took his head out of water and buried it in Yunyang. His body was buried later in Langzhong, another place of Sichuan Province.

B: What a tragedy! His corpse was buried in two places.

A: Follow me please! Next scenic spot is the Corridor of Officials and Generals.

B: Thank you!

Words and Expressions

identity [aɪˈdentətɪ] *n.* 身份,特性
threshold [ˈθreʃhəʊld] *n.* 门槛,入口
majestic [məˈdʒestɪk] *adj.* 宏伟的,庄严的
prisoner [ˈprɪznə(r)] *n.* 战俘
indulge [ɪnˈdʌldʒ] *v.* 纵容
betray [bɪˈtreɪ] *vt.* 出卖,背叛

hierarchy [ˈhaɪərɑːkɪ] *n.* 等级制度,阶层
stumble [ˈstʌmbl] *v.* 绊倒,蹒跚
throne [θrəʊn] *n.* 王座,君主
capture [ˈkæptʃə(r)] *vt.* 俘获,捕获
flirt [flɜːt] *vi.* 调情,玩弄
loyal [ˈlɔɪəl] *adj.* 忠诚的,忠心的

reunification [ˌriːjuːnɪfɪˈkeɪʃn] n. 统一
dedication [ˌdedɪˈkeɪʃn] n. 贡献,奉献
enshrine [ɪnˈʃraɪn] vt. 入庙祀奉,铭记
tragical [ˈtrædʒɪkl] adj. 悲剧的,悲剧性的
mosquito [məˈskiːtəʊ] n. 蚊子
suicide [ˈsuːɪsaɪd] n. 自杀,自毁

exemplar [ɪɡˈzemplɑː(r)] n. 模范,榜样
confer [kənˈfɜː(r)] vt. 赠与,把……赠与
descendant [dɪˈsendənt] n. 子孙,后裔
murder [ˈmɜːdə(r)] vt. 谋杀,凶杀
ironical [aɪˈrɒnɪkl] adj. 讽刺的,用反语的
compromise [ˈkɒmprəmaɪz] n. 妥协,折衷

Proper Nouns

Liu Bei's Hall 刘备殿
Wei Kingdom 魏国
Guan Yu 关羽
Guan Xing 关兴
Emperor Guansheng 关圣大帝
Fan Qiang 范强
Wu Kingdom 吴国
Langzhong 阆中

Liu Chan 刘禅
Luoyang 洛阳
Guan Ping 关平
Northern Song Dynasty 北宋
Zhang Fei 张飞
Zhang Da 张达
Yunyang 云阳

Exercise

Directions: Listen to the dialogue. Imagine that you are the local guide and your classmates are tourists. Do the dialogue again with additional information that the teacher may offer.

Part V Video for Tourism
旅游视频

Dujiangyan Irrigation Project

Words and Expressions

turbulent [ˈtɜːbjələnt] adj. 湍急的
divert [daɪˈvɜːt] v. 使转向
magistrate [ˈmædʒɪstreɪt] n. 地方行政官
irrigate [ˈɪrɪɡeɪt] v. 灌溉
canal [kəˈnæl] n. 运河
prefecture [ˈpriːfektʃə(r)] n. 县,府
regulate [ˈreɡjuleɪt] v. 规定;整顿

tranquil [ˈtræŋkwɪl] adj. 平静的
conservancy [kənˈsɜːvənsi] n. 管理,保护
gigantic [dʒaɪˈɡæntɪk] adj. 巨大的
territory [ˈterətri] n. 领土
confrontation [ˌkɒnfrʌnˈteɪʃn] n. 遭遇;阻碍
channel [ˈtʃænl] n. 通道,隧道

> **Proper Nouns**
>
> Minjiang River 岷江 Chengdu Plain 成都平原
> Li Bing 李冰 Fulong Temple 伏龙观
> King Zhao of Qin 秦昭王 Yulei Mountain 玉垒山
> Precious Bottleneck 宝瓶口 Fish Mouth 鱼嘴
> Flying Sand Dike 飞沙堰

The Dujiangyan is located on the Minjiang River in the western part of the Chengdu Plain. The weir is a water controlled project with the seemingly more regular effect of turning the river's ever too turbulent water tranquil. The Dujiang weir diverts water from the river to large tracks of lands that are in need of irrigation. Astonishingly, the Dujiangyan was built more than 2,200 years ago. The man directing the construction of project was an engineer who specialized in the water conservancy. His name was Li Bing.

But why was it necessary all those years ago to build this gigantic water conservancy project? In the 3rd century BC, China's territory was divided among number of rival states that were at war with one another. In the year 316 BC, the state of Shu which covered the Chengdu Plain was conquered by the state of Qin. This brought Qin into direct confrontation with the state of Chu.

A plan to join up with Qin was to dig a canal to divert the Minjing River so that the strategic supplies could be shipped to the city of Chengdu. Around this time, King Zhao of Qin appointed 30-year-old Li Bing as magistrate of Shu prefecture. One of the new magistrate's main responsibilities was to make sure the prefecture a strategic base from which Qin could unify China.

Li Bing spent 2 years carrying out survey of Minjiang River valley. He concluded that there was only one way to curve the flooding course by the river using a net work of channels and canals on the Chengdu Plain. This scheme had a key additional benefit: The water diverted from the Minjiang River could be used for irrigation. The scheme would work that a channel would have to be cut through the Yulei Mountain.

Li Bing mobilized the local people to do the work. The massive project took 18 years to complete. The three key elements of the project were given the poetic names: Precious Bottleneck, Fish Mouth and Flying Sands Dike. The Flying Sands Dike divides the Minjiang River into two courses, namely the inner river and the outer river. The dike served to regulate the water volume. The inner river flows to the Precious Bottleneck and continues onto irrigate the Chengdu Plain.

Step 1: Watch the video and write down the key words or phrases in the video. You may use the key words or phrases as the reminders when you watch it the second time.

_____
_____
_____
_____

Step 2: Watch the video again and decide whether the statements are True or False.
1. _____ The Dujiangyan is a water conservancy project which has turned the Chengdu Plain into a Land of Abundance.
2. _____ The water diverted from the Minjiang River could be used for irrigation. The State of Qin built Dujiangyan for the purpose of the flood control, not for the military operation.
3. _____ The 30-year-old Li Bing, the magistrate of Qin prefecture believed that a channel would have to be cut through the Yulei Mountain.
4. _____ The three key parts of the project were given the poetic names: Precious Bottleneck, Fish Mouth and Flying Sands Dike.

Part VI Tour Commentary

Mugecuo

Ladies and Gentlemen!

Attention please! Here we are at the Mugecuo Scenic Area in Kangding County, 379 km from Chengdu. It took us five hours to get here. Everybody of us is very tired, but it is worth traveling a long distance. The beautiful landscape with legendary stories in Mugecuo will certainly relax you and let you forget your fatigue. Please remember the banner of our travel service, of course my handsome face as well. Today we'll visit Dujuanxia Valley (Azalea Valley), Seven-colour Lake, Mugecuo and many more. Then we'll have our dinner in a Tibetan family to enjoy the traditional Tibetan food—tsamba and barley wine. Sounds great!

Now, we're walking into the Azalea Valley. It is 6 km long, connects the Seven-colour Lake at its east end and joins Mugecuo at the west end. The streams in the valley are flowing quietly in some section, but roaring in other reach. When they are quiet, they proceed with confidence and composure; when they're roaring, they give rise to waves and splashes, jumping down from rocks and forming beautiful falls layer upon layer. The slopes of the valley are covered with grass, flowers and trees.

Look! It is a sea of azaleas. Can you guess how many species of azalea trees grow here? There are more than 68 types of the azaleas. Now, it is the season of blossom. You can see various kinds of azaleas in full blossom and make the valley a world of flowers. But not all the flowers are azaleas; some of them are wild flowers. You see, the flowers grow on the cliff, some hide contently in dense bushes, some dance joyfully against the wind, while others stand solemnly. The flourishing flowers, red or white, blue or purple, present a panorama of colourful flowers in different postures. Flying birds and roaming animals are found in the woods now and then. It is a landscape picture with birds and wild life, isn't it?

Well, we've reached another end of the Azalea Valley. It is also called Dahaizi, the biggest alpine lake 2,000m above sea level in northwest Sichuan. Look around! Mugecuo is embraced on all sides by mountains, forests and grasslands. The weather constantly changes in a day, and the natural scenery presents different looks. At dawn, fogs hover over the lake, which appears to be a vast expanse of misty, rolling water, mysterious and unfathomable. As the sun rises, the blue ripples twinkle and glitter, fogs and clouds are dyed by rays of sunlight into different hues, a dreamy and fancy sight. Now, it is getting dark. Look at the sky! The remaining rays of the setting sun radiate on the lake, and add its splendour to everything within its reach. It is one of the spectacles in Mugecuo—"Mugecuo Sunset."

Ladies and Gentlemen! Look as far as you can! What have you seen? Not far away from Yerenhai are the surrounding satellite lakes: the Red Sea, the White Sea, the Black Sea, etc, like stars around the moon. Opposite to the Yerenhai is the Red Sea Grassland. Did you see the peak standing to the left of the Yerenhai? It is called the Rhinoceros Peak. When the moon is shinning with few stars, you can see the peak takes a shape of a rhinoceros's horn and gleams with cold silver light.

Well, we're heading for a dinner in a Tibetan family nearby. You can watch the marvellous scene while you're enjoying the buttered tea with our Tibetan friends.

Thank you!

Words and Expressions

roar [rɔː(r)] vi. 吼叫, 怒号, 咆哮
solemn ['sɔləm] adj. 庄严的, 严肃的
posture ['pɒstʃə(r)] n. 姿势, 心境
embrace [ɪm'breɪs] vt. 拥抱, 互相拥抱
misty ['mɪstɪ] adj. 有薄雾的
unfathomable [ʌn'fæðəməbl] adj. 深不可测的
gleam [gliːm] vi. 闪烁

azalea [ə'zeɪlɪə] n. [植]杜鹃花
panorama [ˌpænə'rɑːmə] n. 全景; 全景画
roam [rəʊm] v. 漫游, 闲逛, 徜徉
grassland ['grɑːslænd] n. 牧草地, 草原
mysterious [mɪ'stɪərɪəs] adj. 神秘的
radiate ['reɪdɪeɪt] vi. 发光, 辐射; 流露

Proper Nouns

Mugecuo Scenic Area 木格措风景区
Kangding County 康定县
Seven-colour Lake 七色海

Mugecuo "木格措," 藏语, 意为"野人海"
Dujuanxia Valley (Azalea Valley) 杜鹃峡

tsamba 糌粑		Dahaizi 大海子	
"Mugecuo Sunset" "木格夕照"		Rhinoceros Peak 犀牛峰	

Exercise

Directions: Act as the local guide and show the tourists around the Yerenhai. Try to make your introduction more situational and attractive using the proper body language.

Part VII　Readings

Directions: Read the following passage and fill in the blanks with the words or phrases given below.

hesitation	infected	shimmering	enough
clothes	tale	around	

Du Fu's Thatched Cottage

　　Upon entering the Front Gate, a (1)_____ brook comes into view—the Huanhua Brook, which was frequently mentioned in Du Fu's poetry. There is a wonderful (2)_____ about the origin of the brook's name. It is said that in the Tang Dynasty there lived a beautiful and kind-hearted girl, whose surname was Ren. One day, she was washing (3)_____ over the bank of the brook, when a monk whose body was (4)_____ with sores came and asked the girl to wash his pus-stained kasaya. The girl assented without (5)_____. As soon as the girl immersed the kasaya into the water, numerous lotus flowers appeared in the brook. Surprised, people looked (6)_____ for the monk, but he had disappeared. Then people named the brook Huanhua Brook, which means "washing-flower brook." The brook has fine scenery on each side and used to be a river deep (7)_____ for ships to sail on. Du Fu vividly describes the scene in the following quatrain:

　　Two yellow orioles chirp amid the green willows,
　　White herons flutter in the blue sky in a row.
　　The snow-capped Xiling Mountain glows over my window,
　　And the boats from Dongwu anchor outside my abode.

Words and Expressions

shimmer ['ʃɪmə(r)] n. 微光
pus [pʌs] n. 脓,脓汁
kasaya [keɪ'seɪə] n. 袈裟
kind-hearted [kaɪnd 'hɑːtɪd] adj. 仁慈的,好心肠的
stained [steɪnd] adj. 沾污的,褪色的
assent [ə'sent] n. 赞成 vi. 同意

immerse [ɪˈmɜːs] vt. 沉浸,使陷入
oriole [ˈɔːrɪəʊl] n. 鹂,金莺类
heron [ˈherən] n. 鹭,苍鹭
anchor [ˈæŋkə(r)] v. 抛锚,锚定

quatrain [ˈkwɒtreɪn] n. 四行诗
chirp [tʃɜːp] v. 吱喳而鸣
flutter [ˈflʌtə(r)] vi. 鼓翼,拍(翅)

Proper Nouns

Front Gate 正门   Huanhua Brook 浣花溪

Part VIII   Translation

Mt. Qingcheng

1. Mt. Qingcheng (青城山) is situated 63 kilometers west of Chengdu (成都). Characterized by its secluded and quiet environment, the scenic area is surrounded by ring-shaped peaks (群峰环绕).
2. Mt. Qingcheng enjoys equal fame for steepness with Jianmen (剑门), for elegance with Mt. Emei (峨眉) and for grandeur with Kuimen (夔门). It has been widely acclaimed as the "most secluded mountain under the heaven" ("青城天下幽").
3. In Chinese Qingcheng literally means "green city" ("绿色的城郭"). Mt. Qingcheng gets its name because the main scenic spots such as the Tianshi Cave (天师洞) are all surrounded by 36 mountain peaks which have forests of lush evergreen trees encircling each spot like a city wall.
4. 青城山位于四川省西部,群峰环绕,清幽隐逸(tranquil and secluded),林木清幽,是著名的旅游景点和避暑胜地(summer resort)。
5. 作为一座道教名山(a famous Taoist mountain)、道教的发祥地和道教发展的重要基地,青城山已有两千多年的历史了。青城山以其清幽的环境和深厚的道教文化底蕴而独具一格(unique)。
6. 1982年,青城山被国务院(State Council)评定为全国首批重点风景名胜区(China National Key Tourist Resort)。2000年,青城山和都江堰(Dujiangyan Irrigation Project)联名被联合国教科文组织(UNESCO)列入世界文化遗产名录(List of World Cultural Heritage)。

Unit 5

Touring Anhui

Focus on Learning 学习要点

导游案例　　Checking in the Hotel 入住酒店
导游听力　　1. Hefei City 合肥市
　　　　　　2. Lord Bao Memorial Temple 包公祠
情景对话　　Mt. Jiuhua 九华山
旅游视频　　Hongcun Village 宏村
导　游　词　Mt. Huangshan 黄山
导游阅读　　Tangyue Memorial Archways 棠樾牌坊群
导游翻译　　Ancient Street of Tunxi 屯溪老街

 Part I　Tips for Tour Guides

Case 5

Checking in the Hotel

It was half past nine in the evening. Miss Dai Jia received a tour group from England on behalf of Anhui China International Travel Service. She picked up the tourists and helped them check in the Hefei Shangri-la Hotel. Afterwards, she left with the driver and hurried back to take care of her baby in the hospital. Please evaluate her guiding service and make your comments in the blanks after you listen to the passage.

(1) Miss Dai should not leave the tourists in the hotel without fulfilling the basic _____ as a local guide;
(2) She should ask the porter to _____ to tourists' rooms;
(3) She should tell the tour group about _____;
(4) She should inform the tour group of itinerary _____;
(5) She should arrange _____ for the group;
(6) She must arrange _____ for the tourists.

Words and Expressions

check in 入住酒店 hotel facilities 饭店设施
itinerary 线路 morning call 叫醒服务

Exercise

Directions: Act as Miss Dai, the driver and the tourists. Replay the scene that the tourists checked in the hotel. Ask one of your classmates to act as the general manager of Anhui China International Travel Service and evaluate the service rendered to the tourists according to the basic procedures of the guiding service.

Part II   Listening Activities

Listening 1

Hefei City

Words and Expressions

battlefield [ˈbætlfiːld] n. 战场, 沙场
noted [ˈnəʊtɪd] adj. 著名的
abundant [əˈbʌndənt] adj. 丰富的, 充裕的
stupendous [stjuːˈpendəs] adj. 惊人的, 巨大的
tuck [tʌk] vt. 挤进, 塞, 使隐藏
academic [ˌækəˈdemɪk] adj. 学术的, 理论的
magnificence [mæɡˈnɪfɪsns] n. 华丽, 富丽堂皇
repute [rɪˈpjuːt] v. 认为, 称为

Proper Nouns

Hefei 合肥
Xiaoyaojin 逍遥津
Xinghua (Apricot Flower) Park 杏花公园
Chaohu Lake 巢湖
Mt. Tianzhu 天柱山
Hongcun 宏村
Yixian County 黟县

Bao Zheng 包拯
Jiaonu (Archery Drilling) Terrace 教弩台
Shouxian 寿县
Mt. Jiuhua 九华山
Xidi 西递
Shexian County 歙县
Tangyue Memorial Archway 棠樾牌坊

Exercise ➡ ➡ ➡

Directions: Listen to the passage and decide whether the statements are true or false. If it is true, put "T" in the space provided and "F" if it is false.

1. _____ Hefei, capital of Anhui Province, used to be a battlefield of the Three Kingdoms Period.
2. _____ Mt. Huangshan was also the cradle of one of China's four local academic schools, the school of Anhui Studies.
3. _____ Mt. Jiuhua, one of the three famous Buddhist Mountains in China.
4. _____ Xidi and Hongcun are the well-preserved ancient villages in Yixian County near Mt. Tianzhu.
5. _____ Shexian County is also a must for each visitor to experience fine examples of residential architecture from the Ming and Qing dynasties.

Listening 2

Words and Expressions

imitate ['ɪmɪteɪt] vt. 模仿,仿效,仿造　　display [dɪ'spleɪ] vt. 陈列,展览,显示
waistband ['weɪstbænd] n. 腰带,束腰带　　clench [klentʃ] v. 紧握,(拳头)牢牢地抓住

Proper Nouns

Lord Bao's Memorial Temple 包公祠　　Baohe Park 包河公园
Stele Pavilion 碑亭　　Main Hall 主殿
Second Hall 二殿

Lord Bao's Memorial Temple

Lord Bao's Memorial Temple is located in Baohe Park just (1)_____ of the city center. It was initially built in (2)_____ in memory of Baozheng, a famous upright officer during the Northern Song Dynasty. Lord Bao's Memorial Temple is a typical ancient architectural (3)_____ with style imitating that of the Song Dynasty. Covering an area of one hectare, it mainly consists of (4)_____, the Second Gate, the Stele Pavilion, the Main Hall, the Second Hall and the east and west exhibition rooms. In the main hall, a (5)_____ of Lord Bao, which is (6)_____ in height and 2.5 tons in weight, is displayed. Baozheng sits (7)_____ with his hat and waistband on. One of his hands placed on the chair with the other clenched. The eastern and western halls, using (8)_____ and essays, show visitors many stories and tales about Lord Bao.

Exercise ➡ ➡ ➡

Directions: Listen to the passage and fill in the words or phrases you have heard.

Part III   On-the-Way Introduction

Mt. Jiuhua

(A=Miss Li Lei, a guide; B=Bill)

A: Well, we're going to hike in Mt. Jiuhua today according to our travel schedule. Are you ready?

B: No, not yet. Why not to go sightseeing in Mt. Huangshan? I think Mt. Huangshan is more popular than Mt. Jiuhua.

A: Not exactly. Mt. Jiuhua is also a famous mountain in China.

B: Anything special about the mountain?

A: It is one of the four great Buddhist mountains in China, along with Mt. Wutai in Shanxi, Mt. Emei in Sichuan, and Mt. Putuo in Zhejiang.

B: When did Mt. Jiuhua become a Buddhist mountain?

A: According to historical records, Buddhism was first introduced to Mt. Jiuhua in the year 401. In 719, a Korean monk named Jin Qiaojue arrived and practiced Buddhism here for 75 years.

B: That's great. Jin Qiaojue was a Korean. To my surprise, he practiced Buddhism as long as 75 years.

A: Upon his nirvana in 794, Jin Qiaojue was respected as the Earth Buddha by the locals. Since then, Mt. Jiuhua has become the place where religious rituals are held to worship the God of Earth. Just as a Chinese saying goes, "A mountain is famous not for its height but for its holiness."

B: I've been to Mt. Emei. I know the Wannian Temple is one of the well-known temples on Mt. Emei. What is the most well-known temple on Mt. Jiuhua?

A: Well, I think Huacheng Temple is the oldest and holiest temple on the mountain. It is located in the center of Jiuhua Street. Though it first appears simple and solemn, the structure and decoration of the building are truly artistic.

B: Oh, really?

A: The engravings on lintels, brackets and roofs reinforce the brightness and liveliness of the building. The picture, "Nine Dragons Playing with Pearls" on a panel in the Main Shrine is a consummate piece of ancient Chinese art.

B: Are there any Buddhist relics there?

A: Yes, there are. There is one spectacle you may not expect—a skeleton of the monk that has been well preserved for more than 350 years.

B: Really? What's that?

A: Wu Xia was a venerable monk on Mt. Jiuhua. He once wrote sutras with a mixture of gold powder and his own blood in a cave during the Ming Dynasty. After hard practice of sutras for a hundred years in Mt. Jiuhua, Wu Xia passed away at the age of 126.

B: Unbelievable. He lived such a long life.

A: His body was found in the cave three years after his death, and then his corpse was housed in the Corporeal Body Hall Monks on the mountain believed Wu Xia was the reincarnation of Rinpoche. From then on, Buddhist believers have come here to visit the mountain and to pay homage to the monk.

B: Very good! Then, I'd like to travel to Mt. Jiuhua with you. When shall we start our trip?

A: After you take your breakfast, we'll get there by coach.

B: Thank you!

Words and Expressions

nirvana [nɪəˈvɑːnə] *n.* 涅盘,天堂
holiness [ˈhəʊlɪnəs] *n.* 神圣
engraving [ɪnˈgreɪvɪŋ] *n.* 雕刻,雕版
bracket [ˈbrækɪt] *n.* 支架
skeleton [ˈskelɪtn] *n.* 骨架,骨骼
corporeal [kɔːˈpɔːriəl] *adj.* 肉体的;有形的
consummate [ˈkɒnsəmeɪt] *adj.* 至上的,完美的
venerable [ˈvenərəbl] *adj.* 值得尊敬的;古老的

ritual [ˈrɪtʃʊəl] *n.* 典礼,(宗教)仪式
artistic [ɑːˈtɪstɪk] *adj.* 艺术的,有美感的
lintel [ˈlɪntl] *n.* [建]楣,过梁
reinforce [ˌriːɪnˈfɔːs] *vt.* 加强,修补
sutra [ˈsuːtrə] *n.* 佛经,经典
reincarnation [ˌriːɪnkɑːˈneɪʃn] *n.* 再投胎,化身

Proper Nouns

Mt. Wutai 五台山
Mt. Putuo 普陀山
Jin Qiaojue 金桥觉
Huacheng Temple 化城寺
Wu Xia 无瑕
Corporeal Body Hall Monks 肉身宝殿

Shanxi 山西
Zhejiang 浙江
Earth Buddha 地藏菩萨
Historical Relics Museum of Mt. Jiuhua
九华山文化历史博物馆
Rinpoche 仁波切(莲花生大师)

Exercise ➡ ➡ ➡

Directions: Listen to the dialogue. Imagine that you are the local guide and your classmates are tourists. Do the dialogue again with additional information that the teacher may offer.

Part IV Video for Tourism
旅游视频

Hongcun Village

Words and Expressions

ditch [dɪtʃ] *n.* 沟渠
potential [pəˈtenʃl] *adj.* 潜在的
divert [daɪˈvɜːt] *v.* 转移；使……转向
imply [ɪmˈplaɪ] *v.* 意味，暗示
miracle [ˈmɪrəkl] 奇迹

avert [əˈvɜːt] *v.* 避免
wane [weɪn] *v.* 衰落；退潮
fade [feɪd] *v.* 褪色；凋谢
transparent [trænsˈpærənt] *adj.* 透明的
regulate [ˈreɡjuleɪt] *v.* 调节，规定

Proper Nouns

Hongcun 宏村
He Keda 何可达

Moon Pond 月塘

According to family trees, Hongcun village took shape during the Southern Song Dynasty. In the early days, only the stream flowed in front of the hills. The number of villagers increased year after year. The houses were closed to one another on a narrow strip of land. If a fire broke out from a house, the neighboring houses would be engulfed in the flames, and it means even the entire village could not avert the disaster. The stream was quite distant away from the village. When water was fetched from the stream, some houses had already been burned down. The potential danger would undoubtedly affect the development of the village. During Yongle period of the Ming Dynasty the villagers invited He Keda, a scholar of Huizhou to survey the terrain and make a plan. They hoped the elderly scholar could remove the hidden danger of fire for them.

Accompanied by villagers, He Keda began to survey the terrain of setting of Hongcun village. He carefully examined the trend of the hills, especially, the direction of which the stream flowed. After 10 years' exploration, He Keda decided to divert the stream to the village and let it pass by every house.

According to He Keda's design, the villager dug a broad pond in the village. Traditionally, the local people believe that when flowers bloom, it begins to fade; when the moon reaches the full, it begins to wane, so they dug the pond into shape the half moon to imply that "flowers have not bloomed and the moon has not reached the full." The pond was named the Moon Pond. It stores water for the village and serves the place for women to get together. From the upper section of the stream flowing westwards in front of the hills, the villagers diverted the water southwards and then eastwards and the stream flowed by every house. The water flowed into the Moon Pond and ultimately entered the lower section of the stream. After the water was built, the villagers did washing in front of their houses, but a new problem occurred—when some villagers washed cloth in the upper section of the ditch, others obtain drinking water from the lower section. They claimed to discuss the matter and forced the regulation—the villager should obtain drinking water before 8 o'clock every morning, after that they were allowed to do washing in the ditch.

　　500 years have gone by. Today, the ditch in Hongcun village remains clear and transparent. It is really a miracle. The water system regulates the air and the environment around Hongcun village. The village is known far and wide for its beautiful living environment.

Step 1: Watch the video and write down the key words or phrases in the video. You may use the key words or phrases as the reminders when you watch it the second time.

_____
_____
_____
_____

Step 2: Watch the video again and decide whether the statements are True or False.
1. _____ Hongcun village took shape during the Southern Song Dynasty. The houses were closed to one another on a narrow strip of land far away from the stream which flowed in front of the hills.
2. _____ According to He Keda's design, the villager dug a broad pond which looked like a full moon in the village. The pond was named the Moon Pond.
3. _____ From the upper section of the stream flowing westwards in front of the hills, the villagers diverted the water southwards and then eastwards and the stream flowed into every house.
4. _____ The villagers made a rule that they could wash clothes before 8 o'clock every morning. After that they were not allowed to do washing in the ditch.

✿ Part V　Tour Commentary

Mt. Huangshan

　　Ladies and Gentlemen! Welcome to Mt. Huangshan! Well, to fully experience the beauty of Mt. Huangshan, you have to reach the peak areas. With the assistance of telphers, this is made much easier. The three telphers can take you to different peaks on Mt. Huangshan. Now, we'll take the Cloud Valley Telpher to reach the White Goose Ridge. From here you can visit the Shixin Peak, the Monkey Gazing at the Sea, the Refreshing Terrace and the Flying Stone and more.

Now, we've arrived at the White Goose Ridge. Look afar! What a magnificent landscape! The sun is shining brightly, but the cool wind is blowing. It is hard to resist the charm of the valleys and peaks covered with a green blanket. You can sit here and refresh yourself while enjoying the beautiful scenery with a cooling breeze to sooth you. Listen! Did you hear roaring of the waterfalls somewhere in the mountain? Numerous streams and waterfalls compose an exciting and vigorous symphony. Here the sea of clouds in summer is not as vast as in autumn or winter but it rivals its brightness. If you are really lucky today, you'll see a vivid rainbow flying over two peaks. Besides, sunset is no less enchanting than sunrise.

Everybody! We're heading for North Sea Scenic Area. It has plenty of wonders. Here you can watch three wonders of Mt. Huangshan except for hot springs. They are strange pines, absurd stones and sea of clouds. The North Sea is the most important scenic area. So we'll not miss it. There are a lot of intoxicating scenic spots here: the Shixin Peak, the Lion Peak, the Refreshing Terrace, the Monkey Gazing at the Sea, the Flying Stone and more. If you want to visit them all, you must stay here tonight.

Here we are at the Shixin Peak. It is said that only when you come to Shixin Peak that you will believe the magic of Mt. Huangshan. Look at the towering peak! When you view it from different angles, it presents varied shapes, for the peak is covered with grotesque stones with pines! In Mt. Huangshan the spectacular rocky peaks will inspire your imagination. Some look like human beings, some birds and other animals. Every stone has its own fantastic legend. There are one of four wonders on Mt. Huangshan-absurd stones. The Celestial Basking Boot is the most absurd rock and the story about it is most romantic. Later, I'll tell you the story when we go sightseeing in the Cloud Dispersing Pavilion of the West Sea Scenic Area.

Ladies and Gentlemen! Each of the four seasons on Mt. Huangshan has its respective beauty, but even this can change from day to day because of variations in the weather, light and shade. So please get ready for every moment of the constant changes of the landscape. Take pictures whenever you focus on them!

Have a short rest here. Enjoy!

Words and Expressions

assistance [ə'sɪstəns] n. 协助, 援助
resist [rɪ'zɪst] vt. 抵抗, 反抗
vigorous ['vɪgərəs] adj. 精力旺盛的, 有力的
enchanting [ɪn'tʃɑːntɪŋ] adj. 迷人的, 妩媚的
respective [rɪ'spektɪv] adj. 分别的, 各自的

telpher ['telfə] n. 缆车, 索道
blanket ['blæŋkɪt] n. 毯子
rainbow ['reɪnbəʊ] n. 彩虹; 幻觉
absurd [əb'sɜːd] adj. 荒谬的; 奇异的
variation [ˌveəri'eɪʃn] n. 变更, 变化, 变异

Proper Nouns

Mt. Huangshan 黄山
White Goose Ridge 白鹅岭
Monkey Gazing at the Sea 猴子观海
Flying Stone 飞来石
Celestial Basking Boot "仙人晒靴"
West Sea Scenic Area 西海风景区

Cloud Valley Telpher 云谷索道
Shixin Peak 始信峰
Refreshing Terrace 清凉台
North Sea Scenic Area 北海风景区
Cloud Dispersing Pavilion 排云亭

Exercise ➡ ➡ ➡

Directions: Act as the local guide and take tourists to hike in Mt. Huangshan. Try to make your introduction more situational and attractive using the proper body language.

Part VI   Readings

Directions: Read the following passage and fill in the blanks with the words or phrases given below.

back	execute	cultural	touching
best-preserved	piety	caring	order

Tangyue Memorial Archways

Tangyue Memorial Archways, a complex of seven arches, was listed as a key national (1)_____ protection unit under the approval of the State Council in 1996. Situated in Tangyue Village six kilometers west of the renowned Town of Arches—Shexian County, it is the biggest existing and (2)_____ complex of arches in Anhui Province.

The seven memorial archways were built by the Baos in honor of the merits and virtues of their family members. The seven archways stand in the main street of Tangyue Village in (3)_____ of "loyalty, filial piety, chastity and charity." Three were constructed in the Ming Dynasty (1368—1644), and the other four in the Qing Dynasty (1644—1911). The most ancient archway, which has a long history of over 580 years, can be traced (4)_____ to 1420 during the reign of Yongle in the Ming Dynasty. The latest one was built in 1820 in the reign of Jiaqing.

Behind every archway, there is a (5)_____ story. The Ci Xiao Li Archway was built in honor of Bao Yuyan and Bao Shouxun (father and son). According to historical records, the father and the son were captured by a general, who wanted to (6)_____ one of them. Bao Shouxun wanted to sacrifice his life to save his father, so he begged the general to behead him instead of his father. Whereas, the father was also a loving and (7)_____ father and wanted him to be executed rather than his son. Their action and love moved the general, who finally released them. Later, the court knew the fact and approved the construction of the archway in praise of their filial (8)_____ and self-sacrificial spirit.

Words and Expressions

renowned [rɪˈnaʊnd] *adj.* 著名的
chastity [ˈtʃæstəti] *n.* 忠节

filial [ˈfɪliəl] *adj.* 孝顺的
charity [ˈtʃærəti] *n.* 慈善, 仁义

Proper Nouns

Shexian County 歙县
Bao Yuyan 鲍余岩

Ci Xiao Li Archway 慈孝里坊
Bao Shouxun 鲍寿逊

Part VIII Translation

Ancient Street of Tunxi

1. At the foot of the Mt. Huangshan(黄山), in the bend of Xin'an River(新安江), lies the beautiful mountain town called "Tunxi"("屯溪").
2. The Ancient Street of Tunxi (屯溪老街)is located in the old city. The street starts in the west at Zhenhai Bridge(镇海桥), a stone arch bridge built during the Ming Dynasty, and ends in the east at the Memorial Archway(牌坊碑). Its total length is about 1.5km and the street is laid with slab stones(用石板铺成).
3. There are hundreds of old but well preserved rows of shops, evoking a bygone era in buildings that are simple and elegant(淡雅古朴). The shops, workshops and residences have continued to maintain the special layout of ancient stores such as shop in the front and workshop or house in the back(前店后坊、前店后户).
4. 屯溪老街多数房屋仅为三层, 具有鲜明的徽派(in the distinct Hui style)建筑特色: 白粉墙、小青瓦、雕梁画栋。
5. 老街是一条商业步行街(pedestrians)。安徽、江浙、福建的商人在此聚集, 摩肩接踵(jostle each other), 一派《清明上河图》("Picture of the Spring Festival along the River")的景象。
6. 一位西欧建筑家到老街时说, 在这里他找到了"东方古罗马"("the Eastern Ancient Rome")。

Unit 6

Touring Shandong

Focus on Learning 学习要点

导游案例	Rooms below the Contract Standard 客房低于合同标准
导游听力	1. Jinan City 济南市
	2. Dacheng Hall 大成殿
情景对话	Mt. Taishan 泰山
旅游视频	Qufu 曲阜
导游词	The Confucius Temple 孔庙
导游阅读	Qingdao City 青岛市
导游翻译	Mt. Taishan 泰山

 Part I　Tips for Tour Guides

Case 6

Rooms below the Contract Standard

The Japanese tourists checked in a small hotel in Qingdao, but they found the rooms were below the contract standard. They were so angry that they just stayed in the lobby and refused to take the key cards and enter the rooms. Miss He Xiaoyan, the local guide from Qingdo International Travel Service was at loss what to do with the tourists and the hotel. Listen to the passage and write down your suggestion.

(1) Miss He should negotiate with the manager of the hotel and demand that the rooms should _____ specified in the contract.

(2) If the manager of the hotel agrees that the double rooms replace _____ or pay some money as the settlement, Miss He should consult with _____ to see if they are willing to compromise.

(3) If the manager refuses to do an apology and pay compensation as a settlement, Miss He should lay out _____ and discuss them with the tour group to gain their support and cooperation.

(4) Miss He should lodge a claim against the hotel; meanwhile she should try to arrange another

hotel for the tourists after obtaining instructions _____.

Words and Expressions

below the contract standard 低于合同标准
single room 标准间
lodge a claim against 向……索赔
double room 套房
terms of compensation 赔偿条件

Exercise

Directions: Act as a local guide and the manager of the hotel. Make up a dialogue and role-play it according to the above situation. The teacher is expected to stress the main points and ask the role players to improve their presentation. Other students make comments and evaluate the settlement.

Part II Listening Activities

Listening 1

Jinan City

Words and Expressions

rectangular [rekˈtæŋgjələ(r)] *adj.* 矩形的，成直角的
thunderous [ˈθʌndərəs] *adj.* 打雷的，像打雷的
mellow [ˈmeləʊ] *adj.* 醇香的，甘美的
outlet [ˈaʊtlet] *n.* 出口，出路
spin [spɪn] *v.* 旋转，纺纱
paradise [ˈpærədaɪs] *n.* 天堂

Proper Nouns

Baotu Spring 趵突泉
Qufu 曲阜
Daming Lake 大明湖
Four-Door Pagoda 四门塔
Mt. Laoshan 崂山
Confucius Mansion 孔府
Mt. Taishan 泰山
Thousand-Buddha Mountain 千佛山
Lingyan Temple 灵岩寺
Spring and Autumn Annals《春秋》
Temple and Cemetery of Confucius 孔庙与孔墓

Exercise ➡ ➡ ➡

Directions: Listen to the passage and decide whether the statements are true or false. If it is true, put "T" in the space provided and "F" if it is false.

1. _____ Jinan is situated with Mt. Taishan in the west and the Yellow River in the north.
2. _____ "Black Tiger" is the name of the four best known of the 74 springs in Jinan.
3. _____ Because it is both pure in quality and mellow in taste, the natural spring water could be directly used for drinking.
4. _____ "Pearl" is the "First Spring under Heaven," a symbol of Jinan.
5. _____ Mt Taishan, the Temple and Cemetery of Confucius in Qufu were inscribed on the World Cultural and Natural Heritage List by UNESCO.

Listening 2

Words and Expressions

achievement [əˈtʃiːvmənt] n. 成就, 功绩　　coronet [ˈkɔrənit] n. 宝冠, 小冠冕
ribbon [ˈribən] n. 丝带, 带状物　　apotheosize [əpɒθiˈəʊsaɪz] vi. 神化, 封为神
sacrifice [ˈsækrɪfaɪs] n. 牺牲; 祭品

Proper Nouns

Bianzhong 编钟　　　　　　　　　Bianqing 编磬
Qin 磬　　　　　　　　　　　　　Se 瑟
Xiao 箫　　　　　　　　　　　　Sheng 笙
Xun 埙　　　　　　　　　　　　Drum 鼓
Dacheng Hall 大成殿　　　　　　Gui 圭板
"Most Holy and Perfect Master" "至圣先师"

Dacheng Hall

Dacheng Hall is the main hall of the Confucius Temple at (1)_____. This hall, (2)_____ meters is the highest building in the temple as well as one of the three largest (3)_____ in China. Dacheng means master with (4)_____, which truly describes Confucius. The statue of Confucius, located in the middle of the hall, is 3.35 meters tall. On his head is a coronet with (5)_____ and his "King's Clothes" have 12 decorative patterns. In his hands is a Gui. This shows that Confucius is apotheosized and that in the hearts of the rulers he is as great as (6)_____. In front of the Confucius statue, a memorial (7)_____ of "Most Holy and Perfect Master" is placed. On the sacrifice table are some sacrifice (8)_____, and in front of it pigs, cows and goats are placed. At the two sides are displayed the (9)_____: Bianzhong, Bianqing, Qin, Se, Xiao, Sheng, Xun, Drum and so on, which were used in (10)_____ service.

Exercise ➡ ➡ ➡

Directions: Listen to the passage and fill in the words or phrases you have heard.

Part III   Situational Dialogue

Mt. Taishan

(A=Miss Hu Di, a guide; B=Arthur)

A: Arthur, I'm happy to take you to hike in Mt. Taishan today. In China, there are five famous mountains, collectively called wu yue. Mt. Taishan is not the highest, but the most famous.

B: Why do you say so?

A: Since the Qin Dynasty, Mt. Taishan, as the royal object of cult, was the place where the emperors worshiped Heaven and Earth. Many historical figures also worshiped the mountain here and have left plenty of inscriptions and steles. Mt. Taishan symbolizes the Chinese Spirit. In China, we often use Mt. Taishan to glorify a person's devotion to the country.

B: Which emperors came to worship Heaven and Earth here?

A: Many of them. In 219 BC, the first emperor Qin Shihuang worshiped the God of mountain on Mt. Taishan. When he was halfway down from the mountain, it began to rain cats and dogs. He took shelter under the five pines. Later, he conferred them the titles of "Dafu," the so-called "Five Pines Pavilion." Since then, about 27 emperors in Chinese history came here to offer the sacrifice to God of the mountain.

B: I see. Mt. Taishan is an important holy mountain in China.

A: Arthur, here we're at the Dai Temple. And it was the first stop for the pilgrims on their way to the holy Mt. Taishan.

B: What a grant temple! The Temple, I believe, is more magnificent than the Temple of Heaven in Beijing.

A: I think so. The Dai Temple is the largest ancient building complex on Mt. Taishan. When you watch it from a long distance, you'll feel its grandiosity and magnificence; but when you take a closer view and you will feel astonished by its delicateness and stateliness.

B: I couldn't agree with you less.

A: Here is Tiankuang Hall (the Hall of Celestial Gifts). The hall is built in 1009 AD. It is one of the three palace-style architectures in China. Look at the portrait of God! It is a portrait of big size, 4.4 m high. Around the walls of the east, west and north is an enormous mural. It is 3 meters high and 62 meters long, named "the God of Mt. Taishan on an Inspection Tour."

B: Terrific. It is really a wonderful and grand scene of Mt. Taishan.

A: Well, you can have a rest in courtyard. The old cypress trees in the yard are very valuable.

Five of them were planted by Emperor Wudi himself during the Han Dynasty. After a short rest, we'll take you to visit the Bronze Pavilion. It just lies in the northeast corner of the temple. The pavilion is made of bronze castings and reputed as one of the famous bronze pavilions in China.

B: Ok. Thank you!

A: You're welcome.

Words and Expressions

glorify [ˈglɔːrɪfaɪ] v. 使更壮丽；赞扬
shelter [ˈʃeltə(r)] n. 避身处，庇护所
grandiosity [ˌɡrændəˈɒsɪti] n. 宏伟，堂皇
mural [ˈmjʊərəl] n. 壁画，壁饰

devotion [dɪˈvəʊʃn] n. 热爱，忠诚
confer [kənˈfɜː(r)] vt. 授予(称号、学位等)，赠与
delicateness [ˈdelɪkətnɪs] n. 精巧，精致
inspection [ɪnˈspekʃn] n. 视察，巡视

Proper Nouns

"Dafu" "大夫，"秦朝时的一种爵位   "Five Pines Pavilion" 五松亭
Dai Temple 岱庙   Tiankuang Hall (the Hall of Celestial Gifts) 天贶殿
Emperor Wudi 汉武帝   Bronze Pavilion 铜亭

Exercise ➡ ➡ ➡

Directions: Listen to the dialogue. Imagine that you are the local guide and your classmates are tourists. Do the dialogue again with additional information that the teacher may offer.

Part IV   Video for Tourism
旅游视频

Qufu

Words and Expressions

philosopher [fəˈlɒsəfə(r)] n. 哲学家
compete [kəmˈpiːt] v. 竞争
turbulent [ˈtɜːbjələnt] adj. 骚乱的
proliferation [prəˌlɪfəˈreɪʃn] n. 扩散

series [ˈsɪəriːz] n. 系列
warfare [ˈwɔːfeə] n. 战争；冲突
ensue [ɪnˈsjuː] v. 跟着发生
flourish [ˈflʌrɪʃ] v. 繁荣

pervade [pəˈveɪd] v. 遍及，弥漫
warrior [ˈwɒrɪə(r)] n. 战士，勇士
maid [meɪd] n. 少女

reenactment [riːɪˈnæktmənt] n. 再扮演
weaponry [ˈwepənri] n. 兵器，武器
zip [zɪp] v. 迅速地行动

Proper Nouns

Buddhism [ˈbʊdɪzəm] n. 佛教
Confucius 孔子
Spring and Autumn Period 春秋时期

Confucianism [kənˈfjuːʃənɪzm] n. 儒家思想，孔子学说

China would not be China today if it were not for one person, Confucius. He was a philosopher, a thinker, a teacher in the 6th century BC. And today, in our history and culture series, we are going to explore his hometown of Qufu. Welcome to the Travelogue, I'm Yin. Let's go.

Qufu in southwest Shandong Province was the capital of the Lu Kingdom during the Spring and Autumn Period from 770—476 BC. At that time, Lu Kingdom was just one of the competing 150 kingdoms. Constant warfare meant chaos throughout the land. However, turbulent times were ensued by philosophical proliferation, as the 5th and 6th centuries marked a period of learning around the world. Greek philosophies flourished, Buddhism was founded, and the roots of Confucianism were established in Qufu.

Don't think history is a thing of the past through. Today, the city is still pervaded with traces of the man. For tourists, the town of Qufu serves as a window into the philosophy that still governs Chinese lifestyle today.

It's not all peace and quiet here. Every weekend, a large ceremony is held to open up the gates of the ancient city, it's a reenactment of the past. Watch as the warriors stand tall with their weaponry. And you don't want to forget the palace maids that dance gracefully to traditional music. All this, combined with eager tourists, fills the air with pure excitement. Walk through the gates and zip back into the past.

Step 1: Watch the video and write down the key words or phrases in the video. You may use the key words or phrases as the reminders when you watch it the second time.

_____
_____
_____

Step 2: Watch the video again and decide whether the statements are True or False.

1. _____ China would not be China today if it were not for one person, Confucius. He was

a philosopher, a thinker rather than a teacher in the 6th century BC.

2. _____ Qufu in southwest Shandong Province was the capital of the Lu Kingdom, one of the 50 kingdoms, during the Spring and Autumn Period from 770—476 BC.

3. _____ For tourists, the town of Qufu serves as a window into the Confucianism that still exerts a great impact on Chinese lifestyle today.

4. _____ Every weekend, a large ceremony is held to open up the gates of the ancient city. It is a reenactment of the grand ceremony to commemorate Confucius.

Part V   Tour Commentary

The Confucius Temple

Ladies and Gentlemen!

Now, we're standing in front of the Confucius Temple. The temple is also called the Temple of the Supreme Saint, where people offer sacrifices to Confucius. The Confucius Temple, together with the Forbidden City in Beijing and the Summer Mountain Resort in Chengde of Hebei are called China's three great ancient building complexes. Among these three, the construction of the Confucius Temple enjoys the longest history. There are a lot of temples for Confucius all over the world, especially in Japan, South Korea and Vietnam, but the one in Qufu is the greatest of all.

Attention, please! Here is one stone stele you must see. On the steles writes "officials should dismount here." In the past civil and military officials and people in the street should dismount horses or sedan chairs and walk on foot when they passed by to show their respect for Confucius and his temple. So everybody of us should wear decent clothes. Don't wear slippers and put your hats on sidewise!

Now, here is the Ling Star Gate. This gate was erected in the Ming Dynasty and was rebuilt in 1754. The three characters were written by Emperor Qianlong. The legend has it that there are 28 constellations in the galaxy. The star in charge of culture is called "Ling Star" or "Wenqu Star." The ancient Chinese offered sacrifices to Ling Star before they did to Heaven. Why? Because they believed Confucius was the Ling Star and the reverence to Confucius was the same important as that to Heaven.

After we pass so many gates, halls and steles, we arrive at the Dacheng Hall. This is the main hall of the Confucius Temple. Dacheng means master with great achievement, which truly describes Confucius. Dacheng Hall, together with Supreme Harmony Hall in Beijing and Tiankuang Hall at Daimiao Temple in Tai'an City are called the three greatest halls in China or "the Three Greatest Halls in the East." The hall is surrounded by 28 dragon columns carved out of whole blocks of stone. The 10 dragon columns in front are outstanding. Carved on each column are two dragons twisting and flying. They are made true to life and three is no similarity between each other. The tablets preserved in the hall are those for the five saints and those for 12 sages. The one in the middle is Confucius. The grand ceremony will be held in front of the

Dacheng Hall to show people's respect to Confucius on his birthday which falls on 28th September.

My friends, the Confucius Temple is not only a grand and large history museum, but a sacred hall of arts. As a tour guide, I stroll along this temple every day. I have been thinking, but I still fail to get to the root of the connotation. I'm trying to compliment it with the most beautiful language and I always find myself at the end of the rope and my words always fail to convey my thought. From this respect we can see how great and profound Confucius and the Confucius Temple are, and this also reminds us that there is still much to learn. If you have something to discuss with me about Confucianism, I'm ready to learn from you.

Have a rest! We'll enjoy the commemoration performance here after fifteen minutes.

Words and Expressions

dismount [dɪsˈmaʊnt] v.(使)下马
reverence [ˈrevərəns] n. 尊严,威望
compliment [ˈkɒmplɪmənt] vt. 褒扬,恭维
decent [ˈdiːsnt] adj. 端庄的,有分寸的
connotation [ˌkɒnəˈteɪʃn] n. 含蓄,内涵
convey [kənˈveɪ] vt. 传达;转让

Proper Nouns

Temple of the Supreme Saint 至圣庙(孔庙)
Japan 日本
Vietnam 越南
"Wenqu star" "文曲星"
Daimiao Temple 岱庙
Hebei Province 河北省
South Korea 南朝鲜
Ling Star Gate 棂星门
Supreme Harmony Hall 太和殿
Tai'an City 泰安市

Exercise

Directions: Act as the local guide and take tourists to visit the Confucius Temple. Try to make your introduction more situational and attractive using the proper body language.

Part VI   Readings

Directions: Read the following passage and fill in the blanks with the words or phrases given below.

exhibits	away	water	visiting
freeze	convalescent	industries	

Qingdao City

Qingdao, surrounded on three sides by (1)_____, is a good deepwater port on Jiaozhou Bay of the Yellow Sea. It never silts up, nor does it (2)_____ in winter. With a history of only over eighty years, Qingdao has gradually set up its own textile, machine-building, food, chemical, shipbuilding, rubber and other modern (3)_____. A city with a nice climate all the year round and red-tiled villas spread out on rolling, forested hillside, it is among the nation's best tourist and (4)_____ resorts. Major scenic spots there include the Plank Bridge, Lu Xun Park and the Marine Products Museum, the quiet and secluded Zhongshan Park, the Qingdao Museum with a rich collection of (5)_____, a number of nice bathing beaches and the convalescent quarters of Badaguan tucked (6)_____ in greenwood. Especially noteworthy is Mt. Laoshan to the east of the city. As with all famous mountains, it has plenty of places worth (7)_____.

Words and Expressions

Jiaozhou Bay 胶州湾　　　　Yellow Sea 黄海
Plank Bridge 栈桥　　　　　Lu Xun Park 鲁迅公园
Marine Products Museum 海产博物馆　　Zhongshan Park 中山公园
Qingdao Museum 青岛博物馆　　Badaguan 八大关

Part VII　Translation

Mt. Taishan

1. Mt. Taishan is located in the center of Shandong Province spanning (跨越) the cities of Taian(泰安) and Jinan(济南), extending for total area of 250 kilometers.
2. It boasts of a wealth of natural legacies(自然遗产). A large number of scenic spots were given names since ancient times. They include 112 peaks, 98 precipitous ridges, 18 rock caves, 58 odd shaped rocks, 102 streams and valleys, 56 pools and waterfalls, 64 springs.
3. There are 989 species of plants falling into 114 families, and vegetation coverage (植被覆盖率) of 79.9 percent.
4. 泰山古称岱山(Daishan)，春秋时期被尊为(revered as)东岳(East Sacred Mountain)。其山势磅礴雄伟，峰峦突兀峻拔(abruptly rising)，景色壮丽。
5. 中国历代帝王秦始皇、汉武帝、唐玄宗、清帝乾隆等均曾到泰山封禅(hold grand sacrificial ceremonies)，历代72君主到此祭告天地(offer sacrifices to heaven and earth)。
6. 风景区拥有延续数千年的历史文化遗产。现有古建筑群22处，古遗址97处，历代碑碣(commemorative stone tablets)819块，历代刻石(inscribed rocks) 1800余处。

Unit 7

Touring Henan

Focus on Learning 学习要点

导游案例 Food and Dietary Change 饮食变化
导游听力 1. Zhengzhou City 郑州市
     2. Yellow River Scenic Area 黄河景区
情景对话 Longmen Grottoes 龙门石窟
旅游视频 Shaolin Temple 少林寺
导 游 词 Shaolin Temple 少林寺
导游阅读 Yin Ruins 殷墟
导游翻译 White Horse Temple 白马寺

 Part I Tips for Tour Guides

Case 7

Food and Dietary Change

  It is one o'clock in the afternoon. The tourists come down Mt. Songshan. They just take seats around the table to have the dinner when Mr. Mohammad and his wife propose that they'd like to change the dishes. As a local guide, how do you handle the case? Listen to the passage and fill in the blanks with the missing information.

(1) Generally speaking, restaurants could agree to change the dishes if _____ ahead of mealtime. In such a case, I shall accept their request.

(2) If the request is made just before mealtime, the restaurant may _____ since some of the dishes will have already been _____. In such a case, I would graciously decline the request and give explanations.

(3) However, I shall try my best to _____ if it is related to their religious practice or for health reasons. If they change the menu, _____, I shall tell them they should _____.

(4) I shall arrange _____ for them at the future meals.

Words and Expressions

menu 菜单
beverage 饮料
bear the expense 承担费用

Exercise

Directions: Imagine you are the local guide and your classmates are Mr. Mohammad and his wife. Make up a conversation among them. The teacher put forward more proposals to perfect the service. Other students make comments to see if they could improve their presentation.

Part II   Listening Activities

Listening 1

Zhengzhou City

Words and Expressions

hub [hʌb] n. 中心
jurisdiction [ˌdʒʊərɪsˈdɪkʃn] n. 权限,管辖
observatory [əbˈzɜːvətrɪ] n. 天文台,气象台
masonry [ˈmeɪsənri] n. 石工;石匠职业

sanctuary [ˈsæŋktʃʊərɪ] n. 圣殿,圣地
martial [ˈmɑːʃəl] adj. 军事的,威武的
inscription [ɪnˈskrɪpʃn] n. 题字,碑铭

Proper Nouns

Monument to February 7 Workers' Uprising "二七"工人起义(大罢工)纪念碑
Zhengzhou City 郑州
Guangzhou City 广州市
Lanzhou City 兰州市
Lianyungang City 连云港
Dengfeng 登封
Mt. Songshan 嵩山
Shaolin Temple 少林寺

Taishi Mountain 太室山
Shaoshi Mountain 少室山
Songyue Temple 嵩岳寺
Songyang Academy 嵩阳书院
Northern Wei 北魏
Zen Sect 禅,禅宗(中国佛教宗派)
Gongyi 巩义
Xinzheng City 新郑市

Exercise ➡ ➡ ➡

Directions: Listen to the passage and decide whether the statements are true or false. If it is true, put "T" in the space provided and "F" if it is false.

1. _____ Zhengzhou, capital of Henan Province, is a major railway hub.
2. _____ Mt. Songshan is a holy mountain in north China.
3. _____ The. Songyang Academy is one of the four major academies in ancient China.
4. _____ The Shaolin Temple has made a name for itself for its martial arts, but stone inscriptions of various dynasties, and Ming-dynasty murals are not popular.
5. _____ Xinzheng, a city 40 km south of Zhengzhou, is the native place of the Jade Emperor.

Listening 2

Words and Expressions

aim [eɪm] vt. 瞄准,对准,打算
irrigation [ˌɪrɪˈɡeɪʃn] n. 灌溉,冲洗
enhance [ɪnˈhɑːns] vt. 提高,增强

Proper Nouns

Yellow River Scenic Area 黄河风景区
Mt. Guangwushan 光雾山
Mt. Wulongfeng 五龙峰
Xiang Yu 项羽
Battlefield of King Liu Bang and King Xiang Yu 汉霸二王城(公元前203年刘邦、项羽楚汉争雄时的古战场)
Mt. Yueshan 岳山
Yueshan Temple 岳山寺
Liu Bang 刘邦
Huayuankou 花园口

Yellow River Scenic Area

Yellow River Scenic Area is located in (1)_____ section of Mt. Yueshan, 27 kilometers to the northwest of Zhengzhou City. It covers an area of about (2)_____ square kilometers with Mt. Yueshan and Mt. Guangwushan as its center. About (3)_____, there is still a wilderness. In (4)_____, aiming to solve the problem of water supply and (5)_____, a water project was launched by the government and was completed two years later. After that, another (6)_____ was spent in building a scenic area to (7)_____ the culture of the Yellow River. Cultural scenic spots include Yueshan Temple, Mt. Wulongfeng, Battlefield of King Liu Bang and King Xiang Yu, Huayuankou Scenic Zone and etc, which are different in (8)_____, but reveal the same (9)_____ of the Yellow River culture.

Exercise ➡ ➡ ➡

Directions: Listen to the passage and fill in the words or phrases you have heard.

 Part III   Situational Dialogue

Longmen Grottoes

(A=Miss Li Lei, a guide; B=Joe)

A: OK, let's enter in the Fengxian Temple!

B: It seems this is a very huge cave.

A: Yes, it is the largest cave in Longmen Grottoes. It is 35 meters wide and 39 meters long.

C: Is this cave very old like any others in Longmen?

A: Yes, of course. This cave was carved over 1,300 years ago. When it was first constructed, the entire grotto was covered with a roof. Today the roof is missing and the sculptures stand out in the open air.

B: What's the Buddha carved here in the middle?

A: It's Grand Vairocanna Buddha. The whole sculpture is 17.1 meters tall. Only its head is as long as 4 meters! Please look at her face carefully. She wears a mysterious complexion. Well, Joe, could you please describe her in your own words? I know you're majored in English language and literature.

B: Let me see. This colossal Buddha shows a perfect combination of moral integrity, delicate emotions, broad mind and elegant semblance. Her lips are slightly upturned while her head a little bit lowered; a slight smile makes her look like a sagacious middle-aged woman.

A: Thank you very much, Joe. Your description is so vivid and detailed. It is said that the statue was modeled after the face of Empress Wu Zetian of the Tang Dynasty, so people also call it Empress Wu Zetian's Statue. Also because of her gentler facial expression, this statue is reputed as the "Eastern Mona Lisa," the "Eastern Venus," and the "Mother of China."

C: Fantastic! I think she is more beautiful than Venus.

A: In this cave there are other statues. On each side, the Buddha is flanked by an Ananda, a Bodhisattva, a Heavenly King and a Vajra. Look at the Heavenly King! He stands on a ghost with the Divine Pagoda in his hand.

B: I'm very impressed by his posture. You see, each of them has their distinct expressions. The Bodhisattva looks dignified while the Vajra looks ferocious. I believe they are masterpieces in the world. I'm so sorry I am not allowed to take photos in the cave.

A: What a pity! Longmen Grottoes was listed by UNESCO as a World Cultural Heritage Site in 2000. You may buy a CD of the Grottos in the shop instead.

A: All right.

Words and Expressions

complexion [kəmˈplekʃn] n. 面色,肤色
sagacious [səˈɡeɪʃəs] adj. 有远见的,精明的
emotion [ɪˈməʊʃn] n. 情绪,情感,感情
semblance [ˈsembləns] n. 外表,外貌

colossal [kəˈlɒsl] adj. 巨大的,庞大的
integrity [ɪnˈteɡrəti] n. 正直;完整性
ferocious [fəˈrəʊʃəs] adj. 残忍的,凶猛的
upturned [ʌpˈtɜːnd] adj. 朝上的,翻过来的

Proper Nouns

Longmen Grottoes 龙门石窟
Bodhisattva [ˌbəʊdiˈsætvə] n. 菩萨
Ananda 阿难(释迦牟尼的弟子)
Heavenly King 天王
Vajra 金刚
Divine Pagoda 神塔

"Eastern Venus" "东方的维纳斯"
Fengxian Temple 奉先寺
Grand Vairocanna Buddha 卢舍那大佛
Empress Wu Zetian 武则天女皇
"Eastern Mona Lisa" "东方的蒙娜丽莎"

Exercise ➡ ➡ ➡

Directions: Listen to the dialogue. Imagine that you are the local guide and your classmates are tourists. Do the dialogue again with additional information that the teacher may offer.

 Part IV   Video for Tourism
旅游视频

Shaolin Temple 少林寺

Words and Expressions

warrior-monk n. 武僧
formidable [ˈfɔːmɪdəbl] adj. 庞大的
novice [ˈnɒvɪs] n. 学徒,新手
captivate [ˈkæptɪveɪt] vt. 迷住
kungfu [kʌnˈfuː] 功夫

dazzling [ˈdæzl] adj. 眼花缭乱的
legacy [ˈleɡəsi] n. 遗产
evoke [ɪˈvəʊk] v. 唤起
regime [reɪˈʒiːm] n. 政权;管理体制
drill sergeant 武僧教练

Proper Nouns	
Shaolin Temple 少林寺	Yan Xiu 严修

Shaolin Temple, home of the ancient sect of warrior-monks, proud defenders of a thousand-year-old tradition until now. Today, a new generation is re-inventing Shaolin Temple, as the kungfu monks take on the challenges like none of them.

The Kungfu monks of Shaolin Temple, for more than a thousand years, they protected Chinese emperors and defended their nation with their dazzling fighting skills. A formidable legacy, and a lot to live up to. If you are only ten years old, welcome to boot camp—Shaolin style.

"Two hands on the foot, strengthen the body." This is Lu Zhenzhong, one of Shaolin youngest novice monks. Zhenzhong lived to his parents in Fujian Province, until he was selected for a place at the temple; that was a year ago. Since then he's lived in the Shaolin Temple. With more than 40 other novice monks, all of them had been picked from the kungfu schools all over China, training 3 hours in the morning, 2 and half hours in the afternoon, 365 days a year, always under the watchful eye of Yan Xiu, Shaolin's drill sergeant, "Keep your feet straight," his job to turn these kids into real kungfu monks.

"Keep your back straight! Kick properly! Hurry up! Hurry up! Faster! Faster! Faster!"

The Chinese words kungfu evokes honor and glory, but translating to English, simply as "hard work." It's a punishing regime, even for these boys—the best of the best. That's why Shaolin calls these novices the hopefuls. Back home each of these boys was a star, but now they are all competing with each other. Each hoping he will be one of the few who eventually get what they come here for—a place on the A team. Shaolin performance teams travel the world, captivate the audience with the dazzling Kungfu displays.

Step 1: Watch the video and write down the key words or phrases in the video. You may use the key words or phrases as the reminders when you watch it the second time.

_____
_____
_____
_____

Step 2: Watch the video again and decide whether the statements are True or False.
1. _____ The kungfu monks of Shaolin Temple protected Chinese emperors and defended their nation with the dazzling fighting skills since ancient times.
2. _____ All of them had been picked from the sports schools all over China, training 3 hours in the morning, 2 and half hours in the afternoon, 365 days a year.
3. _____ The Chinese words kungfu evokes honor and glory, but simply means "hard work" in the foreigners' eyes.

4. _____ Back home each of these boys was a star, but now they are all competing with each other, hoping that he would become the best of the best monks.

Part V Tour Commentary

Shaolin Temple

Ladies and Gentlemen! Welcome to the world-famous Shaolin Temple!

Look, this is the Shanmen, the mountain entrance to the temple. It is a three-section architecture with single eaves. A stone staircase leads up to the gate that is flanked by a pair of marble lion statues. On the lintel of the gate hangs a plaque bearing Shao Lin Si in Chinese characters. They are the handwritten work by Emperor Kangxi of the Qing Dynasty. After you enter the gate, you will see the statue of the smiling pot-bellied Maitreya. On each side of the main path are flanked by a dozen of stone tablets that are erected by foreign monks who have completed their studies in the temple.

Here we come to the Hall of Heavenly Kings. There stands two sculptured fierce looking guardian, known as Generals Heng and Ha. According to the legend, whenever they fight, they would win by shouting the sounds of "heng" and "ha." Later, the Shaolin monks shout "heng" and "ha" while they practice martial arts.

Now, we've arrived at the major structure of the temple—Hall of Sakyamuni Buddha. In the hall are enshrined three famous figures of Buddhism, who are in control of three different worlds in terms of space and time. The one on the left is dedicated to Amitabha, the supreme ruler of the Land of Ultimate Bliss. According to Buddhist sutras, this world is full of beautiful scenery and melodic music. The one on the right is the Bhaisajya-guru. He lives in the Eastern Pure Crystal Land. It is said that people living there are free of all kinds of illness. The statue situated in the center is dedicated to Sakyamuni, the ruler of the present world of Saha. Flanking these three statues are sculptures dedicated to 18 Arhats.

Well, we come to the Abbots' Room. Who is enshrined in the center of the room? Right, he is just the Bodhidharma, the founder of the Zen Sect. Bodhidharma reached the Shaolin Temple in 527 and settled down. With his face against the wall, he sat alone in meditation for nine years in a natural stone cave in the back of the temple. As a result, the shadow of his face and body was imprinted on the wall. No wonder people call it the Stone for Facing the Wall. This founder of the Zen Sect developed a set of "Arhat boxing" in an effort to relax himself after prolonged sitting in meditation. Later, his disciples perfected this school of Chinese boxing and made it a must for every monk. In this sense, the Shaolin Temple is also known as a place famous for its martial arts, in addition to the Cradle of Zen Sect.

Ladies and Gentlemen! We haven't visited all the sites of the Shaolin Temple, yet you have seen the essence of the temple. To sum up, it may be said that this temple is famous for four reasons: first, it is the cradle of Zen Sect of Buddhism; second, it is the Shaolin School of Chinese Boxing; third, it is a treasure house full of cultural and religious relics; last but not the least, it is one of the major tourist sites in China which attracts tourists from all over the world.

Now, it's time for a rest. Thank you for your attention.

Words and Expressions

eaves [iːvz] n. 屋檐
pot-bellied ['pɒtˌbelɪd] adj. 大腹便便的
plaque [plæk] n. 匾额, 铭碑
meditation [ˌmedɪ'teɪʃn] n. 沉思, 冥想
disciple [dɪ'saɪpl] n. 弟子, 门徒

staircase ['steəkeɪs] n. 楼梯, 阶梯
erect [ɪ'rekt] vt. 使竖立, 建立
dedicate ['dedɪkeɪt] vt. 献(身), 致力
renovate ['renəveɪt] vt. 革新, 修复
shanmen 山门

Proper Nouns

Bodhidharma ['bəudi'dʌrmə] 菩提达摩
(印度僧人, 中国佛教禅宗的始祖)
Hall of Heavenly Kings 天王殿
Generals Heng and Ha 哼哈二将
Daxiong Baodian (Hall of Sakyamuni Buddha)
　大雄宝殿
Bhaisajya-guru 药师佛

Arhat ['ɑːhət] n. [宗]阿罗汉
Amitabha 阿弥陀佛
Eastern Pure Crystal Land "东方净土琉璃世界"
World of Saha 娑婆世界
"Arhat boxing" "罗汉拳"
Land of Ultimate Bliss "西方极乐世界"

Exercise ➡ ➡ ➡

Directions: Act as the local guide and take tourists to visit the Shaolin Temple. Try to make your introduction more situational and attractive using the proper body language.

Part VI Readings

Directions: Read the following passage and fill in the blanks with the words or phrases given below.

topped	written	historical
excavated	unveiled	capital

Yin Ruins

In 1899, in Anyang City, Henan Province, people found many tortoise shells and bones carved with letters and symbols, which (1)_____ to the world Yin Ruins, an ancient city with a long history and splendid culture. Since then this place has become great interest to worldwide archeologists, because those inscriptions have proved to be the earliest (2)_____ characters of human beings, the Oracles.

About 3,300 years ago, one king of the Shang Dynasty (16th—11th century BC) moved his capital city to Yin, which is today's Anyang City, and since then Yin has been the (3)_____ city for more than 250 years. Today Yin Ruins has proved to be the earliest remains of an ancient capital city in written record.

The large-scale excavation in Yin Ruins has been continued since the last century. Besides the 150,000 pieces of oracles, abundant bronze ware has been (4)_____, and among them, Simuwu Ding, a 4-legged bronze cooking vessel is the biggest and heaviest bronze ware ever found worldwide. Apart from oracles and bronze ware, people have also excavated much pottery ware and jade.

Because of its great value in not only the (5)_____ relics of Chinese culture but also the human civilization of the whole world, Yin Ruins (6)_____ the 100 Greatest Archeological Discoveries of China in the last century and it is now working on being included in the World Cultural Heritage List of UNESCO. Yin Ruins is revealing its beauty to the world.

Words and Expressions

splendid ['splendɪd] adj. 灿烂的
excavate ['ekskəveɪt] v. 挖掘, 开凿
vessel ['vesl] n. 容器, 器皿

inscription [ɪn'skrɪpʃn] n. 铭文
abundant [ə'bʌndənt] adj. 丰富的
heritage ['herɪtɪdʒ] n. 遗产

Proper Nouns

Anyang City 安阳市
Oracles 甲骨文
UNESCO 联合国教科文组织

Simuwu Ding 司母戊鼎
World Cultural Heritage List 世界文化遗产名录

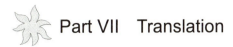
Part VII Translation

White Horse Temple

1. Located 13 kilometers to the east of Luoyang City (洛阳市), the White Horse Temple (白马寺), secluded and elegant, was built with red walls and green tiles(红墙绿瓦).
2. Built in the Eastern Han Dynasty (东汉)over 1,900 years ago, it was originally the place where Liu Zhuang(刘庄), the second emperor of that time, used as a summer resort and study.
3. In the year when two venerable Indian monk brought Buddhist scriptures (佛经)to Luoyang on the back of white horses to preach Buddhism(传教), Liu Zhuang, a devout believer in Buddhism, built the first government-run temple (官办寺院) in China and called it White Horse Temple.
4. 白马寺曾是中国最大的菩提道场(sanctuary for Buddhist rituals)，据说寺内最多有僧人数千。继两位高僧(venerable monks)之后，陆续又有许多西域(the Western Regions)僧侣来到洛阳。
5. 唐代，洛阳玄奘(Xuan Zang)赴西域求法取经(go on a pilgrimage for Buddhist scriptures)，回国后就在白马寺主持佛教、传经讲学(preach the Buddhist scriptures)。
6. 白马寺，令人萦怀的千年古刹(ancient temple)！

Unit 8

Touring Hunan

Focus on Learning 学习要点

导游案例　Shopping 旅游购物
导游听力　1. Changsha City 长沙市
　　　　　2. Tourist Sites in Hunan 湖南旅游景点
情景对话　A Splendid Tour of Hunan 锦绣湖南游
旅游视频　Zhangjiajie 张家界
导 游 词　Dongting Lake 洞庭湖
导游阅读　Phoenix Town 凤凰城
导游翻译　Yueyang Tower 岳阳楼

 Part I　Tips for Tour Guides

Case 8

Shopping

The Japanese and Korean tourists always have a great interest in the Chinese antiques and traditional Chinese medicine. Now it is time to go shopping in the downtown area of Yueyang City. What could you suggest as a local guide? Listen to the passage and write down your suggestion in the blanks.

(1) First, I shall take the tour group to go shopping only at those shops _____. I shall not add extra shops or _____.

(2) If they want to purchase antiques, I shall inform them to keep _____ for the customs check on departure from China. Antique shops will provide such documentation; antiques sold by peddlers usually do not have _____, and may not be taken out of China.

(3) If they want to buy traditional Chinese medicine, I shall recommend _____ to them. I shall inform them of the limit of traditional Chinese medicine one can take out of China for personal use. Some products such as musk, rhinoceros horns and tiger bones are _____.

(4) I shall not buy or _____ for my tourists. If it is impossible to say "no," I shall first report to the manager of my travel agency. After getting approval, I may _____ from my tourists to purchase and deliver the goods. Both the tourists and I should keep _____.

Words and Expressions

go shopping 购物　　　　　　　　antique shop 文物店,古董店
shopping time 购物时间　　　　　traditional Chinese medicine 中医

Exercise

Directions: Act as the local guide showing the tourists around the downtown area of Yueyang City. Make up a dialogue between the guide and the tourists and act it out in the class. Other students are expected to make comments to see if they could improve their presentation.

Part II Listening Activities

Listening 1

Changsha City

Words and Expressions

eye-catching [ˈaɪˌkætʃɪŋ] adj. 引人注目的,耀眼的　　furnish [ˈfɜːnɪʃ] vt. 供应,提供,布置
prefecture [ˈpriːfektʃə(r)] n. 辖区,郡　　　　　　　valuable [ˈvæljuəbl] adj. 贵重的
file [faɪl] n. 文件,档案　　　　　　　　　　　　　poise [pɔɪz] vt. 保持……姿势

Proper Nouns

Changsha 长沙　　　　　　　　　Zhoumalou 走马楼
Yuelu Academy 岳麓书院　　　　　Yueyang City 岳阳市
Mawangdui 马王堆　　　　　　　 Tianxing Pavilion 天兴阁
Sun Quan 孙权

Exercise ➡ ➡ ➡

Directions: Listen to the passage and decide whether the statements are true or false. If it is true, put "T" in the space provided and "F" if it is false.

1. _____ Hunan Embroidery Institute is one of the major tourist attractions in Hunan.
2. _____ Yuelu Academy at the foot of Yuelu Mountain in east Changsha, is China's earliest government-funded institution of higher learning.
3. _____ Han Tombs at Mawangdui achieved world fame overnight in the 1960s.
4. _____ A total of 700,000 bamboo slips were excavated from Zhoumalou, Changsha, in December 1996.
5. _____ Poised atop Yueyang's 30-metre-high ancient city wall, Tianxing Pavilion provides an overview of the entire city.

Listening 2

Words and Expressions

reconstruction [ˌriːkənˈstrʌkʃn] *n.* 重建, 改造　contrast [ˈkɒntrɑːst] *vi.* 和……形成对照
establish [ɪˈstæblɪʃ] *vt.* 建立, 设立, 安置　　serene [səˈriːn] *adj.* 平静的
steep [stiːp] *adj.* 陡峭的, 险峻的

Proper Nouns

Hunan Province 湖南省　　　　　　　　　Mt. Hengshan 衡山
Dongting Lake 洞庭湖　　　　　　　　　　Yuanjiang River 沅江
Yueyang Pavilion 岳阳楼　　　　　　　　　*Peach Blossom Fountainhead*《桃花源记》
Zhangjiajie National Forest Park 张家界国家森林公园

Tourist Sites in Hunan

Hunan is popular for its abundant landscapes and historical interests. Dongting Lake is the (1)_____ largest lake in China. Yueyang City, located on the shore of Dongting Lake, is home to one of China's three famous (2)_____. Yueyang Pavilion was (3)_____ built during the Tang Dynasty. The present pavilion is the work of recent reconstruction, built in (4)_____ of the Song Dynasty. (5)_____ National Forest Park was established in a particular scenic area in northwest Hunan. The park is especially known for its quartz-sandstone rock (6)_____, bare stones sculpted by Nature and set among green trees and frequent clouds. The high and steep (7)_____ is frequently snow-capped in the winter, (8)_____ with the subtropical fields that one sees below it. It is one of the five most famous mountains in China. The region along the Yuanjiang River is especially well known for (9)_____. It takes its name, *The Peach Blossom Fountainhead*, from a work of Chinese literature from the Jin Dynasty. The Yuanjiang River Region has been a (10)_____ since ancient times.

Exercise

Directions: Listen to the passage and fill in the words or phrases you have heard.

Part III Situational Dialogue

A Splendid Tour of Hunan

(A=Miss Li Ren, a manager of travel service; B=Brian)

A: Good morning, sir! What can I do for you?

B: I've just arrived at Changsha from England. I want to travel around Hunan.

A: Well, there are a lot of tourist sites in Hunan. First, I suggest you visit the Hunan Provincial Museum. There you can see a lot of the unearthed relics and better understand the culture of Hunan Province.

B: What can I see there?

A: The museum contains a collection of more than 110,000 objects, including 763 pieces of first class cultural relics. Among all these collections, the relics from Mawangdui Han Tomb are most excellent and miraculous.

B: I've heard of that. What were found in the tombs?

A: Three tombs of the Western Han Dynasty were unearthed in 1972 and open to the public later. The Tomb of Xin Zhui, Li Cang's wife, was the most famous. Countless elegant and elaborate objects such as trappings and decorations were found in her tomb. Of these objects, a T-shaped silk picture, supposedly a banner for the soul is the most fascinating.

B: Where can I enjoy the landscape in Hunan?

A: Mt. Hengshan is one of the five most famous mountains in China, a holy mountain for both Taoists and Buddhists. It is frequently snow-capped in the winter, contrasting with the subtropical fields you can see below it. A fantastic landscape, isn't it?

B: Any other famous landscapes in Hunan?

A: Then, you may go sightseeing in the Zhangjiajie National Forest Park. It is especially known for its quartz-sandstone rock formations, bare stone sculpted by Nature and set among green trees and frequent clouds.

B: I also want to watch the waterscape. Can you recommend any beautiful waterscapes?

A: I'm very proud of the waterscape in my hometown. The Dongting Lake is the second largest fresh lake in China. Yueyang Pavilion, located on the shore of Dongting Lake, is one of China's three famous towers.

B: I heard there was a Chinese Utopia somewhere in Hunan. I also want to pay a visit.

A: The Yuanjiang River Region has been a tourist destination since ancient times. It takes its name, *The Peach Blossom Fountainhead*, from a work of Chinese literature from the Jin Dynasty. Tao Yuanming wrote about an isolated Utopia-like paradise where people had escaped from hustle and bustle of the world.

B: Terrific! I must visit the Utopia in China. Can you offer me a four-day travel package?

A: All right. Wait a moment! I'll offer you the travel schedule and our quotation.

B: Thank you!

Words and Expressions

trappings [ˈtræpɪŋz] *n.* 服饰,马饰　　miraculous [mɪˈrækjələs] *adj.* 奇迹的,不可思议的
subtropical [ˌsʌbˈtrɒpɪkl] *adj.* 亚热带的　Utopia [juːˈtəʊpɪə] *n.* 乌托邦,理想的完美境界
quotation [kwəʊˈteɪʃn] *n.* 价格,行情表

Proper Nouns

Hunan Provincial Museum 湖南省博物馆　　Mawangdui Han Tomb 马王堆汉墓
Western Han Dynasty 西汉　　　　　　　　Xin Zhui 辛追
Li Cang 利仓(西汉初期长沙国丞相)　　　　Tao Yuanming 陶渊明

Exercise ➡ ➡ ➡

Directions: Listen to the dialogue. Imagine that you are the local guide and your classmates are tourists. Do the dialogue again with additional information that the teacher may offer.

Part IV　Video for Tourism
旅游视频

Zhangjiajie

Words and Expressions

immortal [ɪˈmɔːtl] *n.* 神仙　　　　　　　secluded [sɪˈkluːdɪd] *adj.* 隐居的
derive [dɪˈraɪv] *v.* 源于　　　　　　　　consulate [ˈkɒnsjələt] *n.* 谋士

exuberant [ɪgˈzjuːbərənt] *adj.* 生气勃勃的
spectator [spekˈteɪtə] *n.* 观众
designate [ˈdezɪgneɪt] *v.* 指定
quartzite [ˈkwɔːtsaɪt] *n.* 石英岩，硅岩
erode [ɪˈrəʊd] *v.* 腐蚀，侵蚀

primitive [ˈprɪmətɪv] *adj.* 原始的
landscape [ˈlændskeɪp] *n.* 风景
patch [pætʃ] *n.* 小块土地
pillar [ˈpɪlə(r)] *n.* 柱子，柱形物

Proper Nouns

Wulinyuan Scenic Area 武林源风景区
Tianzi Mountain Natural Reserve
　天子山自然保护区
World Geological Park 世界地质公园
Tianmen Mountain 天门山
Suoxiyu Natural Reserve 索溪峪自然保护区
UNESCO 联合国教科文组织
World Heritage Site 世界遗产地
Cathaysian Tectonic System [地质] 华夏构造体系
Gui Guzi 鬼谷子，姓王名诩，春秋战国时期卫国
(今河南鹤壁市淇县)人

　　The ancient Chinese believed that immortal and masters always lived secluded in high mountains and the forests because they derived strength and wisdom from the nature. Zhang Liang, consulate of the first emperor of Han Dynasty, 202BC to 9AD, lived secluded in the mountain area after he helped the emperor establish the empire. From then on, the place where he secluded himself was named Zhangjiajie, which means Zhang Family homeland.

　　Zhangjiajie is located in northwest of Hunan, a province south of the Yangzi River in China. The main tourists' draw in Zhangjiajie is the Wulinyuan Scenic Area, which contains three major areas: Zhangjiajie National Park, Suoxiyu Natural Reserve and Tianzi Mountain Natural Reserve, with the total area of 350 square kilometers. It is covered with hundreds of peaks, clear streams, deep valleys, exuberant forests and fantastic caves which have formed a complete primitive ecological environment. With the changes of seasons and the weather, they constantly present different views to spectators. It is honored as the most fantastic mountain under heaven and a living Chinese landscape painting. In 1992, Wulinyuan Scenic Area in Zhangjiajie has been designated in the UNESCO World Heritage Site. In the year 2004, it was awarded the title of World Geological Park.

　　The unique and beautiful landscape makes Zhangjiajie to become the paradise of photographers and tourists from home and abroad. Normally it takes two days to explore Wulinyuan Scenic Area. Since the scenic area is large and spots are far from each other, public shuttle buses inside the park are provided to connect sights. Cable cars help tourists to reach the summit easily. The longest outdoor elevator in the world was built in 2002 from root to the top of the mountain. It takes two minutes to bring people up to 322.6 meters' high.

　　The pass of ring road on the mountain leads the tourists to view points where they can catch beautiful sights of peaks. The geological formation of Zhangjiajie belongs to the new Cathaysian Tectonic System. About three billion years ago, this place was a large patch of ocean. After a serious of geological changes, the bottom of ocean rose out of the surface, and the quartzite sandstone pillars and peaks took shape after the gradual cutting, eroding and crumbling of nature for millions of years.

A part from Wulinyuan, Tianmen Mountain in Zhangjiajie City is another highlight which is regarded as the symbol and soul of the city. The mountain is named after the natural huge cave half way up the mountain just like the gate to the heaven. The longest passenger cable way in the world, with the length of 7,455 meters, takes about 25 minutes, to lead tourists to the top of the mountain.

After that, people can hike a breath-taking live walk along the 1.5 kilometers of plank road, which is built in cliff at the side of the mountain. When people look back, they can find a cave on the cliff. The legend said that Gui Guzi, an ancient philosopher and master of statesman, a military strategist in Warrior States Period, 403 BC to 221 BC, lived inside the cave for a period of reflection. The master then vanished like the wind, just like he never existed here, but his thought and work remained to help people to understand the basic rule of the world.

Travel with China highlights, we are pleased to share with you the fairyland which is full of legend and stories.

Step 1: Watch the video and write down the key words or phrases in the video. You may use the key words or phrases as the reminders when you watch it the second time.

_____
_____
_____
_____

Step 2: Watch the video again and decide whether the statements are True or False.
1. _____ The place where Zhang Liang lived secluded after he helped the first emperor of the Han Dynasty establish the empire was named Zhangjiajie, which means Zhang Family homeland.
2. _____ It was a large patch of ocean millions of years ago where the bottom of ocean rose out of the surface, and the quartzite sandstone pillars and peaks took shape.
3. _____ Tianmen Mountain is named after the natural huge cave half way up the mountain just like the gate to the heaven.
4. _____ Zhangjiajie is honored as the most fantastic mountain under heaven and a living Chinese landscape painting designated in the UNESCO World Heritage Site.

Part V Tour Commentary

Dongting Lake

Ladies and Gentlemen! Welcome to the Dongting Lake!

Dongting Lake is China's second-largest freshwater lake. It is also known as "eight-hundred Li Dongting Lake." The Li is a Chinese length unit equal to 500 meters. An impressive characteristic of the Lake is its vastness of water and varieties of waterfowl. As the seasons change, concentric ridges of land appear in the lake in many areas. This is because the lake acts as a flood basin for the Yangtze River. The appearance of Dongting Lake changes throughout the different seasons, sometimes even change during the same day.

Ladies and Gentlemen! Dongting Lake is divided into 5 parts: East Dongting Lake, South Dongting Lake, West Dongting Lake, North Dongting Lake, and Datong Lake. Now, we're traveling on the East Dongting Lake. It is the biggest part of the Dongting Lake. The area around the lake has tremendous agricultural production ability with a long history of development. Since the plain is graced with fertile soil, proper temperature and plentiful rain, Dongting Lake is also called "a land flowing with milk and honey."

Look, a row of water ducks are fluttering over the lake. There are abundant animals and plant lives, especially birds and waterfowl here. According to scientists, there are 1,086 kinds of plants, 114 kinds of fresh water fish, and 207 kinds of birds living in the district, and the total number of animals and birds reaches 10 million every year. The large water area, beach, and rich natural resources here provide protected living conditions for many animals that are in danger of extinction. East Dongting Lake is recognized as "a zoology pearl on the middle part of the Yangtze River," and "a hopeful place to save the animals in danger."

Now, we're approaching the Junshan. In fact, Junshan is not a mountain, but an island on the Dongting Lake. The original name of the Junshan Island was Dongting Island, which means the cavity for the immortals to live in. It is said that 4,000 years ago, after Emperor Shun went south to go on a tour of inspection, two of his concubines tried to find him but failed. They began to cry while they grasped bamboo. Their tears dropped onto the bamboo, and the bamboo became mottled from then on. After they died, people built a tomb for them, which is called "two concubines' tomb." To commemorate them, people changed the name of the island from Dongting Island to Junshan Island. The bamboo on the island is well known for its many varieties such as mottled bamboo, arhat bamboo, square bamboo, sincere bamboo, and purple bamboo.

As we're talking about Junshan, it comes into our sight. After 20 minutes, we'll watch the dragon boat race. It is a traditional festivity performance to commemorate a Chinese patriotic poet named Qu Yuan more than 2,000 years ago. Qu Yuan tried to warn the emperor of an increasingly corrupt government, but he failed. In a last desperate protest, he threw himself into the river and drowned. At the news of the poet's death, the local people raced out in boats in an effort to search his body. They beat the water with their oars and scattered rice dumplings wrapped in reed-leaves (zongzi) into the river in the hope that fish in the river would eat the rice dumplings instead of his body. Later the activity became a boat race and the boats gradually developed into dragon-boats. It is a very exciting boat race. I hope all of you'll enjoy it.

Here we are at the Junshan. You see, many dragon boats have been anchored here. Please don't push and get off the boat one by one. Thank you for your attention.

Words and Expressions

freshwater [ˈfreʃwɔːtə(r)] n. 淡水,湖水
waterfowl [ˈwɔːtəfaʊl] n. 水鸟,水禽
agricultural [ˌæɡrɪˈkʌltʃərəl] adj. 农业的
extinction [ɪkˈstɪŋkʃn] n. 消失,消灭
cavity [ˈkævəti] n. 洞,空穴
commemorate [kəˈmeməreɪt] vt. 纪念
festivity [feˈstɪvəti] n. 欢宴,欢庆
corrupt [kəˈrʌpt] adj. 腐败的,贪污的
drown [draʊn] v. 淹死

vastness [vɑːstnəs] n. 巨大
concentric [kənˈsentrɪk] adj. 同中心的
plentiful [ˈplentɪfl] adj. 大量的,丰富的
zoology [zəʊˈɒlədʒi] n. 动物学
concubine [ˈkɒŋkjubaɪn] n. 妾,情妇
anchor [ˈæŋkə(r)] v. 抛锚,锚定
patriotic [ˌpætriˈɒtɪk] adj. 爱国的
desperate [ˈdespərət] adj. 不顾一切的,令人绝望的

Proper Nouns

"eight-hundred Li Dongting Lake" "八百里洞庭"
Emperor Shun 舜帝
mottled bamboo 斑竹
square bamboo 方竹
purple bamboo 紫竹
Junshan 君山
"two concubines' tomb" "二妃墓"
arhat bamboo 罗汉竹
sincere bamboo 实心竹
Qu Yuan 屈原

Exercise ➡ ➡ ➡

Directions: Act as the local guide and take tourists to go sightseeing on the Dongting Lake. Try to make your introduction more situational and attractive using the proper body language.

Part VI   Readings

Directions: Read the following passage and fill in the blanks with the words or phrases given below.

| harmony | hovered | admire | primitive |
| paved | same | flames | gabled |

Phoenix Town

"Feng Huang" is Chinese for "Phoenix," the mythical bird of good omen and longevity that is consumed by fire to be re-born again from the (1)_____. Feng Huang Cheng or Phoenix Town is so called as legend has it that two of these fabulous birds flew over it and found the town so beautiful that they (2)_____ there, reluctant to leave.

The town is situated on the western boundary of Hunan Province in an area of outstanding natural beauty where mountains, water and blue skies prevail. Upon entering the town the visitor will be impressed by its air of mystery, elegance and (3)_____ simplicity. This is a world that is dominated by the colour green. The mountain slopes are covered with green foliage, the fields are green and even the Tuojiang River reflects the greenery. The bridges over the water and unique houses built on stilts display a (4)_____ that is so often portrayed in traditional Chinese paintings. This is particularly true when mist pervades the scene in the early morning or after rain.

Feng Huang Cheng is a wonderful example of what villages were like prior to the onset of modernization. Here dozens of alleys (5)_____ with flagstones run between the houses, each showing wear caused by the feet of generations of local people who have used them when going about their daily business. For the visitors, these alleys are the way to see the typical high (6)_____ wooden houses built on stilts along the banks of the Tuojiang River at close quarters.

Stretching diagonally from the northwest to southeast of the town, Tuojiang River is a life force of the local people. Here in its waters women wash their clothes and the men fish with their nets, while on the bank food is prepared in much the (7)_____ way as it has for centuries. The river also provides a means for boatmen to support their families by ferrying tourists up and down the stream so that they may (8)_____ many splendours of the town.

Words and Expressions

omen ['əʊmən] n. 预兆，征兆
alley ['ælɪ] n. 小巷
fabulous ['fæbjələs] adj. 传说的，寓言的
ferry ['ferɪ] v. 摆渡
foliage ['fəʊliɪdʒ] n. 植物；叶子
diagonally [daɪ'ægənəlɪ] adv. 对角地，斜对地
stilt [stɪlt] n. 高跷；支柱
splendour ['splendə(r)] n. 显赫，光彩壮丽

Proper Nouns

Tuojiang River 沱江

Part VII　Translation

Yueyang Tower

1. Situated at the confluence (交汇处) of the Dongting Lake (洞庭湖) and the Yangtze River (长江) in the north-eastern Hunan Province, Yueyang is an ancient city of culture. It has been known for "the waters of Dongting are well-known across the land; the tower of Yueyang is simply beyond compare" ("洞庭天下水，岳阳天下楼") to the world.
2. Yueyang Tower stands on the west gate of the old city. It is a three-storey wooden structure(纯木结构建筑), 19 meters tall, with upturned eaves and a helmet shaped roof (飞檐盔顶), supported by four pillars. The structure is a unique combination of artistic taste, mechanics, architecture, and craftsmanship. After you ascend the tower you will have a spectacular view of the Dongting Lake.
3. The predecessor (前身) of Yueyang Tower was a structure built by Lu Su (鲁肃) in the three Kingdoms Period (三国时期)for reviewing military parades. It was expanded into a tower in 716 by Zhang Shuo (张说)and given its present name.
4. 1044年，宋代官员滕子京(Teng Zijing)谪守巴陵郡(Baling Prefecture)，重修岳阳楼，并于翌年请当时著名的政治家(statesman)、文学家范仲淹(Fan Zhongyan)撰文以记之。
5. 这篇名为《岳阳楼记》("Notes on Yueyang Tower")的文章语言精美，思想深邃，其文学成就无以伦比(matchless in literary achievement)，因而名扬四方。
6. 文中一幅对子"先天下这忧而忧，后天下之乐而乐"("Be concerned before anyone else becomes concerned; enjoy yourself only after everyone else finds enjoyment.")为每个中国人所熟悉。

Unit 9

Touring Shaanxi

Focus on Learning 学习要点

导游案例	Passports Lost 丢失护照
导游听力	1. Xi'an City 西安市
	2. Xi'an City Wall 西安城墙
情景对话	Mt. Huashan 华山
旅游视频	Huaqing Palace 华清宫
导 游 词	The Terra Cotta Warriors and Horses 兵马俑
导游阅读	Shaanxi History Museum 陕西省历史博物馆
导游翻译	Daci'en Temple 大慈恩寺

 Part I   Tips for Tour Guides

Case 9

Passports Lost

Mr. Smith planned to leave Xi'an for New York at 11:00 o'clock next morning after he visited Museum of the Qin Terra-cotta Warriors and Horses. When he checked out the hotel, he found that his passport was missing. How could you help Mr. Smith search for the passport? Listen to the passage and write down the measures you will take in the blanks.

(1) First of all, I shall ask Mr. Smith to make sure whether he has left the documents with _____ or put it somewhere else.
(2) After he tried to look for _____, but in vain, I shall help search for it.
(3) If the passport is not found, I shall report it to the travel agency and get _____ issued from the travel agency for him.
(4) I shall show him to the local _____ and present the loss report together with the written testimonial made by the travel agency.
(5) With the testimonial issued by the Public Security Bureau, Mr. Smith should apply for _____ in his own country's Embassy or Consulate General in China.

(6) With the newly issued passport, Mr. Smith should apply for _____ in the office of the entry and exit visas for foreigners of the public security.

Words and Expressions

check out 离店结账　　　　　　　　　loss testimonial 遗失证明
Consulate General 总领馆

Exercise

Directions: Act as the local guide and Mr. Smith to demonstrate how you could join your efforts to search for the lost passport. The teacher is expected to give clues and help the role players to solve the problem. Other students can put forward suggestions how the presentation could be improve.

Part II Listening Activities

Listening 1

Xi'an City

Words and Expressions

pockmark [ˈpɒkmɑːk] v. 密集　　　　funeral [ˈfjuːnərəl] n. 葬礼, 出殡
feast [fiːst] n. 节日, 盛宴　　　　　　merit [ˈmerɪt] n. 优点, 价值
departed [dɪˈpɑːtɪd] n. 逝者　　　　　slave [sleɪv] n. 奴隶

Proper Nouns

Xi'an City 西安市　　　　　　　　　Shaanxi Province 陕西省
Chang'an 长安　　　　　　　　　　Silk Road 丝绸之路
Big Wild Goose Pagoda 大雁塔　　　Ci'en Temple 慈恩寺
Small Wild Goose Pagoda 小雁塔　　Jianfu Temple 荐福寺
Lishan Hill 骊山　　　　　　　　　Lintong 临潼
Feng 鄷京　　　　　　　　　　　　Hao 镐京

Western Zhou Dynasty 西周时期

Exercise

Directions: Listen to the passage and decide whether the statements are true or false. If it is true, put "T" in the space provided and "F" if it is false.

1. _____ For 1,062 years the city had been capital for 15 dynasties, and a total of 73 emperors had ruled China there.
2. _____ More than 217 palaces and temples, for example, were built in the Qin Dynasty.
3. _____ The Big Wild Goose Pagoda in Jianfu Temple is one of the well reserved temples in Xi'an.
4. _____ Feng and Hao in the Xi'an area, which were the capitals of the Western Zhou Dynasty, have been acclaimed as "the Home of the Bronze Wares."
5. _____ It was quite popular to put up stone tablets in front of tombs to record the merits and achievements of the dead, in many dynasties.

Listening 2

Words and Expressions

landmark ['lændmɑːk] n. 路标, 标志   enceinte [enˈseɪnt] n. 城廓, 围廓

Proper Nouns

Xi'an City Wall 西安城墙   Hongwu Reign 洪武年间(明皇帝朱元
Changle 长乐门   璋的年号)
Anding 安定门   Yongning 永宁门
Anyuan 安远门   Tower of Shooting Arrow 箭楼

Xi'an City Wall

The Xi'an City Wall is the best preserved, (1)_____ and largest ancient city defense system in China. As one of the most important (2)_____ of the Xi'an city, it was first built from the 3rd to the 11th of the Hongwu reign in the Ming Dynasty on (3)_____ site of the imperial walls of Chang'an in the Tang Dynasty. The city walls are built with yellow earth in separated layers. The bottommost layer is rammed with (4)_____, earth and sticky rice and it is very solid. The eastern wall is (5)_____ meters long; the western one is (6)_____ meters, the southern one is 3,441 meters and the northern one is 3,244 meters. The perimeter of the walls is (7)_____ kilometers and the wall is 12 meters high and 16.5 meters deep. There is an area of 12 square kilometers inside the city. On each side of the city there is (8)_____: the eastern gate is named Changle; the western one is Anding; (9)_____ one is Yongning and the northern one is Anyuan. Outside each gate there is a Tower of Shooting Arrow, inside which there is a city (10)_____. Between them there is an enceinte.

Exercise ➡ ➡ ➡

Directions: Listen to the passage and fill in the words or phrases you have heard.

Part III Situational Dialogue

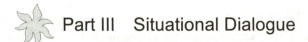

Mt. Huashan

(A=Miss Luo Yaling, a guide; B=Bruce)

A: Well, we're on our way back to Xi'an City. Although you hiked hours in the mountain, you're still in high spirits. A wonderful trip, isn't it?

B: Yes, I'm happy to view such a fascinating landscape.

A: I think it's very interesting to look back at the mountaineering activities we've experienced. Let's share each one's travel experience.

B: Sounds good.

A: Ok, I'd like to ask you some questions about Mt. Huashan. Just to fresh your mind. Bruce, how many peaks are there in Mt. Huashan?

B: There are five peaks. They're East Peak, West Peak, South Peak, North Peak and Middle Peak.

A: What does Mt. Huashan look like?

B: The five peaks of Mt. Huashan look like five petals of a flower. Hua, means flower, and shan means mountain in your language. It also has another name, Taihuashan. Am I right?

A: Right. You really have good memories. What do you think of North Peak?

B: North Peak is a precipitous peak with cliffs on three sides. Only a road here leads to the south. From here I went south to Ca'er Precipice, Sky-leading Ladder, Sun and Moon Precipice along the only path in Mt. Huashan. The cliff path is less than 30 centimeters wide and faces a deep valley, so I had to walk along carefully. Here, you told me a story "Capturing Mt. Huashan Wisely."

A: What do you think of South Peak? Anything special here?

B: Well, along the cliff of South Peak is a planked path equipped with an iron chain. I walked carefully on the frightful path. It is very dangerous. Fortunately I put on gym shoes and gloves as you told me.

A: Very good! My mountaineering experience is always helpful for my guests. How do you feel about West Peak?

B: What strikes me most is a giant rock in front of the Cuiyun Temple on West Peak. As it takes the shape of a lotus flower, the mountain is also called Lotus Peak.

A: Do you still remember the legend about it?

B: Yeah, you told me that Chen Xiang was a filial young man. He once split the mountain and rescued his mother out of it. I saw a crack in a giant rock beside Cuiyun Temple as if an axe made it. The rock is called "Axe-splitting Rock," and a huge axe with a long handle lies beside it.

A: Then, what about East Peak?

B: East Peak is also called Facing Sun Peak. As the sun emerges from the sea of clouds, I cannot help but jump with joy.

A: That's very good. We'll reach Xi'an in fifty minutes. Just take a nap!

B: Thank you!

Words and Expressions

hike [haɪk] v. 远足,步行
petal ['petl] n. 花瓣
frightful ['fraɪtfl] adj. 可怕的
filial ['fɪliəl] adj. 子女的,孝顺的

mountaineering [ˌmaʊntn'iːrɪŋ] n. 登山
precipitous [prɪ'sɪpɪtəs] adj. 陡峭的
gym [dʒɪm] n. 体育馆;体育

Proper Nouns

Mt. Huashan 华山
West Peak 西峰
North Peak 北峰
Taihuashan 太华山
Sky-leading Ladder 天梯
Capturing Mt. Huashan Wisely "智取华山"
Lotus Peak 莲花峰
"Axe-splitting Rock" "斧劈石"

East Peak 东峰
South Peak 南峰
Middle Peak 中峰
Ca'er Precipice 擦耳岩
Sun and Moon Precipice 日月岩
Cuiyun Temple 翠云宫
Chen Xiang 沉香
Facing Sun Peak 朝阳峰

Exercise ➡ ➡ ➡

Directions: Listen to the dialogue. Imagine that you are the local guide and your classmates are tourists. Do the dialogue again with additional information that the teacher may offer.

Part IV Video for Tourism
旅游视频

Huaqing Palace

Words and Expressions

attraction [əˈtrækʃn] *n.* 吸引物
gigantic [dʒaɪˈɡæntɪk] *adj.* 巨大的
concubine [ˈkɒŋkjubaɪn] *n.* 妾,妃子

extraordinary [ɪkˈstrɔːdnri] *adj.* 不平常的
vivid [ˈvɪvɪd] *adj.* 生动的
elevate [ˈelɪveɪt] *v.* 举起

Proper Nouns

Huaqing Pool 华清池
Yang Yuhuan 杨玉环
Lishan Mountain 骊山

Emperor Xuanzong 玄宗皇帝
Nine-dragon Pool 九龙池

It is a well-known fact that the China's northwestern Shaanxi Province is famous for its tourism attractions and the capital city of the province of Xi'an has been the culture center for many dynasties. Today, our story is about Huaqing Pool in Xi'an. The scenic pool is famous for a romance between Tang Dynasty emperor Xuanzong and his favorite concubine Yang Yuhuan. Over the years it has attracted millions of travelers from across the world. But one evening in April 2007 something extraordinary happened, a gigantic structure was lift out of the pool.

The Nine-dragon Pool located at the center of Huaqing Pool scenic area has a frame work over 10 meters high, and a mechanical engineering plate, covering several hundreds of square meters. It looks almost magical rising up from the bottom of the lake. It is difficult to imagine how a royal garden open to tourists in the day can become so colorful at night. Thousands of the green iron bars are hidden in the forests of Lishan Mountain behind Huaqing Pool. In the day time, these are part of the 180-thousand-square-meter mountain forest. But at night, they generate a beautiful vision.

With so many possibilities, what is the scene used for? General Manager of Shaanxi Tourism Cooperation Group Zhang Xiaoke is the man behind all the design.

Lowering the stage is necessary during the daytime when tourists visit the garden, all four flash lights that shine when the stages elevated are dim to make a look like even a smooth surface. The light source shining on the main ancient style stage can move freely. It may seem that the stage is made up of a tile surface, but it is not.

Zhang Xiaoke's aim was to build a vivid backdrop for the show, the song of an unending sorrow. A heart wrenching love story of the Tang Dynasty emperor, Xuanzong and his favorite concubine Yang Yuhuan, pavilions, carvings and elegant buildings in the scenic area would naturally become a part of the background for the musical drama.

Step 1: Watch the video and write down the key words or phrases in the video. You may use the key words or phrases as the reminders when you watch it the second time.

_____
_____
_____
_____

Step 2: Watch the video again and decide whether the statements are True or False.
1. _____ Huaqing Pool is famous for a romance between Emperor Xuanzong and his wife Yang Yuhuan.
2. _____ The Nine-dragon Pool, one of the most famous pools is located at the center of Huaqing Pool Scenic Area.
3. _____ Thousands of the green iron bars hidden in the forests of Lishan Mountain behind Huaqing Pool will generate colorful lights at night.
4. _____ The pavilions, towers and Lishan Mountain will naturally become a part of the background for the musical drama.

Part V Tour Commentary

The Terra Cotta Warriors and Horses

Ladies and Gentlemen! We've arrived at our final destination—the Museum of Qin Terra Cotta Warriors and Horses. The Terra Cotta Warriors and Horses is regarded as one of the eight greatest wonders in the world, and a site not to be missed by any visitor to China. In 1987, it was listed as one of the world cultural heritages by UNESCO. As one of the most famous scenic spots in China, it attracts lots of tourists both at home and from abroad.

Well, I'd like to tell you it will probably take us about 3 hours to visit the Terra Cotta Warriors and Horses. The museum covers an area of 16,300 square meters, and is divided into three sections: No. 1 Pit, No. 2 Pit, and No. 3 Pit respectively. They were tagged in the order of their discoveries. There are columns of soldiers at the front, followed by war chariots at the back. Altogether over 7,000 pottery soldiers, horses, chariots, and even weapons have been unearthed from these pits. Most of them have been restored to their former grandeur. In addition, two bronze chariots are on display in an exhibition room of the museum. They are the national treasures, of course, a must to be appreciated.

Well, my dear friends, now we come to the No. 1 Pit. It was found in 1976. It is the largest, first opened to the public in 1979. Life size terracotta figures of warriors and horses are arranged in battle formations. They are replicas of what the imperial guard should look like in those days of pomp and vigor. It is amazing, isn't it? Well, please look at these tunic infantrymen. Their hair is wound in topknots while some have beards. The warriors wear a knee-length tunic, short trousers, puttees and curved shoes for freedom of movement and fighting. Besides that, the armored soldiers stand 189 cm in height. Each of them has a sword in his left hand. Look at those horses! They have big bright eyes, large nostrils, stout legs and plump waists and hips. Everyone is poised ready to gallop.

After we visit No. 1 Pit, now, we come to No. 3 Pit. It is 25 meters northwest of No. 1 Pit and was excavated in 1976. No. 3 Pit looks like the command center of the armed forces and contains 68 warriors. The terra cotta soldiers here are remarkably realistic sculptures. The lower part of the body is solid while the upper part is hollow. The square faces of the warriors feature broad foreheads and thick-lipped mouths. Their eyes focus on the far distance and some bear a traditional hairstyle. Originally the figures were painted in bright colors. After over two thousand years the color has faded and worn off, but they are still lifelike, aren't they?

Ladies and Gentlemen! We're going to see the amazing discovery—two bronze chariots. They were unearthed in December, 1980, about 20 meters east of Emperor Qin's Mausoleum. They were thought to be half the actual size and were supposed to serve as the vehicle for the emperor's inspection tours in his afterlife. The bronze chariots add to the China's great archeological treasures. They represent the largest finds of earliest delicate fine bronze work anywhere in the world. I think you'll enjoy the wonder, a wonder among wonders.

Words and Expressions

respectively [rɪˈspektɪvli] adv. 分别地, 各个地
chariot [ˈtʃærɪət] n. 战车
replica [ˈreplɪkə] n. 复制品
vigor [ˈvɪɡə] n. 精力, 活力
infantry [ˈɪnfəntri] n. 步兵, 步兵团
puttee [ˈpʌti] n. 布绑腿, 皮绑腿
armored [ˈɑːməd] adj. 披甲的, 装甲的
plump [plʌmp] adj. 圆胖的, 鼓起的
gallop [ˈɡæləp] vi. 飞驰, 急速进行

tag [tæɡ] n. 标签, 名称
pottery [ˈpɒtəri] n. 陶器, 陶器场
pomp [pɒmp] n. 壮丽, 盛况
tunic [ˈtjuːnɪk] n. 束腰外衣
topknot [ˈtɒpnɒt] n. 头饰, 顶髻
curve [kəːv] n. 曲线, 弯曲
nostril [ˈnɒstrəl] n. 鼻孔
waist [weɪst] n. 腰部, 腰; 背心

Proper Nouns
Terra Cotta Warriors and Horses 兵马俑　　　Emperor Qin's Mausoleum 秦陵

Exercise ➡ ➡ ➡

Directions: Act as the local guide and take tourists to visit the Museum of Terra Cotta Warriors and Horses. Try to make your introduction more situational and attractive using the proper body language.

Part VI Readings

Directions: Read the following passage and fill in the blanks with the words or phrases given below.

treasures	specialty	testify	floorage
figurines	opened	exhibitions	

Shaanxi History Museum

Shaanxi History Museum, the construction of which was completed and (1)_____ on June 20th, 1991 is China's first modern museum, covering an area of about 70,000 Sqm. with a (2)_____ of 55,663 Sqm. It has a collection of 375,000 pieces of cultural relics, 762 of which are the national top-grades and 18 are national (3)_____. The museum houses the bronze wares, pottery (4)_____ of various dynasties and gold and silver vessels of the Tang Dynasty style, etc. It is renowned as "the bright pearl of the ancient capital and the treasure house of China." The museum has three types of (5)_____: the permanent exhibition, which is systematic and comprehensive, exhibitions on special subjects, in which (6)_____ is sought among a wide range of topics, and temporary exhibitions which offer freshness to the viewers. The exhibition line of seven galleries lasts for two kilometers with rare treasures which (7)_____ the significance of Shananxi in the ancient Chinese civilization.

Words and Expressions

renowned [rɪˈnaʊnd] *adj.* 有名的
vessel [ˈvesl] *n.* 容器, 器皿
systematic [ˌsɪstəˈmætɪk] *adj.* 系统的
temporary [ˈtemprəri] *adj.* 临时的
figurine [ˌfɪɡjəˈriːn] *n.* 小雕像
permanent [ˈpɜːmənənt] *adj.* 永久的
comprehensive [ˌkɒmprɪˈhensɪv] *adj.* 全面的
testify [ˈtestɪfaɪ] *v.* 证明, 证实

Proper Nouns

Shaanxi History Museum 陕西历史博物馆

Part VII Translation

Daci'en Temple

1. Daci'en Temple (大慈恩寺) was built in 648 A.D. to honor her mother, the Empress Wende (文德皇后) by the crowned prince Li Zhi (李治) during Emperor Taizhong's reign in the Tang Dynasty.
2. The temple which had 13 yards and 1897 rooms occupied an area of more than 360 mu. At that time, it was the biggest temple in Chang'an (长安), where more than 300 monks lived.
3. The original pagoda was constructed with five storeys in Indian style (印度寺庙风格). It was rebuilt to a seven storeyed pagoda during the reign of Empress Wu Zetian (武则天).
4. 大慈恩寺曾是长安最富有盛名的寺庙。公元652年, 大慈恩寺迎请高僧玄奘法师总理事务 (preside over the temple affairs)。玄奘主持在此修建了大雁塔 (Big Wild Goose Pagoda), 以保存印度取回的佛经。
5. 现存的大雁塔为七层佛塔, 塔高64.5米, 塔体为砖混结构 (built of the brick and wood), 唐代佛塔风格。
6. 大雁塔为中国佛塔建筑的优秀代表。1961年, 由国务院公布为全国第一批重点文物保护单位 (the national key cultural relic unit under protection)。

Unit 10

Touring Chongqing

Focus on Learning 学习要点

导游案例　The First Aid 急救
导游听力　1. Chongqing City 重庆市
　　　　　2. Ciqikou 磁器口
情景对话　Dazu Rock Carvings 大足石刻
旅游视频　The Yangtze River Cruise 长江巡游
导 游 词　The Three Gorges 三峡
导游阅读　Northern Hot Spring Park 北泉公园
导游翻译　Baidi City 白帝城

 Part I　Tips for Tour Guides

Case 10

The First Aid

One Irish tourist suffered from a heart attack while he was hiking on the Nanshan Mountain. One tourist took with him the medicine that could alleviate the symptoms. The guide was very worried and took the medicine the tourist offered and helped the patient to take it. Listen to the passage and evaluate the guiding service. Fill in the blanks with the remedies you will take.

(1) The guide should not _____ , for he has no authority to prescribe anything for a patient. The tour guide should not _____ from other tourists to offer the patient if neither the tour guide nor the tourists are doctors.

(2) The tour guide should _____ with his head slightly elevated. If the patient has his own medicine with him, the tour guide should help him take it.

(3) The tour guide should _____ to take the patient to a nearby hospital for first aid.

Words and Expressions

take medicine 服药
first aid 急救
call for an ambulance 叫救护车

Exercise

Directions: Imagine that you are the guide and your desk mate is the Irish tourist. Replay the scene that the guide gave the first aid to the tourist who suffered from the heart attack. The teacher should supervise the first aid and give instructions. Other students are expected to help improve the representation.

Part II Listening Activities

Listening 1

Chongqing City

Words and Expressions

vestige ['vestɪdʒ] n. 遗迹，痕迹
embassy ['embəsɪ] n. 大使馆
nocturnal [nɔk'tɜːnəl] adj. 夜的；夜曲的
glisten ['glɪsn] v. 闪耀；反光
folklore ['fəʊklɔː(r)] n. 民间传说
canyon ['kænjən] n. <美>峡谷，溪谷

mansion ['mænʃn] n. 大厦，官邸
vintage ['vɪntɪdʒ] adj. 古老的；最佳的
inundate ['ɪnʌndeɪt] v. 淹没
spangle ['spæŋgl] v. (使)闪烁
statuesque [ˌstætʃu'esk] adj. 雕像般的；轮廓清晰的

Proper Nouns

Kuomintang (中国)国民党
"provisional capital" "陪都"
Red Crag Village 红岩
Chiang Kai-shek 蒋介石
Pipashan Park 琵琶山公园
Eling Park 鹅岭公园

Chongqing City 重庆市
War of Resistance Against Japan 抗日战争
Zengjiayan 曾家岩
Red Star Pavilion 红星亭
Kansheng Pavilion 瞰胜楼
Yikeshu 一棵树(观景台)

Jinyun Mountain 缙云山　　　　　　　Nanshan Mountain 南山
Yichang 宜昌　　　　　　　　　　　　Three Gorges 三峡
Qutang Gorge 瞿塘峡　　　　　　　　Wuxia Gorge 巫峡
Xiling Gorge 西陵峡　　　　　　　　 Fengdu Mountain 丰都名山（古称平都山）
Baidi City 白帝城　　　　　　　　　　Shibao Village 石宝寨
Zhang Fei's Temple 张飞庙　　　　　　Qu Yuan's Temple 屈原祠
Three Gorges Dam 三峡大坝

Exercise

Directions: Listen to the passage and decide whether the statements are true or false. If it is true, put "T" in the space provided and "F" if it is false.

1. _____ During the War of Resistance Against Japan, Chongqing was the "provisional capital" of China under the Kuomintang rule.
2. _____ The Kansheng Pavilion in the Eling Park, and Yikeshu on the Jinyun Mountain are vintage points for observing the nocturnal scenes of the mountain city.
3. _____ At night the entire city is inundated in an ocean of lights, which form a colorful three-dimensional painting.
4. _____ The 196-km-long Three Gorges, consisting of the majestic Qutangxia, statuesque Wuxia and ferocious Xilingxia gorges, is one of the world's major canyons.
5. _____ Along the way there are such scenic attractions as the Fengdu Mountain, Baidi City, Shibao Village, Zhang Fei's Temple and many more.

Listening 2

Words and Expressions

porcelain [ˈpɔːsəlɪn] n. 瓷器，瓷　　　　　　kiln [kɪln] n. 窑，炉
majority [məˈdʒɒrətɪ] n. 多数，大半　　　　　timber [ˈtɪmbə(r)] n. 木材，木料
notable [ˈnəʊtəbl] adj 显著的，著名的　　　　studio [ˈstjuːdɪəʊ] n. 画室，工作室
workshop [ˈwɜːkʃɒp] n. 车间，工场　　　　　acquaint [əˈkweɪnt] vt. 使熟知，通知

Proper Nouns

Ciqikou 瓷器口　　　　　　　　　　　Longyin 龙隐镇
Shu Embroidery 蜀绣

Ciqikou

Situated on the bank of the Jialingjiang River, not far from (1)_____ with the mighty Yangtze is the ancient village of Ciqikou, formerly known as Long Yin. The history of Ciqikou can be traced back for more than (2)_____. During the Ming and Qing dynasties it was famous for its production of (3)_____. To date, (4)_____ old kiln sites have been discovered there. It is because of the importance of the porcelain industry that the name has been changed from Longyin to Ciqikou which literally means (5)_____. The majority of the houses (6)_____ the Ming and Qing dynasties. Much of the two and three storey construction is of bamboo and (7)_____. The three notable attractions of the village are (8)_____, the artists' studios and the Shu Embroidery workshops. The tea houses offer the opportunity for you to meet (9)_____ and also become acquainted with the unique (10)_____.

Exercise ➡ ➡ ➡

Directions: Listen to the passage and fill in the words or phrases you have heard.

Part III Situational Dialogue

Dazu Rock Carvings

(A=Miss Wang Yiru, a guide; B=Charles)

A: Good morning! Now we are going to visit the Baoding Grotto.

B: Yesterday you just said we would visit Dazu Rock Carvings. Why do you change the site? You should have told me before.

A: I'm afraid you're mistaken. I didn't change the site. The general term of Dazu Rock Carvings refers to all the cliffside carvings in Dazu County. There are more than 50,000 carved stone figures scattered over forty places, mainly in Beishan, Baodingshan, Nanshan, Shizhuanshan and Shimenshan.

B: Wow! So many! I don't think we have enough time to visit all the rock carvings in one day.

A: That's why we can visit one only site today.

B: Why shall we choose to visit Baoding Grotto?

A: A good question! Baoding Grotto is the largest and best preserved site among Dazu Rock Carvings. It is located 15 kilometers northeast of the Dazu County.

B: Are there very old rock carvings?

A: Yes, most of them were carved in the Song Dynasty and have a history over 1,000 years.

B: Can you tell me what kind of rock carvings they are? I think they are all statues of Buddha and Bodhisattva like those in the Yungang and Longmen Grottoes.

A: Not exactly. They are not only the statues of Buddha and Bodhisattva, but also statues of monarchs, ministers, military officials, even jailers and the ordinary people.

B: It sounds interesting. The statuses of the mortals mix with the immortals!

A: Yes, you can also find the Buddhist, Taoist and Confucian rock carvings in Dazu. Many of the carvings reflect religious doctrines and another set of carvings reflects Confucianism, specifically filial piety.

B: Really? I can't expect the sculptures of different religions would exist in the same place.

A: Why not? No wonder Dazu Rock Carvings is regarded as an art treasure house that fully reflected the society, philosophy, religion and folklore of that time. In 1999, UNESCO listed Dazu Rock Carvings as a World Cultural Heritage Site.

B: Then, I think I have a chance to see some masterpieces of the sculptures there.

A: Of course. I think, the statue of Guanyin, the Goddess of Mercy is just one of them. To surprise you, she has more than 1,000 hands.

B: Oh, really? I just watched the dance program "One-Thousand-Arm Guanyin" on TV. It was played by the disables. So beautiful!

A: Yes, in fact, what the carvings offer to us is not only the wonderful enjoyment of the magnificent art but a Buddhist teaching like this: One can free himself from earthly worries by self-cultivation and does not need to go beyond his own inner world to find the truth of Buddhism.

B: I know little about Buddhism. I can't understand what you said.

A: Ok, I explain it with more details when we arrive there.

B: Thank you very much.

Words and Expressions

cliffside [ˈklɪfsaɪd] n. 悬崖边
jailer [ˈdʒeɪlə(r)] n 狱卒
reflect [rɪˈflekt] v. 反射,反映
piety [ˈpaɪəti] n. 虔诚,孝行
earthly [ˈɜːθli] adj. 现世的,俗世的

scatter [ˈskætə(r)] v. 离散,分散
mortal [ˈmɔːtəl] n. 凡人,人类
doctrine [ˈdɒktrɪn] n. 教条,学说
philosophy [fəˈlɒsəfi] n. 哲学
cultivation [ˌkʌltɪˈveɪʃn] n. 培养,教养

Proper Nouns

Dazu Rock Carving 大足石刻
Dazu County 大足县
Baodingshan 宝顶山
Shizhuanshan 石篆山
One-Thousand-Arm Guanyin 千手观音

Baoding Grotto 宝顶山摩崖(石窟)
Beishan 北山
Nanshan 南山
Shimenshan 石门山

Exercise ➡ ➡ ➡

Directions: Listen to the dialogue. Imagine that you are the local guide and your classmates are tourists. Do the dialogue again with additional information that the teacher may offer.

Part IV Video for Tourism
旅游视频

The Yangtze River Cruise

Words and Expressions

pier [pɪə(r)] n. 码头；桥墩
excursion [ɪksˈkəːʃən] n. 旅游观光
depart [dɪˈpɑːt] v. 离开，开出

cruise [kruːz] n. 巡游，漫游
reach [riːtʃ] n. 河段，流域
view [vjuː] v. 观赏；观察

Proper Nouns

Chaotianmen 朝天门
Tanggula Mountain 唐古拉山
Fengdu Ghost City 丰都鬼城
Lesser Three Gorges 小三峡
Three Gorges Dam 三峡大坝

East China Sea 东海
Yichang 宜昌
White Emperor City 白帝城
Shennong Stream 神农溪

    This is Chaotianmen pier in Chongqing City, southwest of China. It is the boarding point for all ships at most of the time. An elevator takes passengers down to the boarding platform. From there, they'll board a ship starting journey on the Yangtze River.

    Yangtze River is the longest river in both China and Asia and the third longest river in the world. It flows about 6,300 kilometers and flows from the south in Tanggula Mountains in Qinghai Province eastwards into the East China Sea in Shanghai. The pass of the Yangtze affects the life of 400 million people in its journey to Shanghai and it is often called "Mother River" of the Chinese people.

    The Three Gorges are named: Qutang Gorge, Wu Gorge and Xiling Gorge. Stretching out along the river between Chongqing and Yichang are the highlights of the trip. Scenic spots, such as Fengdu Ghost City, White Emperor City, Lesser Three Gorges, Shen Nong Stream and Three Gorges Dam lie along the river. Tourists can take a 3-night-downstream Yangtze River cruise from Chongqing to Yichang, or 4-night-upstream cruise from Yichang to Chongqing. Ships of different companies operate different routes and shore excursion.

Apart from the Three Gorges cruise, tourists can also take the 6-night downstream cruise from Chongqing to Shanghai, or 8-night-cruise in the river, a very restful and scenic journey from middle and lower reaches of the Yangtze River.

Now, the boat has departed from Chongqing Cao Tianmen pier for downstream to Yichang. The Three Gorges, Fengdu Ghost City, Lesser Three Gorges and Three Gorges Dam will be viewed on routes.

Experience the beauty on Yangtze River with China highlights.

Step 1: Watch the video and write down the key words or phrases in the video. You may use the key words or phrases as the reminders when you watch it the second time.
_____
_____
_____
_____

Step 2: Watch the video again and decide whether the statements are True or False.
1. _____ Yangtze River originates from the south in Tanggula Mountains in Qinghai Province and flows into East China Sea in Shanghai.
2. _____ The Three Gorges are Qutang Gorge, Wu Gorge and Xiling Gorge. Scenery between Chongqing and Yichang are most beautiful on the Yangtze cruise.
3. _____ Tourists can take a 3-night-upstream Yangtze River cruise from Chongqing to Yichang, or a 4-night-downstream cruise from Yichang to Chongqing.
4. _____ The Three Gorges, Fengdu Ghost City, Lesser Three Gorges, Shen Nong Stream and Three Gorges Dam will be viewed on routes.

 Part V Tour Commentary

The Three Gorges

Ladies and Gentlemen!

Welcome to Chongqing—a famous mountain city in China! I am very glad to be your tour guide! Now we'll start our cruise down the Yangtze River and appreciate the beautiful Three Gorges.

Look! My friends, the marvelous gorge is just ahead.

This is the first gorge of the Yangtze River we come across on our cruise—the Qutang Gorge. The Yangtze River is partially stemmed by the Baidi Mountain here and a bay of 1.6 sq. km is thus formed. It is very much like a weir, so it is named "Qutang Gorge." At the mouth of the gorge there once stood a huge reef. This is the so-called "Yanyudui" which once blocked the throat of the Three Gorges and locked the current. With the ups and downs of the water, it sometimes looks like a horse and sometimes an elephant.

Look ahead! The old construction complex on the mountain on our left is the historical site of the Baidi City. Baidi City is surrounded by water on three sides and mountains on one side. To the east of the gorge and the south of the river stands the 1,415-metre-high Baiyan Mountain. And to the east of the gorge and north of the river erects the 1,400-metre-high Chijia Mountain. These two mountains face each other and lock the river like a door. The magnificent Kuimen is just located here. It is the upper mouth of the Qutang section and it is difficult for boats to pass.

Ladies and Gentlemen! We've passed Qutang Gorge and the travel boat has entered the Wuxia Gorge. Twelve peaks stand on both sides of the Wu Gorge with six on either side. This constitutes the misty "Wuxia Gorge Gallery." Now please look at the left site. This is the Denglong Peak. And it lies 15 km down the lower reach of Wuxia County.

The six peaks on the Denglong Peak seem to wind their way upward as if they were flying dragons soaring towards the sky. The ship is sailing fast. Look far ahead, the Goddess Peak come to our views. It is the highest peak of all 12 peaks in the area, 1,112 meters about sea level. The Goddess stands 6.4 m high like a gentle, slim and graceful maid on the top of the peak. The story goes that Goddess is the incarnation of Yao Ji, the youngest daughter of the Queen Mother of Heaven.

Now, we start visiting the third gorge Xiling Gorge. In Chinese "Xi" stands for "west" while "ling" stands for an ancient city "Yiling." It has been so named just because it lies to the west of Yiling, today's Yichang. Our boat is entering Gorge of Military Books and Sword. Look at the north side and what jumps into your eyes are books on the art of war and a doubled-edged sword. The story goes that when Zhuge Liang entered Sichuan, he hid the books on the art of war and the double-edged sword in the cliff.

Ladies and Gentlemen! Our boat is passing through No. 2 ship lock of Three Gorges Dam. Three days' cruise is drawing to a close. Now we have a profound friendship between us and I will bear it in mind for life. When we say good-bye to each other, please let me, on behalf of all our crew members, extend all our best wishes to you. And I sincerely hope that you will enjoy your visit all the more in Wuhan!

Have a pleasant journey! Good-bye!

Words and Expressions

stem [stem] v. 起源于……
throat [θrəʊt] n. 咽喉,喉咙
soar [sɔː(r)] v. 高飞,滑翔

reef [riːf] n. 暗礁
constitute ['kɒnstɪtjuːt] vt. 组成;任命
incarnation [ˌɪnkɑːˈneɪʃn] n. 赋予肉体,化身

Proper Nouns

Baidi Mountain 白帝山	"Yanyudui" 滟滪堆
Baiyan Mountain 白岩山	Chijia Mountain 赤甲山
Kuimen 夔门	"Wuxia Gorge Gallery" "巫峡画廊"
Denglong Peak 登龙峰	Wuxia County 巫峡县
Goddess Peak 神女峰	Yao Ji 瑶姬
Queen Mother of Heaven 王母娘娘	Yiling 夷陵（宜昌的古称）
Gorge of Military Books and Sword 兵书宝剑峡	Wuhan City 武汉市

Exercise ➡ ➡ ➡

Directions: Act as the local guide and take tourists to cruise on the Three Gorges. Try to make your introduction more situational and attractive using the proper body language.

 Part VI Readings

Directions: Read the following passage and fill in the blanks with the words or phrases given below.

constant	encounter	offer	semitropical
ailments	comprising	compliment	

Northern Hot Spring Park

No stay in Chongqing is complete without a visit to the Northern Hot Spring Park as it has so much to (1)_____ the visitors and is rightly considered to be a pearl of the Jialing River. The park lies at the foot of Jinyun Mountain on the north side of the Jialing River, about 52 kilometers (32miles) from the city center. Here, you can enjoy a beautiful scenic area (2)_____ temples, hills, water, woods, springs, gorges, caves and much else besides.

There are four main palaces at the center of the park where you can feel something of the religious culture. To the east of the four palaces there is the Guxiang Garden as well as the Stone Inscription Garden, Fish Pond and Water Lily Pool. All of the buildings and pavilions have been sited so as to (3)_____ their surroundings so that with the green bamboos, clear water and elegant hills the park is very picturesque.

Naturally, the hot springs are the main feature of the park. There are ten springs altogether in the park and the temperature of the water is a (4)_____ 35℃—37℃. The water contains alkali minerals that are considered as having beneficial medicinal properties. The warm water offers an excellent way to relax from the stresses of day to day existence and it also benefits those who suffer from skin problems, arthritis and many other common (5)_____.

In addition, the park has an abundance of natural flora and fauna. The plants that naturally occur here are mainly tropical and (6)_____ evergreens, horsetail pines and a large area covered by bamboo groves. The park is also home to many species of small animals and birds that you are sure to (7)_____ when you are strolling here. With its many historic sites and fair sceneries, Northern Hot Spring Park offers you a welcome and an escape from the pressures of city life.

Words and Expressions

religious [rɪˈlɪdʒəs] *adj.* 宗教的，虔诚的
arthritis [ɑːˈθraɪtɪs] *n.* 关节炎
beneficial [ˌbenɪˈfɪʃl] *adj.* 有益的，有利的
stroll [strəʊl] *v.* 散步；闲逛

Proper Nouns

Jialing River 嘉陵江
Guxiang Garden 古香园
Fish Pond 观鱼池
Jinyun Mountain 缙云山
Stone Inscription Garden 石刻园
Water Lily Pool 荷花池

Part VII Translation

Baidi City

1. Badi City (White Emperor City) (白帝城)lies on the north bank of the Yangtze River and to the east of Fengjie County(奉节县), guarding the entrance of Qutang Gorge(瞿塘峡). Over 2000 years ago, it was the birth place of the ancient Ba Kingdom(巴国). In the Qin and Han dynasties, a Yufu County (鱼腹县)was set up here.

2. At the end of the Western Han Dynasty(西汉末年), Gongsun Shu (公孙述)made himself ruler of the State of Shu (蜀)and moved his capital from Chengdu to Yufu. As legend goes, Gongsun Shu found a well when the people built the town. From this well emitted white vapor (白气) which he associated with the flying of a white dragon so he renamed himself the White Emperor and the town "White Emperor City."

3. During the Three-Kingdoms Period, Liu Bei(刘备), emperor of the Shu Kingdom was at war with the Wu Kingdom(吴国). Defeated, he withdrew to Baidi City and died of sadness and illness. On his death bed, Liu Bei asked Prime Minister Zhuge Liang (丞相诸葛亮)to take care

of the state affairs and his son Liu Chan(刘禅).
4. 白帝庙青山绿树环抱(nestled among green trees and hills)，绿瓦红墙，亭台楼阁，飞檐画梁，自古以来就是文人墨客(men of letters)流连的胜地。
5. 唐宋著名诗人(the noted poets of the Tang and Song dynasties)李白、杜甫、白居易、刘禹锡、苏轼、陆游、范成大等都在白帝城留有足迹和诗篇。
6. 尤其是杜甫，曾在附近建草堂(thatched cottage)，写诗430多首。因此，白帝城又称"诗城"("Town of Poetry")。

Unit 11

Touring Zhejiang

Focus on Learning 学习要点

导游案例	Hotel on Fire 酒店着火
导游听力	1. Hangzhou City 杭州市
	2. Leifeng Pagoda 雷锋塔
情景对话	Lingyin Temple 灵隐寺
旅游视频	Wuzhen 乌镇
导 游 词	West Lake 西湖
导游阅读	Three Pools Mirroring the Moon Island 三潭印月岛
导游翻译	Melting Snow at Broken Bridge 断桥残雪

 Part I   Tips for Tour Guides

Case 11

Hotel on Fire

It is 4 o'clock in the early morning. All the Japanese tourists are sleeping soundly in the Hangzhou Grand Hotel. Unfortunately the hotel catches a fire. As a national guide, what measures can you take to help the tourist escape from the fire? Listen to the passage and write down the remedies you will take in the blanks.

(1) I must report the fire immediately _____.
(2) I shall lead the tourists to a safe place through a safe _____. I shall warn them not to _____, for they will be trapped in the elevator due to power failure caused by the fire.
(3) If they are surrounded by a big fire or dense smoke, I shall ask them to take the following measures:

   A. They must cover their mouth and nose _____ bend over, and run out of the room;
   B. They should also _____ out the window to signal for help.
   C. If the door is blocked by fire, they should _____ and its frame with wet clothing and splash door with water to keep it cool and wet while waiting for the rescue;
   D. I shall _____ and encourage them to continue with their travel, if it is possible.

E. If tourists are injured in the fire, I shall send them to _____.
F. I shall make _____ to the travel agency and submit _____ after the trip is over.

Words and Expressions

emergency exit 紧急出口 take the elevator 乘电梯
power failure 停电 signal for help 发出求救信号

Exercise

Directions: Act as the national guide and the Japanese tourists. Show your classmates how you could help the tourists escape from the fire. The teacher is expected to supervise the presentation while other students evaluate the remedies taken by the national guide and the tourists.

Part II   Listening Activities

Listening 1

Hangzhou City

Words and Expressions

terminal ['tɜ:mɪnl] n. 终点站,终端
charm [tʃɑ:m] n. 吸引力,魅力
landscape ['lændskeɪp] n. 风景,山水画
illustrate ['ɪləstreɪt] vt. 图解,阐明
mesmerize ['mezməraɪz] v. 施催眠术
picturesque [ˌpɪktʃə'resk] adj. 风景如画的

Proper Nouns

Zhejiang Province 浙江省
Beijing-Hangzhou Grand Canal 京杭大运河
Mt. Putuo 普陀山
Qiandao Lake 千岛湖
Lanting 兰亭
Qiantang River 钱塘江
West Lake 西湖
Mt. Yandang 雁荡山
Mt. Tiantai 天台山
Tianyi Pavilion 天一阁

Xitang 西塘　　　　　　　　　　　　Nanxun 南浔
Wuzhen 乌镇

Exercise ➡ ➡ ➡

Directions: Listen to the passage and decide whether the statements are true or false. If it is true, put "T" in the space provided and "F" if it is false.

1. _____ Hangzhou is also regarded as one of the five ancient capitals in China.
2. _____ There's a saying that illustrates the charm of Hangzhou: "In heaven there is paradise, and on earth there are Hangzhou and Suzhou."
3. _____ The West Lake, one of the most beautiful sites in China, is located right in the outskirts of the city.
4. _____ Mt. Yandang is admired as a "Buddhist Land of South Sea."
5. _____ The three ancient water towns—Xitang, Nanxun and Wuzhen are all scenic spots that delight tourists who visit this region.

Listening 2

Words and Expressions

radiant ['reɪdiənt] *adj.* 发光的　　　　　　bandit ['bændɪt] *n.* 强盗
talisman ['tælɪzmən] *n.* 护身符,法宝

Proper Nouns

Leifeng Pagoda 雷峰塔　　　　　　　　Evening Glow Hill 夕照山
Baochu Pagoda 保俶塔　　　　　　　　"Leifeng Pagoda in Evening Glow"
　　　　　　　　　　　　　　　　　　"雷峰夕照"

Leifeng Pagoda

　　Leifeng Pagoda is situated on the Evening Glow Hill which stands on (1)_____ of the West Lake. The (2)_____ pagoda was a storeyed-pavilion-type structure, built of (3)_____. In the ancient times, Leifeng Pagoda and Baochu Pagoda stood far apart (4)_____. Leifeng Pagoda appeared to be an old gentleman, but Baochu Pagoda appeared to be a (5)_____. When the sun was setting, the pagoda bathed in the evening (6)_____ radiantly beautiful. It was therefore named as "Leifeng Pagoda in Evening Glow." In the Ming Dynasty, the pagoda was (7)_____ by the Japanese bandits and (8)_____ at last on September 25, (9)_____ by the custom of local people to take a brick from its lower storeys as a talisman or (10)_____.

Exercise ➡ ➡ ➡

Directions: Listen to the passage and fill in the words or phrases you have heard.

Part III   Situational Dialogue

Lingyin Temple

(A= Miss Xu Ruijie, a guide; B=Christopher)

A: Well, I'll take you around Hangzhou today. There goes a saying, "Above is Heaven, and below are Suzhou and Hangzhou." Hangzhou is praised as the paradise on the earth.

B: I know. There are so many beautiful gardens and lakes there, especially the West Lake!

A: Apart from West Lake, there are many other famous scenic spots, such as the Lingyin Temple, Tiger Spring, Liuhe Tower (Pagoda of Six Harmonies), Feilaifeng (Peak from Afar), just to name a few.

B: I have a great interest in the Lingyin Temple. Can you take me there?

A: Here we are. The temple is just hidden in the trees. Listen, you may hear the tolls of the bells in the temple.

B: Wow, what a grant temple! By the way, why is it named Lingyin Temple?

A: A good question! The presence of a temple can be traced back to the Eastern Jin Dynasty. According to a local legend, Huili, an Indian monk, was inspired by the spiritual nature of the scenery. To his mind this was a residence of the immortals and so he gave the temple a name Lingyin Temple.

B: I'm still confused about it. What's the implication of the name?

A: It can be translated into English as either "Temple of the Soul's Retreat" or "Temple of Inspired Seclusion," for the environment here has a quiet and beautiful grandeur that encourages a feeling of peace and for contemplation.

B: I see.

A: Let's get into the temple! This is the first hall of Lingyin Temple—Hall of Heavenly Kings. The four characters Yun Lin Chan Si (Cloud Forest Buddhist Temple) on the horizontal board were inscribed by Emperor Kangxi of the Qing Dynasty.

B: I've noticed it. The handwriting is very elegant. I love Chinese calligraphy very much.

A: Please look at the ceiling! The ceiling is decorated with figures of phoenixes and dragons. Look around! The Four Heavenly Kings stand upon either side of the Maitreya. Maitreya is a laughing Buddha with a huge belly.

B: Amazing! What a huge belly he has! Why is he laughing?

A: The laughing Buddha is said to be able to "endure all intolerance and laugh at every laughable person in the world." He is greeting you.

B: Hi, I'm Christopher, from Australia.

A: Now, we'll pass through the hall. After we visit the Hall of Sakyamuni, we'll have a vegetarian lunch at the Lingyin Vegetarian Restaurant. I hope you'll enjoy it.

B: Thank you!

Words and Expressions

spiritual [ˈspɪrɪtʃuəl] adj. 精神上的
retreat [rɪˈtriːt] n. 安泰, 宁静
handwriting [ˈhændraɪtɪŋ] n. 笔迹, 书法
endure [ɪnˈdjʊə(r)] v. 耐久, 忍耐
vegetarian [ˌvedʒəˈteəriən] adj. 素食的

implication [ˌɪmplɪˈkeɪʃn] n. 含意, 暗示
contemplation [ˌkɒntəmˈpleɪʃn] n. 注视, 沉思
belly [ˈbeli] n. 腹部, 胃
intolerance [ɪnˈtɒlərəns] n. 不宽容

Proper Nouns

Lingyin Temple 灵隐寺
Liuhe Tower (Pagoda of Six Harmonies) 六和塔
Eastern Jin Dynasty 东晋时期
Cloud Forest Buddhist Temple 云林禅寺

Tiger Spring 虎跑泉
Feilaifeng (Peak from Afar) 飞来峰
Huili 慧理(印度僧人)
Lingyin Vegetarian Restaurant 灵隐斋堂

Exercise ➡ ➡ ➡

Directions: Listen to the dialogue. Imagine that you are the local guide and your classmates are tourists. Do the dialogue again with additional information that the teacher may offer.

Part IV   Video for Tourism
旅游视频

Words and Expressions

subtle [ˈsʌtl] adj. 微妙的, 精细的
feature [ˈfiːtʃə(r)] n. 特征

masterpiece [ˈmɑːstəpiːs] n. 代表作

Proper Nouns	
Wuzhen 乌镇	Beijing-Hangzhou Grand Canal 京杭大运河
Mao Dun 茅盾	*Lin's Shop*《林家铺子》(茅盾代表作)

Wuzhen, located in the north of Zhejiang Province, is one hour's drive from Hangzhou and two hours' drive from Shanghai. It is embraced by the Beijing-Hangzhou Grand Canal's rivers and canal criss-crossing the whole town. Wuzhen has a history of more than 1,000 years with ancient residential houses, workshops and stores which still standing on the banks of the rivers.

While boating around the water network and wandering boat lanes, one can always favor sincerity and subtle beauty of Eastern China. Wuzhen is famous for its natural beauty and its many talent citizens throughout history, and outstanding modern Chinese writer Mao Dun is one instance. His masterpiece the *Lin's Shop* expresses vividly life of local people in Wuzhen. Wuzhen also boasts its prosperous parts and simple life style. Tradition is still very much alive in Wuzhen. Wandering along the *east-west* sitting room, people enjoy the atmosphere of the traditional cultures and original ancient features at that time that have been preserved intact.

Discover with China Highlight Travel. Let's view the scenery in Wuzhen.

Step 1: Watch the video and write down the key words or phrases in the video. You may use the key words or phrases as the reminders when you watch it the second time.

_____
_____
_____
_____

Step 2: Watch the video again and decide whether the statements are True or False.
1. _____ It takes you one hour to reach Wuzhen by car from Hangzhou and two hours to arrive by boat from Shanghai.
2. _____ Wuzhen is a water town which has a history of more than 1,000 years. Ancient residential houses, workshops and stores are still standing on the banks of the rivers.
3. _____ Wuzhen is not only famous for its natural beauty, but also for its talents throughout history.
4. _____ Although Mao Dun is not the local citizen in Wuzhen he depicts the vivid life of the local people in his masterpiece the *Lin's Shop*.

Part V Tour Commentary

West Lake

Ladies and Gentlemen!

Before you visit Hangzhou, you might have heard of the saying "Above is paradise, and below are Suzhou and Hangzhou." It means Suzhou and Hangzhou are as beautiful as Heaven. Why is Huangzhou compared with the Heaven? Mostly because of the beautiful scenery of the West Lake. Hundreds of years have passed, the West Lake is still as charming as ever. In ancient times, the West Lake was known for its best ten famous sites. Today, we'll visit the West Lake from Yuemiao port.

Now, we are moving from west to east. The scene here is called Gu Hill (Lone Hill). It is connected with the Xiling Bridge in the west and the Bai Embankment in the east. The Gu Hill has been popular since the Tang and Song dynasties. In the Qing Dynasty, Emperor Kangxi took this place as his interim palace. You may ask me: Since the Gu Hill is the biggest isle, why is it called Gu Hill? Well, the emperors of different dynasties reserved the place only for them, so it is called Gu Hill or Lone Hill. The hill is actually a peninsula. The local interesting saying goes like this, "The Lone Hill is not lonely; the Broken Bridge is not broken and the Long Bridge is not long."

Now here is the Bai Embankment. On both sides of the dike are lined with different trees. Especially in spring, it is green and red everywhere. You may feel as if you were traveling in a fairyland. At the east end of the Bai Embankment is the famous Duanqiao Bridge or Broken Bridge. In fact, it was an old stone arch bridge covered with bryophyte. Judging from its appearance, Duanqiao Bridge is a common stone arch bridge. However, it is regarded as the most famous bridge on the West Lake. Why? Because it is connected with *the Tale of White Snake*.

Well, you may ask me a question. Why is Duanqiao Bridge called Broken Bridge since it is not broken. Let me explain it to you. The bridge is facing the mountain and against the city. It is on the joint point between the North Li Lake and the Outer Lake. It is the best place to enjoy snow in winter. When the sun comes out after snowing, the snow on the south side will melt while the other side is still covered with snow. Looking from afar, the bridge is like a broken bridge. Besides, the bridge is the end of the Bai Embankment. In Chinese "duan" also means "ending." Got it?

After we visit the three isles—Three Pools Mirroring Moon, we are heading for the Su Embankment. There are 6 stone arch bridges in the embankment. The Su Embankment always reminds us of Su Dongpo, a very well known poet and scholar in the Song Dynasty. The Su Embankment was built under his leadership when he was the governor of Hangzhou. He used to write a poet to describe the beauty of the West Lake. In his poem, he compared the West Lake with Xi Shi, one of the four most famous ancient beauties in Chinese culture, so the West Lake has another name Xizi Lake. In order to commemorate Su Dongpo, the embankment was called Su Embankment. In the south of the embankment, the Memorial Museum of Su Dongpo was built.

Ladies and Gentlemen! The West Lake is the pearl of Hangzhou, the pearl of the East and the pearl of the world. I hope the lake has left you a wonderful impression. So much for our cruise on the West Lake! See you again.

Words and Expressions

bryophyte [bˈraɪəfaɪt] *n.* 苔藓

Proper Nouns

Gu Hill (Lone Hill) 孤山
Bai Embankment 白堤
Long Bridge 长桥
Three Pools Mirroring Moon 三潭印月
Su Dongpo 苏东坡
Xizi Lake 西子湖

Xiling Bridge 西泠桥
Duanqiao Bridge (Broken Bridge) 断桥
"the Tale of White Snake"《白蛇传》
Su Embankment 苏堤
Xi Shi 西施

Exercise

Directions: Act as the local guide and take tourists to have a cruise on the West Lake. Try to make your introduction more situational and attractive using the proper body language.

Part VI Readings

Directions: Read the following passage and fill in the blanks with the words or phrases given below.

| pagodas | bridge | eye | three | zigzag |
| top | biggest | lake | post | island |

Three Pools Mirroring the Moon Island

Three Pools Mirroring the Moon Island is also called "Lesser Yingzhou." In addition to the Mid-Lake Pavilion and Ruangong Islet, there are (1)_____ islands in West Lake. Among the three islets in the lake, the Lesser Yingzhou is the (2)_____ and finest one. And it is recommended as the "best scenic spot in the West Lake." The islet covers an area of 7 hectares including the water surface and features a "lake within an (3)_____ and an island within a lake." The wonderful garden design made this islet very unique among the ten (4)_____ views. This island was built to create a lake within a (5)_____ in 1607. Afterwards, three small gourd-shaped (6)_____ were built in the south lake of the islet called "Three Pools." At the beginning of Qing Dynasty, a general named Peng Yulin, after retiring from his official (7)_____, built for himself a garden villa on the island and then zigzag bridges, pavilions were added. After you go ashore at the port located on the north of the islet, two buildings will meet your (8)_____ firstly. Then, you will walk along the (9)_____ bridge which is better known as the "Nine-Turn Bridge." There are total four pavilions along this (10)_____ including the Open Net Pavilion, Tingting Pavilion, Emperor Kangxi Stele Pavilion and Heart-to-Heart Pavilion.

Words and Expressions

"Lesser Yingzhou" "小瀛洲"
Ruangong Islet 阮公墩
Peng Yulin 彭玉麟
Open Net Pavilion 开网亭
Emperor Kangxi Stele Pavilion 康熙御碑亭

Mid-Lake Pavilion 湖心亭
"Three Pools" "三潭"
"Nine-Turn Bridge" "九曲平桥"
Tingting Pavilion 亭亭亭
Heart-to-Heart Pavilion 我心相印亭

Part VII Translation

Melting Snow at Broken Bridge

1. The snow scene of the West Lake enjoyed very high praise, and the view of "melting snow at broken bridge" ("断桥残雪")is unique in the winter of the West Lake.
2. Why is it called as "melting snow on the broken bridge"? There are different sayings(众说纷纭). It snows almost every winter in Hangzhou.
3. When the sun comes out after snowfall, the snow on the sunny side of the bridge (桥阳面)melts first, while the snow on the shady side still lingers.
4. 从附近小山上极目远眺,那小桥好似桥断一般(appear to be broken)。
5. 待到冬日雪霁(on fine winter days),伫立桥头,放眼四望,远山银装素裹(clad in white),更加妩媚迷人,是欣赏西湖雪景之佳地(a best venue)。
6. 而中国民间传说"白蛇传"("The Tale of White Snake")又为断桥景物增添了些许浪漫(romance)色彩。

Unit 12

Touring Yunnan

Focus on Learning 学习要点

导游案例	A Breach of Security 治安事故
导游听力	1. Kunming City 昆明市
	2. Dianchi Lake 滇池
情景对话	Stone Forest 石林
旅游视频	Colorful Yunnan 七彩云南
导 游 词	Lijiang Ancient Town 丽江古城
导游阅读	Dali 大理
导游翻译	Yunnan Ethnic Village 云南民族村

 Part I   Tips for Tour Guides

Case 12

A Breach of Security

A group of Danish tourists just came back from the Old Town Lijiang. After they checked in the small inn, one of the tourists found that the facilities of his room were broken and his hand baggage was missing. What is the incident? How do you protect the tourists' security? Listen to the passage and write down the measures you will take as a local guide.

(1) This incident is _____ . It refers that the tourist have suffered theft, robbery, fraud, indecency or murder and their life or property has been endangered on the trip.

(2) First of all, I shall do my best to _____ of tourists and take them only to safe places. If the tourists are injured I should rescue them.

(3) I shall immediately report the incident to the police _____.

(4) I shall also report the incident to _____. When casualties or loss of property occur, I shall request the travel agency to _____ or request that the travel agency staff come and handle the incident.

(5) I shall try to _____, and if possible, continue with the scheduled travel.

(6) I shall _____ to the travel agency and help handle the issues concerned after the trip is over.

Words and Expressions

incident 事故
rescue 救援
handle the incident 处理事故
breach of security 治安事故
casualty 人员伤亡

Exercise

Directions: Imagine you are the local guide and Danish tourists. Replay the scene that the hotel suffered form the theft and the tourist's handbag was stolen. Demonstrate that you help the tourist handle the case. The students are expected to evaluate the remedies and how the presentation could be improved.

Part II　Listening Activities

Listening 1

Kunming City

Words and Expressions

verdure [ˈvɜːdjə(r)] *n.* 新鲜
gateway [ˈgeɪtweɪ] *n.* 门；通路
alluring [əˈljʊərɪŋ] *adj.* 迷人的，吸引人的
exotic [ɪgˈzɒtɪk] *adj.* 异国情调的；奇异的
alpine [ˈælpaɪn] *adj.* 高山的，阿尔卑斯山的
diversity [daɪˈvɜːsətɪ] *n.* 差异，多样性
camellia [kəˈmiːlɪə] *n.* [植]茶属，茶花，山茶
endow [ɪnˈdaʊ] *v.* 捐赠；赋予
celebrated [ˈselɪbreɪtɪd] *adj.* 著名的
bewitching [bɪˈwɪtʃɪŋ] *adj.* 迷人的，使人着迷的
congregation [ˌkɒŋgrɪˈgeɪʃn] *n.* 集合，集会
gig [gɪg] *n.* 特约演奏；旋转物

Proper Nouns

Zhejiang Province 浙江省
Dianchi Lake 滇池
West Hill Forest Park 西山森林公园
Myanmar [mɪˌænˈmɑː(r)] 缅甸，即 Burma
West Hill 西山
Yunnan Ethnic Village 云南民族村

> Grand View Pavilion 大观楼
> Golden Hall 金殿
> Cuihu Park 翠湖公园
> Mingfeng Mountain 鸣凤山
>
> Qiongzhu Temple 筇竹寺
> Yuantong Temple 圆通寺
> Garden of the World Horticultural Exposition 世界园艺博览园

Exercise ➡ ➡ ➡

Directions: Listen to the passage and decide whether the statements are true or false. If it is true, put "T" in the space provided and "F" if it is false.

1. _____ Kunming is nicknamed "city of spring" due to the fact that it is covered all the year round with the rich verdure of trees and plants.
2. _____ Endowed with a pleasant climate, the city is adorned with more than 380 kinds of flowers.
3. _____ In ancient times it was an important gateway to the celebrated Southern Silk Road which conducted to Tibet, Sichuan, Myanmar and India.
4. _____ The 360-square-km Dianchi is Yunnan's largest alpine lake known as a "highland bright pearl" for its vast expanse of liquid silver and graceful scenery.
5. _____ China's largest cast-bronze hall is found in Jindian Scenic Zone on the Mingfeng Mountain to the northeast of Kunming.

Listening 2

Words and Expressions

surface ['sɜːfɪs] n. 表面, 外表, 水面
massive ['mæsɪv] adj. 厚重的, 大块的
silhouette [ˌsɪluˈet] n. 侧面影像; 轮廓
refraction [rɪˈfrækʃn] n. 折光, 折射
fleet [fliːt] vi. 疾驰, 飞逝, 掠过
moonlight ['muːnlaɪt] n. 月光

altitude ['æltɪtjuːd] n. (尤指海拔)高度
cerulean [sɪˈruːliən] adj. 蔚蓝的, 天蓝的
intoxicate [ɪnˈtɒksɪkeɪt] vt. 使陶醉, 醉人
ethereal [iˈθɪəriəl] adj. 轻的, 像空气一样的
brim [brɪm] vi. 满溢

Proper Nouns

"Pearl of the Plateau" "高原明珠"

Dianchi Lake

If you have been to the Dianchi Lake, which is located at the foot of the Western Hills to (1)_____ of Kunming, you know what the "Pearl of the Plateau" means. Being the largest lake in Kunming and (2)_____ largest fresh water lake in China, Dianchi Lake is 300 square kilometers in surface area, (3)_____ meters in altitude and about 40 kilometers in length (from north to south). When the weather is fine, there are white flocculent or massive clouds (4)_____ in the cerulean sky, the cyan water waves under (5)_____ sunshine and the surrounding mountains reflect (6)_____ on the water. If you take a walk on the lake shore you will feel (7)_____ by the beautiful landscape. The most beautiful view of Dianchi Lake appears at dawn and sunset, the refraction of the ethereal rays glitter on (8)_____ surface just like thousands of silver fishes swimming and playing. At night, when the breeze is fleeting over the water and the world is brimming over with (9)_____, Dianchi Lake lies in silence and breathes in peace like (10)_____ beauty.

Exercise ➡ ➡ ➡

Directions: Listen to the passage and fill in the words or phrases you have heard.

Part III Situational Dialogue

Stone Forest

(A=Miss Yin Heng, a guide; B=Daniel)

A: Here we are at the Stone Forest. It is attractive, isn't it?

B: Yeah, I've never seen such a beautiful landscape before.

A: The Stone Forest has been known as the "First Wonder of the Wonder" since the Ming Dynasty. It covers an area of 400 square kilometers and includes both large and small stone forests. They are Major Stone Forest, Minor Stone Forest and Naigu Stone Forest and many more.

B: I don't think you're exaggerating it. It is really a vast forest of stones.

A: You see, each of the stones is lifelike with its own distinct characteristics. Some are elegant, some are rugged. Look, this is like a monkey, and that is like a bear.

B: Amazing! I think nobody dares to walk around at night. They may take the stones for the animals.

A: Yes, it's very dangerous to walk in the Stone Forest at night, but the local people live here for centuries. Of course, they're not afraid of stone animals or real animals here.

B: What are the local people?

A: They're Sani people, a branch of the Yi Ethnic Group in Yunan Province.

B: I heard tourists repeated Ashima. Who is Ashima?

A: She is a beautiful and warm-hearted Sani girl. A long time ago, she fell in love with a poor shepherd, but the landlord forced her to marry his son. At last she turned into a stone and stood majestically in the Stone Forest forever.

B: She is very brave and kind. By the way, how do the Stone Forest take the shape?

A: Geologists say the Stone Forest is a typical example of karst topography. About 270 million years ago the region was a vast expanse of sea.

B: A sea? Unbelievable!

A: The movements of the lithosphere gradually caused a retreat of the waters and the rise of the limestone landscape. Because of constant erosion, the area finally developed into the Stone Forest.

B: I really cannot expect it. It is really a spectacle of Nature.

A: Yes, I think you will marvel at the unique peaks and strange caves, the flying-down spring, and the plateau lakes here.

B: Certainly. I feel as if I were in a merry dreamland.

A: Ok. The road is slippery. Watch your step!

B: Thank you!

Words and Expressions

exaggerate [ɪgˈzædʒəreɪt] *v.* 夸大,夸张
rugged [ˈrʌgɪd] *adj.* 崎岖的
shepherd [ˈʃepəd] *n.* 牧羊人
lithosphere [ˈlɪθəsfɪə(r)] *n.* [地]岩石圈
slippery [ˈslɪpəri] *adj.* 滑的,光滑的

distinct [dɪˈstɪŋkt] *adj.* 截然不同的
warm-hearted [wɔːmˈhɑːtɪd] *adj.* 热诚的,热心的
topography [təˈpɒgrəfi] *n.* 地形
dreamland [ˈdriːmlænd] *n.* 梦境,梦乡

Proper Nouns

Lingyin Temple 灵隐寺
Stone Forest 石林
Major Stone Forest 大石林
Minor Stone Forest 小石林
Sani 撒尼族
Ashima 阿诗玛

Tiger Spring 虎跑泉
"First Wonder of the Wonder" "天下第一奇观"
Naigu Stone Forest 乃古石林
Yi Ethnic 彝族

Exercise ➡ ➡ ➡

Directions: Listen to the dialogue. Imagine that you are the local guide and your classmates are tourists. Do the dialogue again with additional information that the teacher may offer.

Part IV Video for Tourism
旅游视频

Colorful Yunnan

Words and Expressions

remote [rɪˈməʊt] *adj.* 遥远的
carnivals [ˈkɑːnəvəlz] *n.* 嘉年华
idyllic [ɪˈdɪlɪk] *adj.* 牧歌的
infinite [ˈɪnfɪnət] *adj.* 无限的，无穷的
canyons [ˈkænjənz] *n.* 峡谷

diversified [daɪˈvɜːsɪfaɪd] *adj* 多样化的
evolution [ˌiːvəˈluːʃn] *n.* 演变，进化
pastoral [ˈpɑːstərəl] *adj.* 田园生活的
turbulent [ˈtɜːbjələnt] *adj.* 汹涌的
random [ˈrændəm] *adj.* 随机的，任意的

Proper Nouns

Mid-South Peninsula 中南半岛

For her magical sights, mysterious national customs and remote history, Yunnan Province has become the most diversified natural and cultural area in the world. Everything here will go beyond your imagination and her charm will let you experience something new and out of the ordinary.

Come to Yunnan, you may choose an ecological journey from which you may feel nature's purity beauty magic and majesty.

Come to Yunnan and you will be in for a trip of national customs and conditions feeling colorful national customs and being involved in the national festivals and carnivals.

Come to Yunnan, feel her unique history and culture and you will sigh with the feeling, the might of the historical remains formed through two applied forces, passed time and fixes space.

Come to Yunnan, join the journey of scientific exploration and it will open a window of exploring and interpreting the evolution of nature and mankind.

Come to Yunnan, go back to the idyllic and pastoral countryside and her fine natural ecology and simple customs will make you forget to return.

Come to Yunnan, travel along the border and international rivers and you may enjoy Yunnan's specific border conditions and customs as well as experience those foreign sights and cultures of the Mid-south Peninsula.

Come to Yunnan, over 650 hot springs spread all over the province will bring infinite delight and comfort for your healthy journey.

Come to Yunnan, join the golf sports named "wielding the pole for 365 days every year" and you'll experience the satisfaction and excitement of relaxing yourselves in the all-year-spring nature.

Come to Yunnan, you may travel as you please and let your travelling dream fly freely, you can go to drift down those great turbulent rivers and explore them. You can go to climb the rocks of the mountains to explore those caves and challenge nature. You can drive to travel in those great beautiful mountains canyons forests and lakes. You can walk at random to feel the different pleasures as a free visitor.

Step 1: Watch the video and write down the key words or phrases in the video. You may use the key words or phrases as the reminders when you watch it the second time.

_____
_____
_____

Step 2: Watch the video again and decide whether the statements are True or False.
1. _____ Yunnan Province is one of the multi-nationality provinces where you can enjoy her colorful customs, and festivals and carnivals.
2. _____ Yunnan is well-known for the idyllic and pastoral countryside and her fine natural ecology will make you forget to return.
3. _____ You may enjoy Yunnan's specific border conditions and customs as well as experience those foreign sights and cultures of the Mid-south Peninsula.
4. _____ You can go to climb the rocks the mountains, explore those caves and challenge Nature. You can also drive to travel in those great beautiful mountains canyons forests and lakes.

Part V   Tour Commentary

Lijiang Ancient Town

Ladies and Gentlemen! Here we are. Lijiang is a well-preserved ancient town of ethnic minorities with brilliant culture. It is a central town of the Lijiang Autonomous County of Naxi Ethnic Minority in Yunan Province. If you have a bird's view of the ancient town, it looks like a big jade ink slab, therefore it got the nickname Dayanzhen or the Town of Big Ink Slab. You may feel a little bit dizzy, because the old town is located on the plateau, 2,400 meters above the sea level.

Ok, follow me into the ancient town! Here is the center of the ancient town—Sifangjie (the Square Street). Four main streets radiate from Square Street and extend to the four different directions. Countless lanes extending in all directions form a network and connect every corner of the town. Streets in the ancient town are paved by the local bluestones which are neither muddy in the rainy season nor dusty in the dry season. The massive and fine-grained stones add a sense of antiquity and mystery to the ancient town.

Look at the ancient folk houses along the street! The buildings in the town incorporate the best parts of the architectural traits of Han, Bai, and Tibet into a unique Naxi style. The layout of the town is free-style and flexible, the houses are close and diverse, and the lanes are narrow and meandering. The spacious and applied houses are mostly timber and tile structure compound with a garden; each has engraved vivid figures of people and animals on doors and windows, beautiful flowers and trees in the garden. Tonight, we'll live in one of the cottages, far away from the hustle and bustle of the metropolis. It is a real pleasant thing, isn't it?

Well, you may see many streams running through the street and even households. Lijiang Ancient Town is a town that depends on water for existence and water is just like its blood. Heilongtan (Black Dragon Pool) is the main water source of the town and subdivides into many streams which can reach every family and every street in the town. Because of the water channels, willow trees grow everywhere. And there are almost 350 different bridges in the ancient town. The water not only meets the need of the local people, but also gives the town a picture of waterscape. The sluice at the center of the town is opened late in the night and the current of water flushes and washes all the streets to keep the town clean. This practical use of water is part of the daily life of the residents in the ancient town.

Lijiang Ancient Town is praised as the "Oriental Venice" and "Suzhou in Highland," but it is much, much more than this. Once you visit the ancient town, it will capture your heart for the rest of your life.

So much for my introduction! See you next time!

Words and Expressions

minority [maɪˈnɒrətɪ] n. 少数,少数民族
radiate [ˈreɪdɪeɪt] vi. 发光;辐射;流露
muddy [ˈmʌdɪ] adj. 多泥的,泥泞的
sense [sens] n. 感觉,判断力;见识
incorporate [ɪnˈkɔːpəreɪt] vt. 合并,组成
flexible [ˈfleksəbl] adj. 灵活的;柔软的
subdivide [ˈsʌbdɪvaɪd] v. 再分,细分

dizzy [ˈdɪzɪ] adj. 使人晕眩的
bluestone [ˈbluːstəʊn] n. 青石,蓝砂岩
fine-grained [faɪnˈɡreɪnd] adj. 有细密纹理的
antiquity [ænˈtɪkwətɪ] n. 古代,古老
trait [treɪt] n. 特性
meander [mɪˈændə(r)] v. 漫步,蜿蜒而流
sluice [sluːs] n. 水闸;泄水

Proper Nouns

Lijiang 丽江
Dayanzhen (the Town of Big Ink Slab) 大研镇
Heilongtan (Black Dragon Pool) 黑龙潭
"Suzhou in Highland" "高原姑苏"

Naxi 纳西
Sifangjie (Square Street) 四方街
"Oriental Venice" "东方威尼斯"

Exercise ➡ ➡ ➡

Directions: Act as the local guide and take tourists to visit the old Lijiang Ancient Town. Try to make your introduction more situational and attractive using the proper body language.

Part VI   Readings

Directions: Read the following passage and fill in the blanks with the words or phrases given below.

record	west	relic	butterflies	economic
architectural	geographer	panoramic	posts	

Dali

Dali, located between the Erhai Lake and the Cangshan Mountain, is a city 400 km (1)_____ of Kunming. The Erhai Park on the southern bank provides visitors with its ancient-style pavilions, corridors and platforms where one can take a (2)_____ view of the Cangshan Mountain and the Erhai Lake. The Butterfly Spring is another frequent destination of tourists in Dali. The clear water and the flying (3)_____ give people a sense of tranquility and mystery. Built in the 9th century, the three majestic pagodas of Chongsheng Temple present a typical (4)_____ style of ancient China.

Dali is noted for its glorious history and culture. The stone Dehua Tablet of Nanzhao Kingdom is a very important historical (5)_____ for researching the history of the Tang Dynasty and the Nanzhao Kingdom. Another important historical relic is the Stone Table Commemorating Kublai Kham, the earliest (6)_____ that proves Yunnan Province was established in the Yuan Dynasty. In history, Dali used to be one of the important (7)_____ on the road to India and Myanmar. It was once a very prosperous town for cultural and (8)_____ exchanges between China and Southeast Asian countries. Both the well-known Chinese (9)_____ Xu Xiake and the Italian traveler Marco Polo visited Dali and described it in their travels.

Words and Expressions

Dali 大理
Cangshan Mountain 苍山
Chongsheng Temple 崇圣寺
Nanzhao Kingdom 南诏国
Xu Xiake 徐霞客
Marco Polo 马可·波罗

Erhai Lake 洱海
Butterfly Spring 蝴蝶泉
Dehua Tablet of Nanzhao Kingdom 南诏德化碑
Stone Table Commemorating Kublai Kham 世祖皇帝平云南碑

Part VII Translation

Yunnan Ethnic Village

1. Yunnan Ethnic Village(云南民族村), situated six kilometers south of Kunming, is a theme park (主题公园)of 1,250 mu. Each of the 26 ethnic groups of Yunnan has a village built on the premises in a beautiful setting.
2. The Dai Village surrounded by water on three sides is characterized by limpid ripples and shaped like a jade hairpin(玉簪). Among the sub-tropical trees are "the bamboo houses on poles"("干栏式竹楼").
3. The Bai Village was built in a traditional Bai style of "three houses with one screen wall" ("三坊一照壁")and "five patios surrounded by four residences"("四合五天井"). The village boasts an extensive collection of Bai customs and cultures.
4. 彝族村由三虎浮雕墙(the wall of three-tiger relief),展示彝族虎文化的虎山(Tiger Hill)和依山而建的民居组成。村内的太阳历广场(Solar Calendar Plaza)中央耸立着高大的图腾柱(totem pole)。
5. 白族村以风景名胜西山为背景,象征大理苍山(Cangshan Mountain)。民居临水而建,恰似洱海(Erhai Lake)人家。
6. 云南民族村是云南多民族省份的缩影(epitome),是典型的中国南方园艺(horticultural)大花园。

Unit 13

Touring Guizhou

Focus on Learning 学习要点

导游案例　　Traffic Accident 交通事故
导游听力　　1. Guiyang City 贵阳市
　　　　　　2. Zhijin Cave 织金洞
情景对话　　Mt. Fanjing 梵净山
旅游视频　　The Forest of Ten Thousand Peaks 万峰林
导 游 词　　Huangguoshu Waterfall 黄果树瀑布
导游阅读　　Qingyan Ancient Town 青岩古镇
导游翻译　　Xijiang—No.1 Village of Miao Ethnic Group 西江——苗族第一寨

 Part I　Tips for Tour Guides

Case 13

Traffic Accident

It is raining cats and dogs. Miss Tang Shenglan, a local guide of China Kanghui Travel Service, Guiyang Branch, is on the way to the Huangguoshu Waterfall. There is a heavy traffic jam and the guide is informed that the road has been blocked. Miss Tang contacts the head office for instructions. As the deputy manager on duty, what could you instruct her to handle the case? Listen to the passage and write down your instructions in the blanks.

(1) Miss Tang should first analyze the consequence of the interruption and propose _____ to the travel agency.
(2) She should then explain the situation to the tourists and ask for _____.
(3) She should make _____ and report to the head office according to the emergency alternative program by (a) extending the travel in a certain scenic area; (b) shortening the travel; or (c) changing the itinerary.
　(a) Extension of the travel time:
　　　If the guide has to extend the time of travel in a certain scenic area, she should _____, which should make the appropriate arrangements for _____ and modes of

transportation and notify the travel agency at the next stop to make adjustments according to the revised itinerary. Then she may extend the time _____ and add some programs of entertainment.

(b) Shortening of the travel time:

If she has to shorten the visit, she should contact the travel agency to cancel _____, rooms, transportation and _____. If appropriate, she should do her best to complete the sightseeing schedule within the time. If it is not possible, she may take tourists to visit the _____ so as to minimize their disappointment.

(c) Changing part of the travel schedule:

If she has to cancel part or all of a planned visit or _____, as instructed by the organizing travel agency, she should make a realistic and interesting introduction of _____ so as to arouse the tourists' interest and hopefully get their understanding and cooperation.

Words and Expressions

traffic jam 交通堵塞
head office 总部
modes of transportation 交通方式
emergency alternative program 紧急预案
extension of the travel time 延长旅游时间

Exercise ➡ ➡ ➡

Directions: Act as Miss Tang, the local guide and the Deputy Manager of the travel service. Make up a dialogue to discuss the remedies you will take. The teacher is expected to help improve their presentation in the class, putting forward the suggestions according to the situation.

Part II Listening Activities

Listening 1

Guiyang City

Words and Expressions

refreshment [rɪˈfreʃmənt] n. 点心, 饮料
enthrall [ɪnˈθrɔːl] vt. 迷惑, 迷住

aboriginal [ˌæbəˈrɪdʒənl] adj. 土著的，原来的
breathtaking [ˈbreθteɪkɪŋ] adj. 惊人的，惊险的
precipitation [prɪˌsɪpɪˈteɪʃn] n. 沉淀，沉淀作用

unsophisticated [ˌʌnsəˈfɪstɪkeɪtɪd] adj. 不懂世故的，单纯的
costume [ˈkɒstjuːm] n. 装束，服装

Proper Nouns

Guiyang City 贵阳市
Jiaxiu Pavilion 甲秀楼
Huaxi Park 花溪公园
Nanjiao Park 南郊公园
Baihua Lake 百花湖
Huangguoshu Waterfall 黄果树瀑布
Dragon Palace 龙宫
Zhijin Cave 织金洞

Guizhou Province 贵州省
Qianling Park 黔灵公园
Guizhou Botanical Garden 贵州植物园
Tianhe Pool 天河潭
Maolan Karst Forest Natural Conservation
茂兰喀斯特森林自然保护区
Anshun City 安顺市
Hongfeng Lake (Red Maple Lake) 红枫湖

Exercise ➡ ➡ ➡

Directions: Listen to the passage and decide whether the statements are true or false. If it is true, put "T" in the space provided and "F" if it is false.

1. _____ The landscape in Guiyang is elegant, its folkways are rich, and its sites of cultural interest are numerous.
2. _____ Local dishes and refreshments, prepared in a distinctive Guizhou style, hold Chinese and foreign visitors enthralled.
3. _____ Huangguoshu Waterfall is the second biggest in China and among the world's famous waterfalls.
4. _____ Dragon Palace, about 25 miles southwest of Anshun City, is a splendid underground karst type cave.
5. _____ There are over 100 islands in the clear blue water lake of the Hongfeng Lake Scenic Area.

Listening 2

Words and Expressions

imposing [ɪmˈpəʊzɪŋ] adj. 壮丽的
sway [sweɪ] v. 摇摆，摇动
clint [klɪnt] n. 石芽

dazzling [ˈdæzl] adj. 眼花缭乱的
jungle [ˈdʒʌŋgl] n. 丛林
akin [əˈkɪn] adj. 同族的，类似的

Proper Nouns

Zhijin County 织金县
"Museum of Limestone Caves" "岩溶博物馆"
"King of Caves" "溶洞之王"
Zhijin Cave Scenic Area 织金洞风景名胜区

Zhijin Cave

Situated in northeast Zhijin County, Zhijin Cave is an (1)_____ cave whose (2)_____ -square-metre floor sets the stage for numerous dazzling scenes and sights. In between clusters of pools and by a swaying (3)_____ lake is a jungle of stalagtite, clints and stalagmites akin to (4)_____, pillars and hills. For the 40 or so (5)_____ formations, the cave is honored as the "King of Caves" or the "Museum of Limestone Caves." A 6.6-km section of it has been divided into (6)_____ for public viewing. Zhijin Cave Scenic Area is famous for its massive, scale, (7)_____, stone pillars and stone pagodas in unbelievable heights and numbers. In addition to enjoying the scenery, (8)_____ can discover the rich and varied folk customs and cultures of the ethnic groups. Numerous festivals, strong but (9)_____ customs, architectures with unique style and the exotic and colorful (10)_____, will make tourists feel everything is new and fresh.

Exercise ➡ ➡ ➡

Directions: Listen to the passage and fill in the words or phrases you have heard.

Part III   Situational Dialogue

Mt. Fanjing

(A=Miss Gong Ling, a staff of travel service; B=Donald)

A: What can I do for you, sir?

B: I'm going to hike in Mt. Fanjing. Can you give me some advice?

A: Ok. First of all, I'd like to give you some basic information about the mountain, and then you can make preparations for your trip.

B: Good! What is the height of the mountain?

A: The highest peak of Mt. Fanjing is 2,572 meters above sea level. It is not only the highest mountain in Guizhou but also is the highest peak in all of the Wuling Mountain Range.

B: I heard Mt. Fanjing is a national natural reserve and joined the Man and Biosphere Nature Reserve network of UNESCO in 1986. I think there are a lot of flowers and plants. Are there any animals there?

A: Favorable nature conditions also provide an ideal habitat for wild animals. Over 382 species of vertebrate animals were identified here. Among them 14 species are national protected animals, including the Golden Snub-nosed Monkeys and Tigers of South China.

B: Terrific. I want to catch some wild animals for a barbecue.

A: As a tourist, you cannot hunt any animals in the scenic area.

B: All right. I shall not go hunting, but what else can I see in Mt. Fanjing?

A: Mt. Fanjing is a Buddhist mountain. In the Qing Dynasty, there were 48 Buddhist temples. Many relics of temples and precious stone tablets still remain; you can feel the celestial atmosphere of that time.

B: I'm not interested in the man-made sites. I'm a mountaineer. I love hiking in the mountain.

A: All right. The top of Buddhist mountains is called the "golden summit." Generally speaking, each mountain has one "golden summit," but Mt. Fanjing has three "gold summits." So you can climb the "golden summits."

B: Wonderful! What are they?

A: The first one is the main peak of Mt. Fenghuang, 2,572 meters above sea level. The second one is the Old Golden Summit on Mt. Laoshan, 2,493 meters above sea level. The third one is called New Golden Summit, 2,336 meters above sea level. It is a 94-meter-high huge rock between Mt. Fenghuang and Mt. Laoshan. The top of the New Golden Summit is often shrouded in colorful clouds, so people give it the name Hongyun Summit or Red Cloud Summit.

B: I'll climb Mt. Fenghuang, the highest peak.

A: I suggest you climb Hongyun Summit because you may see the Buddhist Halo. In the halo, you can find enlarged shadows of yours and other objects. Local people regard it as an auspicious sign.

B: Thank you for your advice! I shall start my trip tomorrow morning. Can you provide a guide for me?

A: Certainly. Are you going to travel alone or with your friends?

B: With my two friends.

A: Ok. Please sign the contract and pay in the cashier. We'll pick you up in your hotel 7:00 o'clock in the morning.

B: Thank you very much!

Words and Expressions

habitat [ˈhæbɪtæt] n. 产地，栖息地
identify [aɪˈdentɪfaɪ] vt. 识别，鉴别
celestial [səˈlestiəl] adj. 天上的

vertebrate [ˈvɜːtəbrɪt] adj. 有脊椎的
barbecue [ˈbɑːbɪkjuː] n. 烤烧野餐
auspicious [ɔːˈspɪʃəs] adj. 吉兆的，幸运的

Proper Nouns

Mt. Fanjing 梵净山
Man and Biosphere Nature Reserve "人与生物圈保护区"
Old Golden Summit 老金顶
Hongyun Summit (Red Cloud Summit) 红云金顶
Wuling Mountain Range 武陵山脉
Mt. Fenghuang 凤凰山
Mt. Laoshan 老山
New Golden Summit 新金顶

Exercise

Directions: Listen to the dialogue. Imagine that you are the local guide and your classmates are tourists. Do the dialogue again with additional information that the teacher may offer.

Part IV　Video for Tourism
旅游视频

The Forest of Ten Thousand Peaks

Words and Expressions

sinkholes [ˈsɪŋkhəʊl] n. 灰岩坑，落水洞
tectonic [tekˈtɒnɪk] adj. 地壳构造上的
acid limestone 石灰岩
banyan [ˈbænjən] n. 榕树；菩提树
triangle [ˈtraɪæŋgl] n. 三角形
conical [ˈkɒnɪkl] adj. 圆锥形的
dioxide [daɪˈɒksaɪd] n. 二氧化物
karst [kɑːst] n. 喀斯特地形
evaporate [ɪˈvæpəreɪt] v. 蒸发
auspicious [ɔːˈspɪʃəs] adj. 吉利的

Proper Nouns

Forest of Ten Thousand Peaks 万峰林
Buyi Ethnic 布依族
Yijing《易经》
Xingyi City 兴义市
Bagua Tian 八卦田

　　Everybody, Nihao! Here we are at the entrance of The Forest of Ten Thousand Peaks. And it's basically a mountain and all these kind of things. We are gonna learn about it.
　　Let's go! Check it out. Come on！ Go!
　　"Wanfenglin," or The Forest of Ten Thousand Peaks in English, is located in Xingyi city of

Guizhou Province. Guizhou is known as the mountain kingdom, since 92.5% of Guizhou is covered by mountains and hills.

The unique landscape of The Forest of Ten Thousand Peaks is characterized by karst formations. The combination of sinkholes and limestone caves that make up these formations creates the conical mountains, approximately, the same height and width that stretch for miles in all directions.

So here we are. We are riding this very little car to the top here. We are gonna check out a little bit further what this whole idea of The Forest of Ten Thousand Peaks actually means. Are there really ten thousand of them? I don't know if I can count that far.

About 360 million years ago, this area was completely under water. 280 million years ago, as the result of intense tectonic movement, the earth crossroads and the land started to take shape. Carbon dioxide and organic acids eroded the limestone to create sinkholes, streams, caves, peaks, underground rivers, valleys and other such characteristics of this landscape.

So here we are. We've got some of the peaks of this Ten Thousand Peaks Forest. Down below you can see one of the ethnic minorities of China, called the Buyi ethnic minority, and they've created this nice very little village around here that surrounds these karst formations.

The Buyi ethnicity have a great respect for Nature and living harmony with their natural environment. For example, because banyan trees prevent erosion and create shade, the Buyi people will make offerings to the trees as the display of respect and reference for their ruin in the natural environment.

So down below, we've picked up this Buyi village and it's called the Upper Nahui village of the Buyi ethnicity. And in Feb.,2005, president of the People's Republic of China Hu Jintao came here to have a little dinner, so it's a kind famous now.

President Hu visited the Buyi villagers during the Spring Festival that year, China's most important holiday.

So down below is called the Bagua Tian or the eight triangle field. It's a kind of special field in that it helps regulate the water within the Buyi village down below. Basically, when the water level is higher in the beginning of the summer, it can keep it from overflowing in order to save water from evaporating. And then when the water is lower like right now cause there's a drought going on, it's still nice water with a world down below, sort of a natural part of the water table there. And then they use a pipe to serve sucked out use for irrigation.

And then No.2. This 8 triangle field is from the Yijing, sort of an ancient Chinese book that explains the changes of natural things.

"Dashun Feng" is a cluster of six mountains, and it is considered very auspicious because six is a lucky number in China.

Six peaks. Check it out. Lucky!

Step 1: Watch the video and write down the key words or phrases in the video. You may use the key words or phrases as the reminders when you watch it the second time.

_____
_____
_____
_____

Step 2: Watch the video again and decide whether the statements are True or False.
1. _____ The Forest of Ten Thousand Peaks is famous for its karst formations.
2. _____ Carbon dioxide and organic acids eroded the limestone to create sinkholes, streams, caves, peaks and valleys because of intense tectonic movement.
3. _____ The Buyi people will make offerings to the flowers as the display of respect and reverence for their ruin in the natural environment.
4. _____ Bagua Tian is a kind of special field which has eight triangles where Taoists can help regulate the water running in the Buyi village.

Part V　Tour Commentary

Huangguoshu Waterfall

Ladies and Gentlemen!

Here we are. This is the world-famous Huangguoshu Waterfall. It is 68 meters high and 81 meters wide. The Waterfall has special feature of thunderous roars and heavy mist. In winter and spring, the water flows light like satin hanging down. Many tourists could not help but marvel at this magnificent spectacle. Listen, the roar is like thunders and you can hear the thunderous roars as far as several kilometers away. Look, the mist stretches several hundred meters and nearby farmers' houses are enshrouded by the mist.

Now, we proceed to a place where the flow sinks into the Xiniu Pond (Rhino Pond). As legend has it that a heavenly rhino hid itself underneath the water, and enshrouded the pond in a veil of myth. At such a mysterious place, I'd like to tell you the origin of the name about Huangguoshu Waterfall. According to a legend, there used to be a large orchard by the waterfall where pomelo, or "huangguo" in the local dialect, was planted, so the waterfall got its name.

Everybody! Watch the waterfall carefully! Are they any different features from other waterfalls you've seen? Right! It is a karst fall. Unlike waterfalls in other countries, this cataract is unique. It is the largest waterfall found in a background of karst topography. Among the numerous scenic spots here, the Water Curtain Cavern is the most mysterious.

The Water Curtain Cavern is 134 meters long and consists of 6 caverns, 6 halls, 3 fountains and 6 passageways. A scene from the Chinese TV drama *Monkey King* was shot in the caverns. Well, this is the first cavern. It is the lowest, 40 meters above the surface of the Xiniu Pond. High above in midair in the front of this cavern, there hangs a group of calcific rocks, known as the

Miniature Garden. The surfaces of the rocks are covered with aquatic plants and colorful flowers in blossom.

Everybody! Now we are going to visit a chain of scenes of Xiniu Pond. The cataract consists of a chain of drops and ponds downstream. The Xiniu Pond, the biggest of its kind, is 17.7 meters deep. It is constantly shrouded by a thin veil of mist and watery fog. With the reflection of sunshine, a spectacular rainbow emerges midair in morning and afternoon. If you're patient enough, you may see the rainbow at four o'clock this afternoon.

Ladies and Gentlemen! I think the Huangguoshu Waterfall has left you with lovely impression. This beautiful scenery belongs to China as well as to the world. Have a good time! See you again!

Words and Expressions

enshroud [ɪnˈʃraʊd] vt. 掩盖，隐蔽
dialect [ˈdaɪəlekt] n. 方言，语调
miniature [ˈmɪnətʃə(r)] adj. 微型的，缩小的
cataract [ˈkætərækt] n. 大瀑布，奔流
orchard [ˈɔːtʃəd] n. 果园
calcific [kælˈsɪfɪk] adj. 石灰质的，钙化的
aquatic [əˈkwætɪk] adj. 水生的，水栖的

Proper Nouns

Xiniu Pond (Rhino Pond) 犀牛潭
Miniature Garden 袖珍花园
Water Curtain Cavern 水帘洞

Exercise

Directions: Act as the local guide and take tourists to visit the Huangguoshu Waterfall. Try to make your introduction more situational and attractive using the proper body language.

Part VI   Readings

Directions: Read the following passage and fill in the blanks with the words or phrases given below.

original	archways	town	by	scattered
nationalities	continued	if	conquer	

Qingyan Ancient Town

The ancient town is located south to the Huaxi District of Guiyang City. The inhabitants are not more than one thousand, including Han, Miao and Buyi (1)_____. Qingyan was established as a (2)_____ in 1378 and has a history of 600 years. It was called Qingyan Station in local annals. In 1381, Zhu Yuanzhang—the first emperor of the Ming Dynasty sent an army of 300,000 soldiers to (3)_____ Yunnan and Guizhou provinces. After the campaigns the soldiers remained and stationed there to open up the place. As time went (4)_____, the place in the past turned to be the town at the present. Only the (5)_____ appearance and the structural style can show how long its history is.

The architectures in the town have a peculiar style due to historical accumulation of the town. Its construction first began from the Ming Dynasty and (6)_____ up to the year of Emperor Daoguang in the Qing Dynasty. In a period of its great prosperity there were 9 temples, 8 mosques, 3 caves, 2 shrines, 1 compound, 1 residence and 8 memorial (7)_____. When you enter the Qingyan Ancient Town in Guizhou Province, you'll feel excited to see the civilian buildings of the Ming and Qing dynasties (8)_____ in a peaceful environment. Every tree and bush, each hill and river make you feel relaxed, as (9)_____ you were at home.

Words and Expressions

annals ['ænlz] n. 编年史, 县志
campaign [kæm'peɪn] n. [军]战
mosque [mɔsk] n. 清真寺
accumulation [əˌkjuːmjə'leɪʃn] n. 积聚, 堆积物

conquer ['kɒŋkə(r)] vt. 征服, 战胜, 占领
peculiar [pɪ'kjuːlɪə(r)] adj. 奇特的, 罕见的
prosperity [prɒ'sperətɪ] n. 繁荣

Proper Nouns

Qingyan Ancient Town 青岩古镇
Miao 苗族
Qingyan Station 青岩屯
Zhu Yuanzhang 朱元璋

Huaxi District 花溪区
Buyi 布依族
Emperor Daoguang 道光皇帝

Part VII　Translation

Xijiang —No.1 Village of Miao Ethnic Group

1. Xijiang Town (西江镇)lies northeast of Leishan County(雷山县), Guizhou Province. It is 81 kilometers from the capital of Kaili Prefecture(凯里州). The Baishui River(白水) is running through the town where 12 villages are established.
2. There are over 1,200 households and Miao nationality takes up about 99.2%. It is No. 1 Village of Miao Ethnic Group (苗族第一寨)in Guizhou, even in China.
3. The primitive and ecological environment in the Miao villages has been perfectly preserved. The stilted houses(吊脚楼) built of China fir(衫木), have a special exotic feature. The houses are usually built on the slope of about 30—70 degree.
4. 从雷公坪俯瞰(take a bird's-eye view)整个苗寨，山里是鳞次栉比的木制吊脚楼(row upon row of the wooden stilted houses)。
5. 吊脚楼楼高三层。一层圈养牲畜(livestock)，二层居住，三层作储物之用。客厅位于二楼正中，内供有祖宗牌位(altar)，同时也作为会客之所。
6. "美人靠"("a beauty couch")是一张长椅，放置在客厅前方，人们可坐在这长长的椅子上把酒言欢，欣赏远处的美丽风景。难怪有人把西江称为一座"露天博物馆"("an open museum")。

Unit 14

Touring Guangxi

Focus on Learning 学习要点

导游案例	Policies and Religions 政策与宗教
导游听力	1. Nanning City 南宁市
	2. Elephant Trunk Hill 象鼻山
情景对话	West Street 西街
旅游视频	Yangshuo 阳朔
导 游 词	Lijiang River 丽江
导游阅读	Seven-Star Park 七星岩
导游翻译	Mt. Fubo (Wave-Subduing Hill) 伏波山

Part I Tips for Tour Guides

Case 14

Policies and Religions

A group of foreign tourists are cruising on the Lijiang River. One of them distributed some religious pamphlets to other tourists and spoke ill of Chinese police while another try to seek for the prostitutes because he believes that prostitution is the acceptable service. How do you handle the case as a local guide? Listen to the passage and fill in the blanks with the information which may help you to handle the case.

(1) Handle the matter factually: I shall _____ about China so that they have better understanding.

(2) Handle the matter sensitively: I may simply express my own idea, but _____ to maintain an amicable atmosphere.

(3) Handle the matter with restraint: I may graciously refute the criticisms made by the tourist who _____, but I should continue to provide warm service to _____.

(4) According to the policies and regulations of China, foreign tourists are forbidden to preach, preside over _____ or distribute religious materials _____. I shall tell him of our policies and ask him not to do so.

(5) I shall tell the tourists that _____ is prohibited in China and every foreign tourist should respect _____. If he persists, I should report him to the local police.

Words and Expressions	
religious pamphlet 宗教小册子	speak ill of 诽谤
prostitution 卖淫	policy and regulation 政策和规定

Exercise ➡ ➡ ➡

Directions: Act as the guide and the tourists. Make up a dialogue to demonstrate how you could solve the problem. The rest of the class will make comments on their presentation. The teacher is expected to put forward some suggestions and help them to make progress in the class presentation.

Part II   Listening Activities

Listening 1

Nanning City

Words and Expressions	
autonomous [ɔːˈtɒnəməs] adj. 自治的	industrial [ɪnˈdʌstriəl] adj. 工业的, 产业的
extol [ɪkˈstəʊl] v. 赞美	outskirts [ˈaʊtskɜːts] n. 市郊
slanting [slɑːnt] adj. 倾斜的	Vietnamese [ˌvjetnəˈmiːz] adj. 越南人的
stunning [ˈstʌnɪŋ] adj. 极好的	paddy [ˈpædi] n. 稻, 谷
patrol [pəˈtrəʊl] v. 出巡, 巡逻	

Proper Nouns	
Nanning City 南宁市	Guangxi Zhuang Autonomous Region 广西壮族自治区
Guangxi Museum 广西博物馆	
Guangxi Ethnic Artefact Garden 广西民族文物苑	Guangxi Medical Botanical Garden 广西药用植物园

Yiling Cave 伊岭岩
Chongzuo 崇左市
Ningming County 宁明县
Pingxiang 凭祥
Guilin 桂林
West Street 西街
Wuming County 武鸣县
Huashan Mural 华山壁画
Daxin County 大新县
Lijiang River 漓江
Yangshuo 阳朔

Exercise ➡ ➡ ➡

Directions: Listen to the passage and decide whether the statements are true or false. If it is true, put "T" in the space provided and "F" if it is false.

1. _____ Under a subtropical climate, Nanning is a tourist city that is extolled as an "evergreen metropolis."
2. _____ This garden city has so much to offer its visitors, such as Guangxi Museum, Guangxi Ethnic Artefact Garden and Guangxi Medical Botanical Garden.
3. _____ The border tour is also popular between Guangxi and Vietnam.
4. _____ Very few foreign tourists know the picturesque karst scenery along the Lijiang River down from Guilin to Yangshuo.
5. _____ West Street is known as "the Earth Village in China," for foreigners from all over the world do business here.

Listening 2

Words and Expressions

leisurely [ˈliːʒəli:] adv. 从容不迫
penetrate [ˈpenətreɪt] vt. 穿透, 渗透
suck [sʌk] v. 吸, 吮, 吸取
exceedingly [ɪkˈsiːdɪŋli] adv. 非常地, 极度地

Proper Nouns

Elephant Trunk Hill 象鼻山
Yi Hill 仪山
Moon-over-Water Cave 水月洞
Li Hill 漓山
Chenshui Hill 沉水山

Elephant Trunk Hill

Situated majestically at the southeast of Guilin City and (1)_____ of Lijiang River, Elephant Trunk Hill is regarded as the symbol of Guilin landscape. Originally named "Li Hill," "Yi Hill" and "Chenshui Hill," the hill has a history of (2)_____ years. Resembling an elephant leisurely (3)_____ from the river with its long (4)_____, this hill is famous as the Elephant Trunk Hill for hundreds of years. With an elevation of (5)_____, the hill towers 55m above the water, measuring (6)_____ in length and 100m in width. Between the trunk and the legs of the elephant is a (7)_____, in the shape of a full moon, penetrating the hill from side to side. People named it "Moon-over-Water Cave." When the waters wave and the moonlight (8)_____, the scene is exceedingly (9)_____. On the walls in and around this cave, over (10)_____ from the Tang and Song dynasties were found, praising the beauty of hills and waters nearby.

Exercise ➡ ➡ ➡

Directions: Listen to the passage and fill in the words or phrases you have heard.

Part III Situational Dialogue

West Street

(A=Miss Zhang Xi, a guide, B=Tom)

A: We're walking along the West Street. It is completely paved with marble, 517 meters long and 8 meters wide. It is typical of a south China street with a simple style and courtyard-like setting.

B: Miss Zhang, I see a lot of foreigners here. I feel as if I were not walking in China, but in the Wall Street.

A: You may not know every now and then foreigners outnumber Chinese here, so the West Street is also called "foreigners' street." But don't be surprised if you hear an old Chinese woman speaks English.

B: I do marvel at the people here. Everyone I met could speak English as if I entered "the global village."

A: Yes, it is. Since the 1980's, the West Street has become a window of eastern and western culture and the biggest "foreign language center" in China. Each year, about 100,000 foreigners come here to travel or to attend advanced studies. Visitors are attracted to the West Street by its unique mix of cultures.

B: Terrific. I'm happy to see almost every store has bilingual shop signs. It's convenient for our foreigners to go shopping.

A: Right. The West Street is old, but also modern and fashionable. More than 20 stores have been opened by foreigners who have settled here.

B: Wow! So many foreigners do business in such a small town!

A: Why are you so surprised? Chinese who travel here may think they are in a foreign country, while foreigners come here to search for the ancient civilization of China. However, whether you are Chinese or a foreigner, the West Street is a terrific place to take a rest, both physical and psychological.

B: I couldn't agree with you less. Traveling on the West Street is an experience to be with the landscape, with the people and with the soul. I don't feel tired at all.

A: I hope so. Tom, just now you said you would go shopping. You see, here are various folk-custom stores, painting and calligraphy stores, backpack shops and Chinese Kung Fu academies. What do you want?

B: I want to go shopping in a craftwork shop. My girlfriend asked me to buy her the Chinese embroidered shoes.

A: Now, we come to the craftworks shop. You can choose lots of items, from embroidered silk, wax-painted cloth, to tiny shoes worn by women before 1949.

B: Thank you.

A: This way, please.

Words and Expressions

outnumber [ˌaʊtˈnʌmbə(r)] *vt.* 数目超过
fashionable [ˈfæʃnəbl] *adj.* 流行的,时髦的
backpack [ˈbækpæk] *n.* 挑运,背包
embroider [ɪmˈbrɔɪdə(r)] *vt.* 刺绣,镶边

bilingual [ˌbaɪˈlɪŋgwəl] *adj.* 能说两种语言的
psychological [ˌsaɪkəˈlɒdʒɪkl] *adj.* 心理(上)的
craftwork [ˈkrɑːftwɜːk] *n.* 工艺品

Proper Nouns

Mt. Fanjing 梵净山
West Street 西街

Wuling Mountain Range 武陵山脉
Wall Street 华尔街

Exercise

Directions: Listen to the dialogue. Imagine that you are the local guide and your classmates are tourists. Do the dialogue again with additional information that the teacher may offer.

Part IV Video for Tourism
旅游视频

Yangshuo

Words and Expressions

inspiring [ɪnˈspaɪərɪŋ] *adj.* 鼓舞人心的
proclaim [prəˈkleɪm] *v.* 公布；声称
adage [ˈædɪdʒ] *n.* 格言
premier [ˈpremɪə(r)] *adj.* 首位的，最先的
laid-back [ˌleɪdˈbæk] *adj.* 懒散的，悠闲的

glamour [ˈglæmə(r)] *n.* 迷人
backpacker [ˈbækpækə(r)] *n.* 背包族
multitudinous [ˌmʌltɪˈtjuːdɪnəs] *adj.* 大量的
imbue [ɪmˈbjuː] *v.* 使感染；使渗透

Proper Nouns

Yangshuo 阳朔
Zhuang 壮族
Miao 苗族
Hui 回族
Yao 瑶族

Picture an impossibly steep hill site rising from a valley with heavy mist, teaming with some birds, trees and vines. Perhaps you came across this scene before in traditional Chinese water colors the last time you visited in a museum and like me thought: what an inspiring example of the artistic license. If only a place is as beautiful as that truly existed! Well, it does exist. It's called Yangshuo, 65 km south of the major city of Guilin in southern China's Guangxi Province. The Chinese has long been glamour with a natural beauty of this place. And ancient adage in China proclaims Guilin landscapes are the most beautiful of any in China, but Yangshuo landscapes top even those in Guilin.

But Yangshuo was only popularized recently amongst foreign travelers in the 1980s *by Lonely Planet,* the guide book recommendation, which was first through the backpackers. However the features of dominate the horizon are the multitudinous lime stone towers jutting straight up above the valley. Yangshuo is the heart of the karst which fans the southern Chinese provinces of Guangxi, Guizhou and Yunnan. So Yangshuo is the premier rock-climbing destination in all of China. And the international climbing festival is held here every year. You can also tour many caves hidden below including the water cave, complete with hot springs and natural mud baths.

The special geography provides with eye-catching beauty while over 1400 years of history imbued with the deep traditional culture. The diverse ethnic minority groups found here included the Hui, Zhuang, Yao, Miao and others who enrich Yangshuo with special folk cultures represented by their various festivals. Adding many foreigner residents to this create a fascinating and diverse global community. The streets in Yangshuo are well kept in an original and ancient style. West Street is the most exciting one that locals called the global village. There are not only many foreign tourists but also quite a number of foreign residents managing cafes and restaurants like The VOTOLE restaurant owned by French brothers. So it's easy to find one's favorite restaurant in vegetarian, Indian, Italian and French style as well as the local style. Luckily Yangshuo was also one of the cheapest with prices generally 1/3 that of the southern China's coast areas. Exotic favors combined the traditional culture made Yangshuo world famous. With no doubt, Yangshuo is one of the most laid-back towns in China. We hope to see you soon here in Yangshuo.

Safe travels.

Step 1: Watch the video and write down the key words or phrases in the video. You may use the key words or phrases as the reminders when you watch it the second time.

_____
_____
_____
_____

Step 2: Watch the video again and decide whether the statements are True or False.
1. _____ The landscapes in Guilin are beautiful in China, but Yangshuo landscapes top even those in Guilin.
2. _____ The backpackers from foreign countries made Yangshuo famous in 1980s and more and more foreign tourists come to enjoy its unique landscapes.
3. _____ Yangshuo is well-known for its eye-catching natural beauty, but few visitors would enjoy its traditional cultures of the ethnic minority groups.
4. _____. West Street is called the global village and people from all over the world come to manage cafes and restaurants here.

Part V   Tour Commentary

Lijiang River

Ladies and Gentlemen!

Welcome on board for cruising the beautiful Lijiang River. Please sit back and relax. Our boat is going to leave Zhujiang Port. This cruise will take us about 4 hours to reach Yangshuo. I believe gorgeous karst peaks will give you surprises at each bend of the limpid river under the blue sky. You'll see water buffalo patrol the fields, peasants reap rice paddies, school kids and fishermen float by on bamboo rafts. The scenery along the Lijiang River is a taste of life far from the concrete jungle of the city. And the ever-ceasing landscape and country scenery will never disappoint you.

Now we can see the river rushing to the steep Bat Hill. The 2 peaks with flat yellow cliffs look like 2 flying bats. The 9 peaks on the right look like 9 cattle plowing the land. The 5 peaks on the left look like 5 running horses. If you look carefully, you will find out that the 2 peaks ahead look like 2 lions playing with an embroidered ball and looking around the 3 islets.

Ladies and Gentlemen! Our boat is entering the Caoping Scenic Area. The mountain in front looks like a golden crown of the Han Dynasty, so it is called Crown Hill. There is a grotto called Guanyan Grotto at the foot of the hill. It is the exit of an underground river with a different source from the Lijiang River. Some people had tried to look for its source. In 1987 Sino-British team dived 24 meters underwater and found that the fish there were more than one meter long. But they still failed to discover the source of the underground river. It remains a mystery of the Lijiang River.

Now, our boat is going to arrive at Yangdi. The stretch of river from Yangdi to Xingping is the most excellent part of our cruise. It is the climax of the musical movement we are enjoying. Down stream from Yangdi to Xingping, the river passes an endless procession of distinct peaks and bamboo groves and the stunning landscape.

Look ahead! On the upper right, the steep peaks and flowing clouds create a mysterious atmosphere. The eight peaks over there are eight immortals in a famous Chinese legend. The immortals originally lived in Penglai, Shandong Province. But why did they come here? It is said that the eight immortals came to Guilin and were attracted so much by the beauty of the place that they decided to stay here. So the scene is named "Eight Immortals Across the River."

Ladies and Gentlemen! The most exciting memento on our cruise is coming. The hill in front of us is the famous scenic spot—the Nine-Horse Painting Hill. The huge cliff with rich colors looks like an enormous piece of Chinese landscape painting. Now the boat is coming close to the hill. You will be surprised to find out that nine handsome horses were painted on the cliff.

Now, our boat is entering Yangshuo. Please get ready to get off the boat. We'll go shopping in the West Street. At 4:00 pm we'll take coach back to Guilin.

Have a good time!

Words and Expressions

buffalo [ˈbʌfələʊ] n. [动]水牛
cattle [ˈkætl] n. 牛，家养牲畜
stunning [ˈstʌnɪŋ] adj. 足以使人晕倒的，极好的
reap [riːp] v. 收割，收获
procession [prəˈseʃn] n. 行列，队伍
memento [məˈmentəʊ] n. 纪念品

Proper Nouns	
Zhujiang Port 竹江码头	Bat Hill 蝙蝠山
Caoping Scenic Area 草坪风景区	Crown Hill 冠山
Guanyan Grotto 冠岩	Yangdi 杨堤
Xingping 兴坪	Penglai 蓬莱
Eight Immortals Across the River 八仙过江	Nine-Horse Painting Hill 九马画山

Exercise ➡ ➡ ➡

Directions: Act as the local guide and take tourists to cruise on the Lijiang River. Try to make your introduction more situational and attractive using the proper body language.

Part VI   Readings

Directions: Read the following passage and fill in the blanks with the words or phrases given below.

rocky	scenes	foot	centre	stalactites
tales	inscriptions	environment		

Seven-Star Park

Seven-Star Park on the eastern bank of the Lijiang, only two kilometers from the city (1)_____ , is the largest comprehensive park with the most attractive natural (2)_____ in the city of Guilin. Covering more than 40 hectares of land, the park is named after Seven-Star Hill and Seven-Star Cave.

Seven-Star Cave is 800 meters long. There are a countless number of colourful (3)_____ and stalagmites of all shapes in the underground maze. With some imagination, visitors may see such (4)_____ as "An Ancient Banyan Greeting Guests," "A Bridge of Magpies Spanning the Milky" and "A Peacock Displaying Its Feathers." These mysterious scenes and some 40 others in this underground maze take the visitors to a world of fairy (5)_____.

There are nearly 2,000 carvings and sculptures to be found on the (6)_____ faces of the hills and caves in Guilin. The largest number of them is concentrated in the Dragon Refuge Cave at the (7)_____ of Seven-Star Hill's Yaoguang Peak. A Stelae Preservation Pavilion was built in 1963 at the entrance to Dragon Refuge Cave, where the rubbings of all the important (8)_____ carved on stelae on the hills and in the caves are displayed. The pavilion thus becomes known as "A Forest of Stelae in a Sea of Osmanthus."

Words and Expressions

annals ['ænlz] *n.* 编年史,县志
Seven-Star Park 七星公园
Seven-Star Cave 七星岩
"A Bridge of Magpies Spanning the Milky" "银河鹊桥"
Dragon Refuge Cave 龙隐岩
Stelae Preservation Pavillion 藏碑阁

conquer ['kɒŋkə(r)] *vt.* 征服,战胜,占领
Seven-Star Hill 七星山
"An Ancient Banyan Greeting Guests" "古榕迎宾"
"A Peacock Displaying Its Feathers" "孔雀开屏"
Yaoguang Peak 瑶光峰
"A Forest of Stelae in a Sea of Osmanthus" "桂海碑林"

Part VII   Translation

Mt. Fubo (Wave-Subduing Hill)

1. Mt. Fubo (Wave-Subduing Hill) (伏波山) stands like a giant stone pillar by the Lijiang to the north of the Guilin City proper. It is said that the general Ma Yuan(马援) of the Han Dynasty, known as the Wave-Subduing General(伏波将军), once stood on the hill and shot an arrow, which pierced three hills. From then on, the hill was named Wave-Subduing Hill.

2. A cave at the foot of the hill near the river is called Pearl-Returning Cave(还珠洞). According to a popular legend, an old dragon often came to the cave to toy with a pearl. One day while he was sleeping soundly, a curious fisher boy (渔童)came to the cave and took the pearl away.

3. Later, when the boy learned that the dragon was very sad about the loss of his pearl, he returned the pearl to the dragon. Thereafter, people called the cave the Pearl-Returning Cave.

4. 洞中有一石柱(stalactite)悬挂于洞顶石壁,离地仅二寸,好像被斧砍断(cut with an axe),相传是伏波将军试剑留下的痕迹。

5. 还珠洞口有五千多斤重的大铁钟(a huge iron bel),铸(cast)于清康熙八年,有三百多年历史。

6. 洞中还有历代石刻(stone inscriptions)百余件,壁龛(niches)中造像二百五十余尊,多是唐宋时代的作品,是研究桂林佛教与印度佛教关系的重要资料。

Unit 15

Touring Guangdong

Focus on Learning 学习要点

导游案例	Sending off the Tourists 离站送客
导游听力	1. Guangzhou City 广州市
	2. The Five-Ram Sculpture 五羊雕塑
情景对话	Yuexiu Park 越秀公园
旅游视频	Danxia Mountain 丹霞山
导 游 词	The Sun Yat-sen Memorial Hall 孙中山纪念堂
导游阅读	Splendid China Miniature Tourist Site 锦绣中华微缩景区
导游翻译	Window of the World 世界之窗

 Part I　Tips for Tour Guides

Case 15

Sending off the Tourists

　　It was seven o'clock in the evening. Miss Yin Le was taking the Canadian tourists to the Guangzhou Railway Station by coach. They were leaving for Hong Kong. However, an accident occurred on the way to the station, and the group was held up by the traffic jam. When they arrived at the station, the train had already left. What proper measures could she take to handle the case? Listen to the passage and write down in the blanks the measures she should take.

(1) Miss Yin should first _____ the travel agency, and try to appease the tourists.
(2) She should consider _____ for sending off the tourists. Upon endorsement by the travel agency she may rent a coach, or _____ to send off the tourists and resume their travel schedule.
(3) If it is impossible for the tourists to leave Guangzhou in a short time, Miss Yin or the manager should do an apology to them on behalf of _____, and make arrangements for _____ and necessary services during their stay in Guangzhou.
(4) The travel agency should send by fax _____ to the manager of the next stop who receives the tourists and inform the related parties of its own travel service.

Words and Expressions

endorsement 批准   travel schedule 旅行计划

Exercise

Directions: Act as the tour guide and the logistics staff of the travel service. Make up a dialogue among them and discuss how you could send off the tourists. Make the presentation in the class while the teacher mentions the basic procedures as the guide should perform. The rest of the class may put forward suggestions to improve the presentation.

Part II Listening Activities

Listening 1

Guangzhou City

Words and Expressions

blooming ['blu:mɪŋ] *adj.* 盛开的
stalk [stɔ:k] *n.* 茎, 柄, 梗
colony ['kɒləni] *n.* 殖民地

ram [ræm] *n.* 公羊
literally ['lɪtərəli] *adv.* 照字面意义
Portuguese [ˌpɔ:tʃu'gi:z] *adj.* 葡萄牙人的

Proper Nouns

"Goat City" "羊城"
Sun Yat-sen Memorial Hall 孙中山纪念堂
Yuexiu Park 越秀公园
Pearl River 珠江
Shaoguan 韶关
Hong Kong 香港
Zhuhai 珠海
Splendid China 锦绣中华
China Folk Culture Villages 中国民俗文化村

Ancestral Temple of the Chen Family 陈家祠(陈氏书院)
Baiyun Shan (White Cloud Mountain) 白云山
Nanhua Temple 南华寺
Shantou 汕头
Shenzhen 深圳
Macau 澳门
Window of the World 世界之窗

Exercise ➡ ➡ ➡

Directions: Listen to the passage and decide whether the statements are true or false. If it is true, put "T" in the space provided and "F" if it is false.

1. _____ It is true that Guangzhou was founded by five immortals riding five rams.
2. _____ Guangzhou is an ancient city with a history of almost 3,000 years.
3. _____ You could cruise on the Pearl River and appreciate the Nanhua Temple.
4. _____ You can visit the China Folk Culture Villages in the downtown area of Guangzhou.
5. _____ At Shenzhen, you can complete a round-the-world trip in one day by visiting the Splendid China and Window of the World.

Listening 2

Words and Expressions

barren ['bærən] *adj.* 不生育的, 不孕的; 贫瘠的
garment ['gɑ:mənt] *n.* 衣服, 外衣, 外表
famine ['fæmɪn] *n.* 饥荒, 严重的缺乏
blessing ['blesɪŋ] *n.* 祝福

Proper Nouns

Five-Ram Sculpture 五羊雕塑

The Five-Ram Sculpture

The Five-Ram Sculpture is one of the most famous structures in Guangzhou. It has become the (1)_____ of Guangzhou City. Legend has it that more than (2)_____, Guangzhou was a barren land with people who despite hard work were suffering from (3)_____. One day (4)_____ in five-color garments came riding on five rams, playing their legendary music. The rams held sheaves of rice in their (5)_____. The immortals left the sheaves of rice for the Guangzhou people, gave (6)_____ the city and left. The rams turned into the (7)_____ and the city of Guangzhou became a rich and populous place. Guangzhou got the name of the City of Rams and the City of (8)_____.

Exercise ➡ ➡ ➡

Directions: Listen to the passage and fill in the words or phrases you have heard.

Part III Situational Dialogue

Yuexiu Park

(A=Miss Wu Li, a guide; B=Edward; C=Eric)

A: Good morning, ladies and gentlemen! Did you have a sound sleep last night?

B: Oh, yes!

A: Good! I am happy to hear that. You know, a good sleep can help you restore your energy for today's sightseeing. This morning we'll go sightseeing in the Yuexiu Park. It is the largest park in the downtown area of Guangzhou.

B: Are there anything special in the park?

A: The park is made up of three lakes and seven hills of Yuexiu Mountain. So it is called Yuexiu Park.

C: Excellent! It would be a wonderful journey!

A: Yes, I am sure it is. Well, anybody of you knows Guangzhou's nickname?

C: I don't know.

B: The Goat City.

A: Right, you got it. In the park stands a famous sculpture, the Five-Ram Sculpture. It was built according to a legend. Now it has become the emblem of the city. Later you can enjoy it in the park.

B: Wonderful! I hope to see it right now.

A: All right. Now we've arrived at the Xuexiu Park. In front of us is the famous tower—Zhenhai Tower. The locals call it Five-Story Tower. It is one of the landmarks of Guangzhou City.

C: What a magnificent tower! The striking contrast of green glazed titles and red walls makes the tower elegant and delicate.

A: Yes, Zhenhai Tower now is 28 meters high and 16 meters wide. Over the past 600 years, the tower has been destroyed five times and set up five times. Now it is the Guangzhou Museum.

C: That's great. I bet it is one of the most famous towers in Guangzhou.

A: More famous than this. It is known as the first tower in Lingnan (South of Nanling Mountain). After we visit the Museum, we'll go boating on the lake. I hope you'll enjoy it.

C: A good idea! I think the landscape here is very charming. I heard birds chirping in the trees.

A: Singing birds and exuberant plants add vigor and natural beauty to the park. The three lakes, Dongxiu Lake, Beixiu Lake and Nanxiu Lake are all tranquil and elegant. The lakes are connected with arch bridges and decorated with pavilions and corridors in the Lingnan Style. Now, we'll go boating in the Beixiu Lake.

C: Terrific. Shall we go?

A: Yeah!

Words and Expressions

glaze [gleɪz] v. 上釉,使表面光滑
exuberant [ɪɡˈzjuːbərənt] adj. 繁茂的
destroy [dɪˈstrɔɪ] vt. 破坏,毁坏

Proper Nouns

Yuexiu Mountain 越秀山
Five-Storey Tower 五层楼
Lingnan (South of Nanling Mountain) 岭南地区(南岭山以南地区)
Nanxiu Lake 南秀湖
Zhenhai Tower 镇海楼
Guangzhou Museum 广州博物馆
Dongxiu Lake 东秀湖
Beixiu Lake 北秀湖

Exercise ➡ ➡ ➡

Directions: Listen to the dialogue. Imagine that you are the local guide and your classmates are tourists. Do the dialogue again with additional information that the teacher may offer.

Part IV　Video for Tourism
旅游视频

Danxia Mountain

Words and Expressions

sculptor [ˈskʌlptə(r)] n. 雕刻家
resembling [rɪˈzembl] n. 类似,相似
balance [ˈbæləns] n. 平衡
fertility [fəˈtɪləti] n. 多产
striking [ˈstraɪkɪŋ] adj. 显著的
exaggerate [ɪɡˈzædʒəreɪt] v. 夸张
cysthus [ˈsɪsθəs] n. 女阴
captivating [ˈkæptɪveɪtɪŋ] adj. 迷人的,有魅力的

Proper Nouns

Dan Xia Mountain 丹霞山　　　　　Shaoguan city 韶关市
Ying 阴　　　　　　　　　　　　　Yang 阳
Dan Xia Landform 丹霞地貌

Still, the main attraction here is the famous Danxia Mountain, known as the red stone park in China. It is a one hour's drive from Shaoguan City in the north-eastern suburbs. The red rocks and red cliffs of strange shapes and sizes seem to be the work of the skilled sculptor. It's hard to imagine that they actually come from mysterious hand of Nature.

Danxia Mountain is particularly famous because of the red color of the rocks. And you see, even from the two characters—Dan Xia, you can get that hint: Dan literally means dark red and Xia means brightening of the clouds. So off the distance, you can see the striking resembling. The mountains look like clouds floating in the air.

Danxia Mountains' red trace to the sand stone has given rise to the name: Danxia Landform. In fact, there are over one thousand places in the world with Danxia Landform. But Danxia Mountain is the largest and most characteristic of them. The layers and layers of red under the rise of sunlight particular exaggerate its unique structure and beauty. You need to explore the mountain for at least two days. And on my first day, I couldn't wait to get on a boat and get a complete view. And this boat will take you to all the right places.

Can you guess what that is? Well, I think that you're thinking exactly what I'm thinking. You see, because of the natural shape of this rock, people have called it: the male rock and may mean symbol that of this. You see male means Yang in Chinese, a part of yin and yang. Yang is male and yin is female. And as with everything else of Nature, there's a balance in everything. There's yin and yang, male and female. There's hardest and softness. And there's also big and small. This is an example.

The mountain's real claim to fame is this rare geological formation. And the shape really does for example a male sex organ. Although, many mountains have the shape what you need is the corresponding female stone. Many people see this structure as cysthus and they come here wish for love, happy marriage and fertility. Shaoguan organizes international group weddings with dozens of couples at the top of this mountain. And it believes the symbols of male and female structures will bring a certain balance in their relationship. As well as long lasting love, who knows what particular power this mountain has? But just the scenery itself, it's captivating enough.

Step 1: Watch the video and write down the key words or phrases in the video. You may use the key words or phrases as the reminders when you watch it the second time.

_____

_____

Step 2: Watch the video again and decide whether the statements are True or False.

1. _____ Danxia Mountain is particularly featured by its red color of the rocks. Dan literally means dark red and Xia means brightening of the clouds.
2. _____ Danxia Landform in Guangdong is famous all over the world because it is unique to Shaoguan city, Guangdong Province.
3. _____ Because of the natural shape of this rock, people have called it: the male rock. Male means Yang in Chinese while female means Ying.
4. _____ Young couples come here to hold wedding ceremony because they believe that the symbols of male and female structures will bring a certain balance in their relationship as well as long lasting love.

Part V Tour Commentary

The Sun Yat-sen Memorial Hall

Good Morning, ladies and gentlemen! Sun Yat-sen Memorial Hall is situated in the original site of Sun Yat-sen's Presidential Office at No.18 Dongsha Street, Fangzhi Road in Guangzhou. The original building was built in 1931 with the funds raised by the Guangzhou people and overseas Chinese in memory of Sun Yat-sen, the pioneer of China's bourgeois democratic revolution.

Dear friends, when you pay homage to Dr. Sun Yat-sen in the memorial hall. You should know his extraordinary life, so let me briefly tell you his early days in Guangzhou. Dr. Sun's original name was Sun Wen and styled himself Yat-sen, so foreign friends called him "Dr. Sun Yat-sen." Since he took "Woodcutter in Zhongshan" as his alias when he took part in the revolutionary activities, he was respectfully and widely called Mr. Sun Zhongshan in China. On October 12, 1866, he was born in a farmer's family in the Cuiheng Village of Xiangshan County, today's Zhongshan City, Guangdong Province. When he was still young, he had great expectations. He studied medicine in Honolulu, Hong Kong and some other places. After graduation he worked as a practitioner in Guangzhou and Macao. Later he gave up medicine as his profession to take part in political activities.

Dear friends, Sun Yat-sen Memorial Hall is one of the symbolic buildings of Guangzhou, and a key place for the large-scale meetings and performances. It was put under state protection 1996. The building was built with a mixture of Chinese and western architectural styles. The designer skillfully applied the structural theory of architectural mechanics and took full advantage of the benefits of reinforced concrete. When you look far, the memorial hall looks elegant, indicative of the old days when China suffered from the civil wars and invasion of foreign countries.

Look at the plaque above the entrance of the memorial hall! It bears in gold the words "Sun Yat-sen Memorial Hall." They were inscribed by Liao Chengzhi, the vice chairman of the standing committee of the National People's Congress. At the central up-layer wall of the small hall hangs another plaque with the words "The Whole World as a Community." They were inscribed by Sun Yat-sen himself. This plaque expresses his drive to unify China and to establish a society where all nationalities in China lived equally and harmoniously under the heaven.

Ladies and Gentlemen! Let's get into the memorial hall. Here are a lot of precious pictures, photos, and documents in the exhibition rooms. Numerous objects, full and accurate historical data all reveal the great life of Dr. Sun Yat-sen. On display are many important data which especially show his revolutionary activities in Guangzhou. After Yuan Shikai acclaimed himself an emperor, Dr. Sun fought hard against Yuan and the succeeding warlords, but his wish to unify China didn't come true. As he said, "The revolution is far from success and we should continue working hard."

Thank you for your attention. I hope you enjoy your trip in Guangzhou.

Words and Expressions

mechanics [mɪˈkænɪks] n. 力学；技巧；结构
invasion [ɪnˈveɪʒn] n. 入侵
reinforce [ˌriːɪnˈfɔːs] vt. 加强，修补，加固
accurate [ˈækjərət] adj. 正确的，精确的

Proper Nouns

Xiniu Pond (Rhino Pond) 犀牛潭
Sun Yat-sen Memorial Hall 孙中山纪念堂
Fangzhi Road 纺织路
Cuiheng Village 翠亨村
Honolulu 檀香山
Macao 澳门
"The Whole World as a Community" "世界大同"
Water Curtain Cavern 水帘洞
Dongsha Street 东沙街
Sun Wen 孙文
Xiangshan County 香山县
Hong Kong 香港
Liao Chengzhi 廖承志
Yuan Shikai 袁世凯

Exercise ➡ ➡ ➡

Directions: Act as the local guide and take tourists to visit the Sun Yat-sen Memorial Hall. Try to make your introduction more situational and attractive using the proper body language.

Part VI Readings

Directions: Read the following passage and fill in the blanks with the words or phrases given below.

| palace | history | observatory | karst | civilized |
| fresco | Warriors | harvest | wonders | |

Splendid China Miniature Tourist Site

Located by the picturesque Shenzhen Bay, Splendid China Miniature Tourist Site is the epitome of China's long-standing (1)_____, brilliant culture as well as beautiful scenery and rich historical sites. Here you can find the Great Wall, life-size Terra Cotta (2)_____ and Horses of Emperor Qin Shihuang's Mausoleum, which are among world's eight (3)_____. And there are many world's "top"—the world's oldest stone arch bridge (Zhaozhou Bridge), astronomical (4)_____ (Ancient Star Observatory), and wooden pagoda (Yingxian Wooden Pagoda); the world's largest (5)_____ and Buddha statue (the Imperial Palace and Leshan Giant Buddha Statue); the biggest imperial garden (Yuanmingyuan—"the garden of all gardens"); the world's longest (6)_____ (Dunhuang Mogao Grottoes); the world's most splendid building located at the highest land above sea level (Potala Palace); the world's most wonderful (7)_____ landscape (the Stone Forest); the world's most unique peaks (Mt. Huangshan); one of the world's biggest waterfalls (Huangguoshu Falls). Besides, you can enjoy the scenes of emperors praying for good (8)_____, the wedding of Emperor Guang Xu, a memorial ceremony at Confucius Temple and the local conditions and customs of wedding and funeral. In a word, you will get a good idea of the ancient (9)_____ country with a history of five thousand years and travel over numerous famous rivers and mountains all over China only in one day.

Words and Expressions

Shenzhen Bay 深圳湾
Qinling Mausoleum 秦陵
Zhaozhou Bridge 赵州桥
Yingxian Wooden Pagoda 应县木塔
Dunhuang Mogao Grottoes 敦煌莫高窟

Splendid China Miniature Tourist Site 锦绣中华微缩景区
Ancient Star Observatory 古观象台
"the garden of all gardens" "万园之园"
Potala Palace 布达拉宫

Part VII Translation

Window of the World

1. The Window of the World (世界之窗) is a new large tourist site in Shenzhen(深圳), covering an area of 480,000 sq. m.
2. Here the marvelous sites, historical interests(历史遗迹) in the world, the ancient and modern natural landscapes and attractions, the dwelling houses(民居), sculptures, drawings and even folklore and theatrical performances are integrated into one site, which reveals a very wonderful land to the tourists.
3. In accordance with the geographical position and category of the sightseeing activities, the tourist site is divide into nine scenic areas (景区), totaling 118 scenic spots(景点).
4. 它们是世界广场(World Square)、亚洲区(the Area of Asia)、大洋洲区、欧洲区、非洲区、美洲区、现代科技娱乐区(Recreational centre of Modern Science & Technology)、世界雕塑园(World Sculpture Park)、国际街(International Street)。
5. 其中包括世界著名奇观,如埃及金字塔(Pyramid)、卡拉克·阿蒙神庙(Amon Temple of Karnak)、柬埔寨吴哥窟(Angkor Wat)、美国大峡谷(Grand Canyon)、巴黎凯旋门(L'Arc de Triomple)、梵蒂冈圣彼得大教堂(ST. Peter's Cathedral)、印度泰姬·玛哈尔陵(Taj Mahal)、澳大利亚悉尼歌剧院(Sydney Opera House)、意大利比萨斜塔(Leaning Tower of Pisa)等等。
6. 世界之窗是世界历史之窗(a window of the world history)、世界文明之窗(a window of the world civilization)、世界旅游景点之窗。

Listening Scripts

Unit 1   Touring Beijing

Part I Tips for Tour Guides
Case 1 Preparations for Meeting Tour Group
Mr. Wang will meet a tour group from Nanjing. He is sorting out the documents before he goes to the airport. Listen to the passage and remind him of the documents he must take with him. Fill in the blanks with the missing information.

(1) Mr. Wang must wear his tour guide certificate and take with him a copy of the certificate, as well as the operation schedule of the tour group.
(2) He should accomplish the required formalities if he works for a travel agency other than his own travel agency.
(3) He is required to take with him a tour banner if he takes a group of more than 10 members.
(4) He should take with him copies of the insurance policies, various vouchers, travel schedule and a loudspeaker.

Part II Listening Activities
Listening 1

Beijing City

The venerated Chinese history has strewn the land of Beijing with sites of cultural and historical interest. Some of them, such as the Great Wall, Imperial Palace Museum, Temple of Heaven, Summer Palace, and the ruins of Peking Man at Zhoukoudian, are UNESCO-endorsed world cultural heritage sites. Imperial palaces, mansions, gardens and tombs are epitomes of classical Chinese architecture. Among the massive number of ancient buildings that have remained to this day are quite a few Buddhist monasteries, Taoist temples and Catholic churches, such as Yonghegong Lamasery and Big Bell Temple. There are 120 museums worth seeing, including Museum of Chinese History and China Art Gallery. Over 100 gardens are open to the public.

The Tian'anmen Square in the center of Beijing is the world's largest city square. Tian'anmen Gate on the northern edge of the square used to be the front gate of the Ming and Qing Imperial Palace. The Palace Museum, better known as "Forbidden City," was the imperial palace for the Ming and Qing. Built during the 1406—1420 period, it is the largest royal palatial complex in existence in China. China's largest temple and altar are found in Temple of Heaven. Built in 1420, it was where Ming and Qing monarchs prayed for good harvests. As an emblem of Chinese civilization, another world cultural heritage site, the Great Wall was in China's feudal years a defense works that wound its way across mountains and valleys in the northern part of the country. The Summer Palace in the northwestern suburb of Beijing was built in 1750. As a paragon of Chinese gardens, this place is a de facto museum of China's classical architecture. Housed in these buildings are an immense collection of treasures and cultural artifacts.

Listening 2

Beijing Opera

Acting in Beijing Opera is not subjected to the limitations of time and space; here symbolism is essential. Since some activities in everyday life cannot possibly be reproduced on the stage, Beijing Opera gives expression to them in a stylized, symbolic manner. Thus, particular bodily movements signify opening a door, entering or leaving a room, going upstairs or down, climbing a mountain or wading across a stream. Circling the stage, whip in hand, suggests riding a horse; riding in a carriage is represented by an attendant holding flags painted with a wheel design on either side of the performers; walking in a circle indicates a long journey; four soldiers and four generals flanking both sides of the stage represent an army several thousand strong; two men somersaulting under a spotlight shows the audience how they are groping and fighting in the dark; and on a stage bare of scenery, a performer holding an oar or paddle and doing knee-bends to simulate a heavy swell, demonstrates traveling on a boat.

Unit 2   Touring Shanghai

Part I Tips for Tour Guides
Case 2 Meeting Tourist at the Airport

Mr. He Yan is a trainee tour guide from the Shanghai Oriental Travel Service. He has taken with him all the papers necessary for meeting the tour group. What else could you advise him to meet the tourists at the airport? Situation 1: prior to his arrival at the airport; Situation 2: upon the arrival of the tour group. Listen to the passage and write down your advice in the blanks.

(1) Prior to arrival:
   A. Confirm expected arrival time;
   B. Arrive at the airport 30 minutes prior to expected arrival time and confirm the exact parking place of the coach in parking lot;
   C. Reconfirm exact arrival time;
   D. Contact the porter and inform him of the luggage claim area;
   E. Stand at a highly visible location in the lobby, in full view of the arriving tourists with an identifying cardboard sign.

(2) Upon the arrival of tour group:
   A. Meet the tour group and check the nationality, group code, number of tourists and name of the tour leader;
   B. Make sure that all luggage has been claimed and collected by porter to transfer to coach;
   C. Lead the tour group to the coach and assist them in boarding. The guide should stand by the door to politely greet tourists and confirm the number of the group.

Part II Listening Activities
Listening 1

Shanghai City

Shanghai, also named "Hu" or "Shen" in short, is a famous historical and cultural city, a gate to the Yangtze River delta. It is a municipality under the direct jurisdiction of the central government, the largest economic and trade center, a comprehensive industrial base and the leading port in China. Shanghai has made an effort to develop the city tourism mainly featuring "city scenery," "city culture," and "city commerce." The architecture of Shanghai has its own characters. The Bund, the Stone-gate buildings, the different kinds of Shanghai style constructions, the modern installations which make an assemblage of different styles of architecture are worth visiting.

Modern Shanghai has three key areas of interest to the visitors. These comprise sightseeing, business and shopping centered upon People's Square and along the Huangpu River. The city's cultural center with its public activities and community facilities and finally the main entertainment and holiday tourism area located at Mt. Sheshan, Chongming Island, Dingshan Lake and Shenshuigang Area. Known as "the Oriental Paris," Shanghai is a shopper's paradise. One of the musts for tourists is Nanjing Road. Huaihai Road intrigues those with modern and fashionable tastes, while Sichuan North Road meets the demands of ordinary folk. In addition, Xujiahui Shopping Center, Yuyuan Shopping City, Jiali Sleepless City are thriving and popular destinations for those who are seeking to buy something special as a memento of their visit.

Listening 2

Huangpu River Cruise

Huangpu River cruise is a traditional tourist item in Shanghai's tours. It is significant not only because Huangpu River is Shanghai's mother river but also of the collection of the quintessences of Shanghai scenes. Here, one can find the expression of Shanghai's past, present and prospects for a brilliant future. The cruise begins at the Bund towards south against the current up to the Nanpu Bridge and turns back towards the north, passing the Yangpu Bridge to reach Wusong Mouth and then back to the Bund. During the cruise, one can see both the Nanpu Bridge and the Yangpu Bridge and the 468m tall Oriental Pearl TV Tower. The two bridges are like two dragons sprawling on the Huangpu River while the Oriental Pearl TV Tower in between like "two dragons playing with a pearl." On the west bank of the river, rows of magnificent tall buildings of different foreign architectural styles are in contrast with the modern high-risers on the east bank, presenting an attractive view to visitors.

Unit 3 Touring Jiangsu

Part I Tips for Tour Guides
Case 3 Taking Tourists by Mistake

Mr. Liu Zhenghong was assigned to receive a tour group from the United States this morning. He arrived at the Nanjing International Airport on time. After all the tourists disembarked the plane, he did not expect the arrival of his tour group. He met the tourists other than his own. Later he was told that his tourists have been picked up by another guide. What happened to him? How could he avoid such an incident in the future? Listen to the passage and write down in the blanks the reasons why he failed to meet his tour group and what lessons he should learn from.

I think Mr. Liu is held responsible for such a serious mistake. He should have followed the basic procedures, such as checking the name of the organizing travel agency, the group code, the number of tourists and the name of the tour leader, etc. Mr. Liu should learn from this lesson and take the proper measures under circumstance such as:
(1) If he mistakes the tour group of another travel agency for his group, he should first report to his own agency and hand it over to the other travel agency. Meanwhile he should do an apology to the tourists.

(2) If his own tour group remains at the airport, he should meet them immediately and accomplish the formalities concerned.

(3) If the tour group he receives belongs to the same agency that he works for, but he is not supposed to be their guide, he may make the best of the mistake by acting as their guide.

Part II Listening Activities
Listening 1

Nanjing City

Known as Jinling in old days, Nanjing is the capital of Jiangsu. Strategically situated on the Yangtze, with a moist climate, its terrain renders majesty by the mountains in the background. It is also the province's political, economic, cultural and transportation center. Nanjing today looks new and old—new due to the ongoing modernization drive, and old because it is already 2,460 years old. As one of the nation's seven ancient capitals, it was the capital city for ten feudal dynasties or regimes.

Nanjing is well-known for a wealth of its scenic sites and historical interests. The Qinhuai River is a trunk waterway as well as a famed scenic belt in Nanjing as it is on both banks with a host of places of historical and cultural interests. One of them is the Confucian Temple, where the great thinker is worshipped. Night cruise on the river and visiting the night fair at the Confucian Temple are unique tourist programs available for visitors to Nanjing. The Mausoleum for Sun Yat-sen, forerunner of Chinese democratic revolution, was built during the 1926—1929 period. The entire layout, covering 80,000 square meters, takes the shape of a giant bell. A famous Buddhist establishment, the Linggu Temple 2km east of Sun Yat-sen Mausoleum is known for its 22-metre-high Wuliang (Beamless) Hall, constructed without a single inch of wood, pillar or beam. Ming Xiaoling Mausoleum built for Zhu Yuanzhang, the founder of the Ming Dynasty, is one of the largest ancient imperial tombs in China. The Yangtze River Bridge in Nanjing is very famous and impressive.

Listening 2

Yangzhou City

Yangzhou, situated at the juncture of the Yangtze River and the Grand Canal, has made a name for itself with a wealth of sites of historical interest and elegant gardens. These include the Lean West Lake (actually a natural waterway feeding mountain runoffs into the Grand Canal), Geyuan Garden (whose forte is artificial rockwork), and Lesser Pangu Garden. During their repeated visits to Yangzhou, emperors Kangxi and Qianlong left a succession of historical sites on the land of Yangzhou. This has prompted local travel agencies to invent the "Emperor Qianlong Cruise," which transports visitors to a string of local attractions. Cruise on the ancient Grand Canal is another popular tourist program. Other places worth seeing: Tianning Temple Museum, Daming Temple, Monk Jianzhen Memorial Hall, and Memorial Hall of Eight Yangzhou Eccentrics.

Unit 4　Touring Sichuan

Part I Tips for Tour Guides
Case 4 The Luggage Lost

Mr. Tian Qiang is picking up the tourists in the Chengdu Shuangliu International Airport. All luggage had been claimed, but Mr. Qiao's baggage is not found. Mr. Qiao is so worried that he is reluctant to leave the airport while other tourists are waiting impatiently in the coach. Any suggestions you can put forward to Mr. Yang? Listen to the passage and write down your suggestion in the blanks.

(1) Mr. Tian should try his best to look for the luggage and register the loss for the tourist though he is not responsible for the loss.

(2) He could take Mr. Qiao to register the lost property in the lost-and-found office. With his ticket and luggage tag in hand, Mr. Qiao can specify the number of pieces, the exterior characteristics of the luggage, and leave a phone number for further contact.

(3) He should write down the address and phone number of the airline office and the lost-and-found office at the airport. In this way, he can keep contact with the people concerned for any further information during the travel. Mr. Qiao could buy some daily necessities and submit receipts for reimbursement later.

(4) If Mr. Qiao still cannot find the luggage before he leaves, Mr. Yang should help the tourist to lodge a claim against the airline company, meanwhile inform the administrative staff of the next stop about the address and phone number of the airline company so that they could continue to keep in touch.

Part II Listening Activities

Listening 1

Chengdu City

As one of the 24 China Key Historical and Cultural Cities, Chengdu, the capital of Sichuan Province, has many tourism resources. UNESCO lists Mt. Qingcheng, one of the birthplaces of Taoism, together with the Dujiangyan Irrigation Project, as the world cultural heritage. In the downtown areas of Chengdu, are a number of historic sites and relics, such as: Du Fu's Thatched Cottage, Wuhou Temple, Wangjian's Tomb, Yangsheng-an Temple, Mausoleum of Prince Xiwang of the Ming Dynasty and Jinsha Ruins, etc. In the surrounding districts and counties there are: Mt. Qingcheng and the Dujiangyan Irrigation Project, the world cultural heritage; the Snow-capped Xiling Mountain, a national key tourist resort; and other provincial key scenic spots like: Chaoyanghu Lake, Mt. Tiantai, Mt. Jiufeng, Yunding Stone City, etc. The Snow-capped Xiling Mountain and Mt. Qingcheng near Chengdu are ideal summer resorts. Longchi Forest Park and the Xiling Snow-capped Mountain are places where people in Chengdu and tourists from other southern provinces can appreciate winter snow. Since ancient times, Chengdu has been known as the "Land of Abundance." Today it is also world famous for the giant pandas, and is recognized as the hometown of pandas.

Listening 2

Tourism Resources in Sichuan

Sichuan is a province well known for its rich tourism resources of natural landscapes, historical relics and ethnic customs. As the old saying goes, "Mountains and waters in Shu are best under the heaven." Speaking of tourism resources, Sichuan has: (1) two sites included in the List of World Natural Heritages: Jiuzhaigou Valley, the "fairyland" on the earth; and Huanglong (or Yellow Dragon), the "jasper lake in the mundane world"; (2) one site included in the World Cultural and Natural Heritages: Mt. E'mei with the Leshan Giant Buddha, a sacred site of Buddhism; (3) one site included in the List of World Cultural Heritages: Dujiangyan Irrigation Project & Mt. Qingcheng; (4) 20 State 4A-level or 3A-level Scenic Zones; (5)10 National Key Scenery Resorts; (6) 67 Provincial Scenic Zones; (7) 13 National Nature Reserves; (8) 45 Provincial Nature Reserves; (9) 25 National Forest Parks; (10) 51 Provincial Forest Parks; and (11) 4 National Geological Parks. Among them, the following are promising candidates for the "List of World Heritages": the Sanxingdui Ruins of Guanghan, the Jinsha Ruins of Chengdu, the Qiang Stockaded Village of Taoping in Aba, the Giant Panda Nature Reserve of Wolong, and the Shangri-la of Yading-Daocheng of Ganzi.

Unit 5 Touring Anhui

Part I Tips for Tour Guides
Case 5 Checking in the Hotel

It was half past nine in the evening. Miss Dai Jia received a tour group from England on behalf of Anhui China International Travel Service. She picked up the tourists and helped them check in the Hefei Shangri-la Hotel. Afterwards, she left with the driver and hurried back to take care of her baby in the hospital. Please evaluate her guiding service and make your comments in the blanks after you listen to the passage.

(1) Miss Dai should not leave the tourists in the hotel without fulfilling the basic guiding service as a local guide;
(2) She should ask the porter to deliver the luggage to tourists' rooms;
(3) She should tell the tour group about the hotel facilities and services;
(4) She should inform the tour group of itinerary for the next day;
(5) She should arrange the first meal for the group;
(6) She must arrange the morning call for the tourists.

Part II Listening Activities
Listening 1

Hefei City

Hefei, capital of Anhui Province, was a battlefield of the Three Kingdoms Period, hometown of the upright Song official Bao Zheng, and a bone of contention among warring strategists. Surrounded by wooded mountains and tucked away under the shadows of green trees, Hefei is also a garden city with a pleasant environment. Major attractions are the temple and tomb of Bao Zheng, the battlefield at Xiaoyaojin, Jiaonu (Archery Drilling) Terrace, Xinghua (Apricot Flower) Park, and Chaohu Amusement Park-on-the-Water. Shouxian, a famous historical and cultural city, and the picturesque Chaohu Lake are also in the tourist zone.

A major international tourist city in south Anhui, Mt. Huangshan is noted for its statuesque mountains and rich cultural heritage. It was also the cradle of one of China's three local academic schools, the School of Anhui Studies. Besides Mt. Huangshan Anhui boasts of abundant tourism resources, such as Mt. Jiuhua, one of the four famous Buddhist Mountains in China; Mt. Tianzhu, also a well-known scenic spot. The magnificence of these peaks is simply stupendous. In addition to the beautiful mountain scenery, the well-preserved ancient villages in south Anhui are derived from the Ming and Qing dynasties. Most impressive ones are in Xidi and Hongcun in Yixian County near Mt. Huangshan. It is really a sight worth seeing and a must for visitors who are keen to learn more about life during those years. Shexian County, reputed as Town of Arches, is also a must for each visitor to experience fine examples of residential architecture from the Ming and Qing dynasties and the unique Tangyue Memorial Archway.

Listening 2

Lord Bao's Memorial Temple

Lord Bao's Memorial Temple is located in Baohe Park just southwest of the city center. It was initially built in 1066 in memory of Baozheng, a famous upright officer during the Northern Song Dynasty. Lord Bao's Memorial Temple is a typical ancient architectural complex with style imitating that of the Song Dynasty.

Covering an area of one hectare, it mainly consists of Entrance Gate, the Second Gate, the Stele Pavilion, the Main Hall, the Second Hall and the east and west exhibition rooms. In the main hall, a bronze statue of Lord Bao, which is 3 meters in height and 2.5 tons in weight, is displayed. Baozheng sits upright with his hat and waistband on. One of his hands placed on the chair with the other clenched. The eastern and western halls, using some pictures and essays, show visitors many stories and tales about Lord Bao.

Unit 6 Touring Shandong

Part I Tips for Tour Guides

Case 6 Rooms below the Contract Standard

The Japanese tourists checked in a small hotel in Qingdao, but they found the rooms were below the contract standard. They were so angry that they just stayed in the lobby and refused to take the key cards and enter the rooms. Miss He Xiaoyan, the local guide from Qingdao Travel Service International was at loss what to do with the tourists and the hotel. Listen to the passage and write down your suggestion.

(1) Miss He should negotiate with the manager of the hotel and demand that the rooms should conform to the standard specified in the contract.

(2) If the manager of the hotel agrees that the double rooms replace the single rooms or pay some money as the settlement, Miss He should consult with the tourists to see if they are willing to compromise.

(3) If the manager refuses to do an apology and pay compensation as a settlement, Miss He should lay out the terms of compensation and discuss them with my tour group to gain their support and cooperation.

(4) Miss He should lodge a claim against the hotel; meanwhile she should try to arrange another hotel for the tourists after obtaining instructions from the travel agency.

Part II Listening Activities

Listening 1

Jinan City

Jinan, capital of Shandong Province, is a famous historical and cultural city known as the "City of Springs" since ancient times. "Baotu," "Black Tiger," "Pearl," and "Five-Dragon" are the names of the four best known of the 72 springs in this charming city, which is situated with Mt. Taishan in the south and the Yellow River in the north. Other attractions are Thousand-Buddha Mountain, Daming Lake, and Lingyan Temple with the Four-Door Pagoda.

Baotu Spring, the symbol of Jinan, is known not only as the first of the 72 springs in Jinan but as the "First Spring under Heaven." With its earliest account in *Spring and Autumn Annals*, it has a long history of more than 2,600 years. Because it is both pure in quality and mellow in taste, the natural spring water could be directly used for drinking. When water bursts out through the three outlets, the spring gives thunderous sounds, and water columns surge upward, looking like spinning wheels. The landscape presents a picturesque view of a paradise on earth.

Shandong is also blessed with beautiful landscapes. The most famous scenic spots are Mt. Taishan, Mt. Laoshan and the seaside of the Jiaodong Peninsula. In 1987 and 1994, Mt. Taishan, the Temple and Cemetery of Confucius and the Confucius Mansion in Qufu were inscribed on the China World Cultural and Natural Heritage List by UNESCO.

Listening 2

Dacheng Hall

Dacheng Hall is the main hall of the Confucius Temple at its core. This hall, 24.8 meters is the highest building in the temple as well as one of the three largest ancient halls in China. Dacheng means master with great achievement, which truly describes Confucius. The statue of Confucius, located in the middle of the hall, is 3.35 meters tall. On his head is a coronet with 12 ribbons and his "King's Clothes" have 12 decorative patterns. In his hands is a Gui. This shows that Confucius is apotheosized and that in the hearts of the rulers he is as great as a king. In front of the Confucius statue, a memorial tablet of "Most Holy and Perfect Master" is placed. On the sacrifice table are some sacrifice utensils, and in front of it pigs, cows and goats are placed. At the two sides are displayed the musical instrument: Bianzhong, Bianqing, Qin, Se, Xiao, Sheng, Xun, Drum and so on, which were used in the sacrifice service.

Unit 7　Touring Henan

Part I Tips for Tour Guides
Case 7 Food and Dietary Change

It is one o'clock in the afternoon. The tourists come down Mt. Songshan. They just take seats around the table to have the dinner when Mr. Mohammad and his wife propose that they'd like to change the dishes. As a local guide, how do you handle the case? Listen to the passage and fill in the blanks with the missing information.

(1) Generally speaking, restaurants could agree to change the dishes if informed three hours ahead of mealtime. In such a case, I shall accept their request.
(2) If the request is made just before mealtime, the restaurant may refuse to make any changes since some of the dishes will have already been prepared. In such a case, I would graciously decline the request and give explanations.
(3) However, I shall try my best to meet their requirements if it is related to their religious practice or for health reasons. If they change the menu, add dishes or a beverage, I shall tell them they should bear the expense.
(4) I shall arrange special dishes for them at the future meals.

Part II Listening Activities
Listening 1

Zhengzhou City

Zhengzhou, capital of Henan Province, has a venerated history of over 3,000 years. The Beijing-Guangzhou and Lanzhou-Lianyungang railways cross their ways in Zhengzhou, turning it into a major railway hub. Major attractions are the ruins of a Shang-Dynasty city, Henan Museum, Yellow River Tourist Zone, and Monument to February 7 Workers' Uprising. Dengfeng, a city under Zhengzhou's jurisdiction, is known for Mt. Songshan, a holy mountain in central China, and Shaolin Temple. Mt. Songshan comprises Taishi and Shaoshi mountains, and among its sites of historical and cultural interest are a Yuan-Dynasty observatory built some 700 years ago, China's oldest brick pagoda in Songyue Temple, and the Songyang Academy, one of the four major academies in ancient

China. Built in 495 during the Northern Wei as the ancestral sanctuary of the Zen Sect of Chinese Buddhism, Shaolin Temple on the northern side of Shaoshi Mountain has made a name for itself for its martial arts, stone inscriptions of various dynasties, and Ming-Dynasty murals. To the west of the temple is a forest of 243 brick-and-masonry pagodas built during 1,000-year span from the Tang to Qing dynasties. Gongyi, a city 80km west of Zhengzhou, is the site of a mausoleum buried with the remains of 7 emperors in Northern Song Dynasty. Xinzheng, a city 40km south of Zhengzhou, is the native place of the Yellow Emperor.

Listening 2

Yellow River Scenic Area

Yellow River Scenic Area is located in the eastern section of Mt. Yueshan, 27 kilometers to the northwest of Zhengzhou City. It covers an area of about 27 square kilometers with Mt. Yueshan and Mt. Guangwushan as its center. About 20 years ago, there is still a wilderness. In 1970, aiming to solve the problem of water supply and irrigation, a water project was launched by the government and was completed two years later. After that, another seven years was spent in building a scenic area to enhance the culture of the Yellow River. Cultural scenic spots include Yueshan Temple, Mt. Wulongfeng, Battlefield of King Liu Bang and King Xiang Yu, Huayuankou Scenic Zone and etc, which are different in styles, but reveal the same tune of the Yellow River culture.

Unit 8   Touring Hunan

Part I Tips for Tour Guides
Case 8 Shopping

The Japanese and Korean tourists always have a great interest in the Chinese antiques and traditional Chinese medicine. Now it is time to go shopping in the downtown area of Yueyang City. What could you suggest as a local guide? Listen to the passage and write down your suggestion in the blanks.

(1) First, I shall take the tour group to go shopping only at those shops designated by the contract. I shall not add extra shops or shopping time.

(2) If they want to purchase antiques, I shall inform them to keep the sales receipt for the customs check on departure from China. Antique shops will provide such documentation; antiques sold by peddlers usually do not have signs of authenticity, and may not be taken out of China.

(3) If they want to buy traditional Chinese medicine, I shall recommend reliable drugstores to them. I shall inform them of the limit of traditional Chinese medicine one can take out of China for personal use. Some products such as musk, rhinoceros horns and tiger bones are forbidden exports.

(4) I shall not buy or mail any goods for my tourists. If it is impossible to say "no," I shall first report to the manager of my travel agency. After getting approval, I may receive enough money from my tourists to purchase and deliver the goods. Both the tourists and I should keep a copy of the receipt.

Part II Listening Activities
Listening 1

Changsha City

Historic Changsha, one of China's famous cultural centers, is the capital of Hunan Province. It is also a tourism center, offering its visitors many historical sites and other places of interest. Among about 20 major attractions in the city are Yuelu Academy, Han Tombs at Mawangdui, government archives on bamboo slips found at Zhoumalou, and Hunan Embroidery Institute.

Yuelu Academy at the foot of Yuelu Mountain in west Changsha, was the most important of all the four academies of the Song Dynasty as well as China's earliest government-funded institution of higher learning. The buildings extant on the premises are mostly a Qing legacy. Since the Song Dynasty many famous scholars had lectured and studied in this academy.

Han Tombs at Mawangdui achieved world fame overnight in the 1970s with the discovery of precious cultural relics from three large Han tombs. Most eye-catching of these finds was a woman's corpse well preserved despite the passage of 2,100 years. A total of 170,000 bamboo slips were excavated from Zhoumalou, Changsha, in December 1996. Inscribed on these slips were official documents of Changsha Prefecture during the reign of the Wu Kingdom. These files have furnished valuable material for research into the history of the Three Kingdoms Period. Poised atop Changsha's 30-metre-high ancient city wall, Tianxing Pavilion provides an overview of the entire city.

Listening 2

Tourist Sites in Hunan

Hunan is popular for its abundant landscapes and historical interests. Dongting Lake is the second largest lake in China. Yueyang City, located on the shore of Dongting Lake, is home to one of China's three famous towers. Yueyang Pavilion was originally built during the Tang Dynasty. The present pavilion is the work of recent reconstruction, built in the style of the Song Dynasty. Zhangjiajie National Forest Park was established in a particular scenic area in northwest Hunan. The park is especially known for its quartz-sandstone rock formations, bare stones sculpted by Nature and set among green trees and frequent clouds. The high and steep Mt. Hengshan is frequently snow-capped in the winter, contrasting with the subtropical fields that one sees below it. It is one of the five most famous mountains in China. The region along the Yuanjiang River is especially well known for its serene beauty. It takes its name, *The Peach Blossom Fountainhead*, from a work of Chinese literature from the Jin Dynasty. The Yuanjiang River Region has been a tourist destination since ancient times.

Unit 9 Touring Shaanxi

Part I Tips for Tour Guides
Case 9 Passports Lost

Mr. Smith planned to leave Xi'an for New York at 11:00 o'clock next morning after he visited Museum of Qin Terra-cotta Warriors and Horses. When he checked out the hotel, he found that his passport was missing. How could you help Mr. Smith search for the passport? Listen to the passage and write down the measures you will take in the blanks.

(1) First of all, I shall ask Mr. Smith to make sure whether he has left the documents with someone else or put it somewhere else.
(2) After he tried to look for the lost documents, but in vain, I shall help search for it.
(3) If the passport is not found, I shall report it to the travel agency and get a loss testimonial issued from the travel agency for him.
(4) I shall show him to the local Public Security Bureau and present the loss report together with the written

testimonial made by the travel agency.
(5) With the testimonial issued by the Public Security Bureau, Mr. Smith should apply for the new passport in his own country's Embassy or Consulate General in China.
(6) With the newly issued passport, Mr. Smith should apply for a new visa in the office of the entry and exit visas for foreigners of the public security.

Part II Listening Activities

Listening 1

Xi'an City

Xi'an, capital of Shaanxi Province with a 3,000-year history, was known as Chang'an in ancient times. For 1,062 years the city had been capital for 13 dynasties, and a total of 73 emperors had ruled China there. It became the oriental cultural center of the Silk Road. That is why the land of the city is pockmarked with cultural relics and historical ruins. Many dynasties kept the city beautiful and magnificent. More than 270 palaces and temples, for example, were built in the Qin Dynasty. Now, from these architectural sites people still can imagine the general picture of what Chang'an City was like, then.

Some of the temples constructed in many dynasties have remained well preserved, including the most famous ones, as the Big Wild Goose Pagoda in Ci'en Temple and the Small Wild Goose Pagoda in Jianfu Temple. The bronze wares in Xi'an are an important example of the splendid culture that reflects this slave society. Feng and Hao in the Xi'an area, which were the capitals of the Western Zhou Dynasty, have been acclaimed as "the Home of the Bronze Wares," as a wealth of bronze items unearthed from there, over the years.

All the emperors of the Qin, Han, Tang and other dynasties had their magnificent mausoleums built. Qin Shihuang's mausoleum at the foot of Lishan Hill in Lintong county, for example, is the earliest example of a grand mausoleum for an emperor in ancient China. In front of these mausoleums were erected huge stone carvings, while inside them were exquisite funeral objects and colorful murals, a feast for one's eyes. It was quite popular to put up stone tablets in front of tombs to record the merits and achievements of the departed, in many dynasties, and a great deal of stone tablets and calligraphy data remain to this day. So Xi'an is also famous for being "the Home of Calligraphy."

Listening 2

Xi'an City Wall

The Xi'an City Wall is the best preserved, oldest and largest ancient city defense system in China. As one of the most important landmarks of the Xi'an city, it was first built from the 3rd to the 11th of the Hongwu reign in the Ming Dynasty on the original site of the imperial walls of Chang'an in the Tang Dynasty. The city walls are built with yellow earth in separated layers. The bottommost layer is rammed with limes, earth and sticky rice and it is very solid. The eastern wall is 2,590 meters long; the western one is 2,631 meters, the southern one is 3,441 meters and the northern one is 3,244 meters. The perimeter of the walls is 11.9 kilometers and the wall is 12 meters high and 16.5 meters deep. There is an area of 12 square kilometers inside the city. On each side of the city there is a gate: the eastern gate is named Changle; the western one is Anding; the southern one is Yongning and the northern one is Anyuan. Outside each gate there is a Tower of Shooting Arrow, inside which there is a city tower. Between them there is an enceinte.

Unit 10　Touring Chongqin

Part I Tips for Tour Guides
Case 10 The First Aid

One Irish tourist suffered from a heart attack while he was hiking on the Nanshan Mountain. One tourist took with him the medicine that could alleviate the symptoms. The guide was very worried and took the medicine the tourist offered and helped the patient to take it. Listen to the passage and evaluate the guiding service. Fill in the blanks with the remedies you hear from the tape.

(1) The guide should not offer the patient his own medicine, for he has no authority to prescribe anything for a patient. The tour guide should not take any medicine from other tourists to offer the patient if neither the tour guide nor the tourists are doctors.

(2) The tour guide should have the patient lie down with his head slightly elevated. If the patient has his own medicine with him, the tour guide should help him take it.

(3) The tour guide should call for an ambulance to take the patient to a nearby hospital for first aid.

Part II Listening Activities
Listening 1

Chongqing City

Chongqing figured importantly in modem Chinese history. During the War of Resistance Against Japan, it was the "provisional capital" of China under the Kuomintang rule. Vestiges of that period are still there in and around the city. These include the Red Crag Village, Chiang Kai-shek's mansion, the embassies of various countries to China, as well as former residences of important politicians, generals and cultural figures. The Red Star Pavilion in the Pipashan Park, the Kansheng Pavilion in the Eling Park, and a place called Yikeshu on the Nanshan Mountain are vintage points for observing the nocturnal scenes of the mountain city of Chongqing. At night the entire city is inundated in an ocean of lights, which form a colorful three-dimensional painting, with waves of the Yangtze and Jialing rivers glistening against the moonlit, star spangled sky.

Sailing down the Yangtze from Chongqing to Yichang allows visitors to see the spectacular scenery of the Three Gorges along with its splendid cultural heritage and fabled local folklore. The cruise, which combines sightseeing with scientific, artistic and folklore exploration, is a national-caliber tourist program. The 193km long Three Gorges, consisting of the majestic Qutang Gorge, statuesque Wuxia Gorge and ferocious Xiling Gorge, is one of the world's major canyons. Along the way there are such scenic attractions as the Fengdu Mountain. Baidi City, Shibao Village, Zhang Fei's Temple, Qu Yuan's Temple, and the Three Gorges Dam.

Listening 2

Ciqikou

Situated on the bank of the Jialingjiang River, not far from its confluence with the mighty Yangtze is the ancient village of Ciqikou, formerly known as Long Yin. The history of Ciqikou can be traced back for more than 1,700 years. During the Ming and Qing dynasties it was famous for its production of porcelain. To date, over twenty old kiln sites have been discovered there. It is because of the importance of the porcelain industry that the name has been changed from Long Yin to Ciqikou which literally means Porcelain Village. The majority of the houses date from the Ming and Qing dynasties. Much of the two and three storey construction is of bamboo and timber. The three notable attractions of the village are the tea houses, the artists' studios and the Shu Embroidery workshops. The tea houses offer the opportunity for you to meet the locals and also become acquainted with the unique folk opera.

Unit 11   Touring Zhejiang

Part I Tips for Tour Guides
Case 11 Hotel on Fire

It is 4 o'clock in the early morning. All the Japanese tourists are sleeping soundly in the Hangzhou Grand Hotel. Unfortunately the hotel catches a fire. As a national guide, what measures you should take to help the tourist escape from the fire? Listen to the passage and write down the remedies you will take in the blanks.

(1) I must report the fire immediately to the police.
(2) I shall lead the tourists to a safe place through a safe emergency exit. I shall warn them not to take the elevator, for they will be trapped in the elevator due to power failure caused by the fire.
(3) If they are surrounded by a big fire or dense smoke, I shall ask them to take the following measures:
   A. They must cover their mouth and nose with a wet towel, bend over and run out of the room;
   B. They should also wave colorful clothing out the window to signal for help.
   C. If the door is blocked by fire, they should seal the cracks between the door and its frame with wet clothing and splash door with water to keep it cool and wet while waiting for the rescue;
   D. I shall comfort tourists and encourage them to continue with their travel, if it is possible.
   E. If tourists are injured in the fire, I shall send them to the hospital.
   F. I shall make a verbal report to the travel agency and submit a written report after the trip is over.

Part II Listening Activities
Listening 1

Hangzhou City

The capital of Zhejiang Province is poised on the lower reaches of Qiantang River and the southern terminal of the Beijing-Hangzhou Grand Canal. Hangzhou is also regarded as one of the six ancient capitals in China (The other five are Beijing, Xi'an, Nanjing, Luoyang and Kaifeng). There's a saying that illustrates the charm of Hangzhou: "In heaven there is paradise, and on earth there are Hangzhou and Suzhou." A mesmerizing landscape and a rich cultural legacy combine to make Hangzhou a famed scenic and historical and cultural city. As a key national tourist city, Hangzhou is picturesque all year round. The West Lake, one of the most beautiful sights in China, is located right in the heart of the city. West Lake is as beautiful as a painting. There are many other must-see natural beauties in Zhejiang Province which include the Putuo Mountain, admired as a "Buddhist Land of South Sea." The First Mountain in southeast China—Yandang Mountain, the most elegant Qiandaohu Lake, and the famous Buddhist mountain—Mt. Tiantai are well worth seeing. There is the sacred Chinese calligraphy place—Lanting and the oldest private library in Asia—Tianyi Pavilion. The greatest water conservancy project in ancient China—Beijing-Hangzhou Grand Canal and the three ancient water towns—Xitang, Nanxun and Wuzhen are all scenic spots that delight tourists who visit this region.

Listening 2

Leifeng Pagoda

Leifeng Pagoda is situated on the Evening Glow Hill which stands on the south shore of the West Lake. The 7 storied pagoda was a storey-pavilion-type structure, built of brick and wood. In the ancient times, Leifeng Pagoda and Baochu Pagoda stood far apart facing each other. Leifeng Pagoda appeared to be an old gentleman, but Baochu Pagoda appeared to be a beauty. When the sun was setting, the pagoda bathed in the evening glow looked radiantly beautiful. It was therefore named as "Leifeng Pagoda in Evening Glow." In the Ming Dynasty, the pagoda was fired by the Japanese bandits and collapsed at last on September 25, 1924 by the custom of local people to take a brick from its lower storeys as a talisman or souvenir.

Unit 12 Touring Yunnan

Part I Tips for Tour Guides
Case 12 A Breach of Security

A group of Danish tourists just came back from the Old Town Lijiang. After they checked in the small inn, one of the tourists found that his room was broken down and his hand baggage was missing. What is the incident? How do you protect the tourists' security? Listen to the passage and write down the measures you will take as a local guide in the blanks.

(1) This incident is the breach of security. It refers that the tourist have suffered theft, robbery, fraud, indecency or murder and their life or property has been endangered on the trip.
(2) First of all, I shall do my best to protect the safety and property of tourists and take them only to safe places. If the tourists are injured I should rescue them.
(3) I shall immediately report the incident to the police for investigation.
(4) I shall also report the incident to the travel agency. When casualties or loss of property occur, I shall request the travel agency to give me instructions or request that the travel agency staff come and handle the incident.
(5) I shall try to console the tourists, and if possible, continue with the scheduled travel.
(6) I shall submit a written report to the travel agency and help handle the issues concerned after the trip is over.

Part II Listening Activities
Listening 1

Kunming City

It is spring all year round in Kunming, capital of Yunnan Province and a famous historical and cultural city. The city is nicknamed "city of spring" due to the fact that it is covered all the year round with the rich verdure of trees and plants. Endowed with a pleasant climate, the city's 15,000 square kilometers of land is adorned with more than 400 kinds of flowers. In ancient times it was an important gateway to the celebrated Southern Silk Road which conducted to Tibet, Sichuan, Myanmar and India. The city's highland scenery is alluring; its karst landform is bewitching. Its people are known for their varied and exotic habits and customs, and its land is pockmarked with historical artifacts, places of cultural interest, and gardens landscaped with a picturesque taste.

As a world-famous tourist resort, Kunming holds such major attractions as Dianchi Lake, West Hill, West

Hill Forest Park, Yunnan Ethnic Village, Grand View Pavilion, Qiongzhu Temple, Golden Hall, Yuantong Temple, Cuihu Park, and the Garden of the World Horticultural Exposition. The 300-square-km Dianchi is Yunnan's largest alpine lake known as a "highland bright pearl" for its vast expanse of liquid silver and graceful scenery. Standing by the Dianchi Lake is Yunnan Ethnic Village, a huge congregation of ethnic villages in which visitors are entertained with a diversity of folk singing and dancing and folklore gigs. Dianchi itself is surrounded by many scenic attractions, including Dianchi National Holiday Resort, West Hill Forest Park, and Grand View Pavilion. China's largest cast-bronze hall is found in Jindian (Golden Hall) Scenic Zone on the camellia-covered Mingfeng Mountain to the northeast of Kunming.

Listening 2

Dianchi Lake

If you have been to Dianchi Lake, which is located at the foot of the Western Hills to the southwest of Kunming, you know what the "Pearl of the Plateau" means. Being the largest lake in Kunming and the sixth largest fresh water lake in China, Dianchi Lake is 300 square kilometers in surface area, 1,885 meters in altitude and about 40 kilometers in length (from north to south). When the weather is fine, there are white flocculent or massive clouds floating in the cerulean sky, the cyan water waves under the golden sunshine and the surrounding mountains reflect their silhouettes on the water. If you take a walk on the lake shore you will feel intoxicated by the beautiful landscape. The most beautiful view of Dianchi Lake appears at dawn and sunset, the refraction of the ethereal rays glitter on the water surface just like thousands of silver fishes swimming and playing. At night, when the breeze is fleeting over the water and the world is brimming over with hazy moonlight, Dianchi Lake lies in silence and breathes in peace like a sleeping beauty.

Unit 13　Touring Guizhou

Part I Tips for Tour Guides
Case 13 Traffic Accident

It is raining cats and dogs. Miss Tang Shenglan, a local guide of China Kanghui Travel Service, Guiyang Branch, is on the way to the Huangguoshu Waterfall. There is a heavy traffic jam and the guide is informed that the road has been blocked. Miss Tang contacts the head office for the instructions. As the deputy manager on duty, what could you instruct her to handle the case? Listen to the passage and write down your instructions in the blanks.

(1) Miss Tang should first analyze the consequence of the interruption and propose an emergency alternative program to the travel agency.
(2) She should then explain the situation to the tourists and ask for their support and cooperation.
(3) She should make appropriate adjustments to the itinerary and report to the head office according to the emergency alternative program by (a) extending the travel in a certain scenic area; (b) shortening the travel; or (c) changing the itinerary.
    (a) Extension of the travel time:
        If the guide has to extend the time of travel in a certain scenic area, she should contact the travel agency, which should make the appropriate arrangements for meals, accommodation and modes of transportation and notify the travel agency at the next stop to make adjustments according to the revised itinerary. Then she may extend the time for sightseeing and add some programs of entertainment.

(b) Shortening of the travel time:

If she has to shorten the visit, she should contact the travel agency to cancel the reserved meals, rooms, transportation and entertainment items. If appropriate, she should do her best to complete the sightseeing schedule within the time. If it is not possible, she may take tourists to visit the main scenic spots so as to minimize their disappointment.

(c) Changing part of the travel schedule:

If she has to cancel part or all of a planned visit or replace it with another site, as instructed by the organizing travel agency, she should make a realistic and interesting introduction of the alternative scenic spot so as to arouse the tourists' interest and hopefully get their understanding and cooperation.

Part II Listening Activities

Listening 1

Guiyang City

Guiyang is the capital of Guizhou Province. The landscape here is elegant; its folkways are rich, and its sites of cultural interest are numerous. Major attractions are Jiaxiu Pavilion, Qianling Park, Huaxi Park, Guizhou Botanical Garden, Nanjiao Park, Forest Park, Tianhe Pool and Baihua Lake. Local dishes and refreshments, prepared in a distinctive Guizhou style, never fail to hold Chinese and foreign visitors enthralled.

In addition, more unique, aboriginal, unsophisticated and mysterious landscapes in Guizhou attract tourists, both domestic and international. Maolan Karst Forest Natural Conservation, which contains mountains, water, forests and caves, is charming and breathtaking. Huangguoshu Waterfall is the biggest in China and among the world's famous waterfalls. Dragon Palace, which is located nearly 20 miles southwest of Anshun City, is a splendid underground karst type cave. Zhijin Cave is another highlight. Over forty kinds of karst precipitation formations are found in the cave. There are over 100 islands in the clear blue water lake of the Hongfeng Lake Scenic Area. The karst land formations, fascinating water and hills, as well as the spectacular caves make this area a state ranked key scenic location.

Listening 2

Zhijin Cave

Situated in northeast Zhijin County, Zhijin Cave is an imposing cave whose 300,000-square-metre floor sets the stage for numerous dazzling scenes and sights. In between clusters of pools and by a swaying underground lake is a jungle of stalactite, clints and stalagmites akin to pagodas, pillars and hills. For the 40 or so limestone formations, the cave is honored as the "King of Caves" or the "Museum of Limestone Caves." A 6.6-km section of it has been divided into ten zones for public viewing. Zhijin Cave Scenic Spot is famous for its massive, scale, stalagmites, stone pillars and stone pagodas in unbelievable heights and numbers. In addition to enjoying the scenery, visitors can discover the rich and varied folk customs and cultures of the ethnic groups. Numerous festivals, strong but unsophisticated customs, architectures with unique style and the exotic and colorful costumes, will make tourists feel everything is new and fresh.

Unit 14 Touring Guangxi

Part I Tips for Tour Guides
Case 14 Policies and Religions

A group of foreign tourists are cruising on the Lijiang River. One of them distributed some religious pamphlets to other tourists and spoke ill of Chinese police while another try to seek for the prostitutes because he believes that prostitution is the acceptable service. How do you handle the case as a local guide? Listen to the passage and fill in the blanks with the information which could help you to handle the case.

(1) Handle the matter factually: I shall tell them the facts about China so that they have better understanding.

(2) Handle the matter sensitively: I may simply express my own idea, but not argue with them, to maintain an amicable atmosphere.

(3) Handle the matter with restraint: I may graciously refute the criticisms made by the tourist who intentionally speaks ill of China, but I should continue to provide warm service to all the tourists.

(4) According to the policies and regulations of China, foreign tourists are forbidden to preach, preside over any religious service or distribute religious materials without permission. I shall tell him of our policies and ask him not to do so.

(5) I shall tell the tourists that prostitution is prohibited in China and every foreign tourist should respect our regulations and customs. If he persists, I should report him to the local police.

Part II Listening Activities
Listening 1

Nanning City

Nanning is the capital of Guangxi Zhuang Autonomous Region, and a rising industrial city. Under a subtropical climate, it is a tourist city that is extolled as an "evergreen metropolis." This garden city has so much to offer its visitors, such as Guangxi Museum, Guangxi Ethnic Artefact Garden, and Guangxi Medical Botanical Garden. Its outskirts are clustered with attractions as well. These include the Yiling Cave of Wuming County, Stone Forest and one of the world's eight major slanting pagodas in Chongzuo, the mysterious Huashan Murals in Ningming County, the waterfall that crosses the Sino-Vietnamese border in Daxin County, Friendship pass at Pingxiang, as well as the exotic folklore on the Sino-Vietnamese borderline.

Besides, you can also enjoy more landscapes beyond Nanning. The picturesque karst scenery along the Lijiang River down from Guilin to Yangshuo is well known to foreigners. The cruise is an unforgettable experience for tourists. Yangshuo, the end of the Lijiang River cruise, is a small but peaceful town with stunning country scenery. The town's West Street, lined with western cafes, restaurants and hotels has welcomed countless foreigners from all over the world and is known as "the Earth Village in China." Small villages hide behind paddies, water buffalos patrol the fields while fishermen boat on the river. Each provides a feeling of tranquility far removed from the cement jungle of the large cities.

Listening 2

Elephant Trunk Hill

Situated majestically at the southeast of Guilin City and west bank of Lijiang River, Elephant Trunk Hill is regarded as the symbol of Guilin landscape. Originally named "Li Hill," "Yi Hill" and "Chenshui Hill," the hill has a history of 3.6 hundred million years. Resembling an elephant leisurely sucking water from the river with its long trunk, this hill is famous as the Elephant Trunk Hill for hundreds of years. With an elevation of 200m, the hill towers 55m above the water, measuring 108m in length and 100m in width. Between the trunk and the legs of the elephant is a cave, in the shape of a full moon, penetrating the hill from side to side. People named it "Moon-over-Water Cave." When the water wave and the moonlight gleams, the scene is exceedingly enchanting. On the walls in and around this cave, over 70 inscriptions from the Tang and Song dynasties were found, praising the beauty of hills and waters nearby.

Unit 15 Touring Guangdong

Part I Tips for Tour Guides
Case 15 Sending off the Tourists

It was seven o'clock in the evening. Miss Yin Le was taking the Canadian tourists to the Guangzhou Railway Station by the coach. They were leaving for Hong Kong. However, an accident occurred on the way to the station, and the group was held up by the traffic jam. When they arrived at the station, the train had already left. What proper measures could she take to handle the case? Listen to the passage and write down in the blanks the measures she should take.

(1) Miss Yin should first report the incident to the travel agency, and try to appease the tourists.
(2) She should consider other modes of transport for sending off the tourists. Upon endorsement by the travel agency she may rent a coach, or even an airplane to send off the tourists and resume their travel schedule.
(3) If it is impossible for the tourists to leave Guangzhou in a short time, Miss Yin or the manager should do an apology to them on behalf of the travel agency, and make arrangements for their accommodation and necessary services during their stay in Guangzhou.
(4) The travel agency should send by fax the modified travel schedule to the manager of the next stop who receives the tourists and inform the related parties of its own travel service.

Part II Listening Activities
Listening 1

Guangzhou City

Guangzhou is an ancient city with a history of 2,800 years. It is named the "spring city" because with long summer the city is always with green plants and blooming with fresh flowers all years round. Myth legend tells of Guangzhou was founded by five immortals riding five rams, each ram planted a stalk of rice grain which symbolized abundant harvest or prosperity. And this is how Guangzhou got its nickname, "Yang Cheng" literally means "Goat City." Guangzhou provides travelers with their first taste of mainland China, thus resulting in also being the first place of mainland China where foreign influences enters into the country.

You could cruise on the Pearl River and appreciate the landscape of the city. Ancestral Temple of the Chen Family, Sun Yat-sen Memorial Hall, Yuexiu Park, Baiyunshan (White Cloud Mountain) and the Pearl River water front could be enjoyed in Guangzhou. In addition, Guangdong has many picturesque tourist places of attractions. Traveling north, you can see the Nanhua Temple in Shaoguan. Journeying to the east from Shantou you may see much beautiful countryside scenery. To the west may lead you to Guangxi Province with picturesque lakes and hill landscapes. At the south is China's Special Economic Zone with the two well-known cities of Shenzhen just north of the former British colony of Hong Kong and Zhuhai on the border with the former Portuguese enclave of Macau. At Shenzhen, you can complete a round-the-world trip in one day by visiting Splendid China and Window of the World. Downtown in Shenzhen you may find the China Folk Culture Villages.

Listening 2

The Five-Ram Sculpture

The Five-Ram Sculpture is one of the most famous structures in Guangzhou. It has become the emblem of Guangzhou City. Legend has it that more than 2,000 years ago, Guangzhou was a barren land and people suffered from famine. One day five immortals in five-color garments came riding on five rams, playing their legendary music. The rams held sheaves of rice in their mouths. The immortals left the sheaves of rice for the Guangzhou people, gave blessings to the city and left. The rams turned into the stone and the city of Guangzhou became a rich and populous place. Guangzhou got the name of the City of Rams and the City of Ears.

Bibliography

1. 纪世昌.中国旅游指南.湖南:湖南地图出版社,1999年。
2. 毕洪英.敢说导游服务英语.北京:机械工业出版社,2004年。
3. 朱华.英语导游实务教程.北京:北京大学出版社,2004年。
4. 朱华.四川英语导游景点讲解.北京:中国旅游出版社,2004年。
5. 朱华.赖宇红.西南旅游实务英文教程.北京:北京大学出版社,2004年。
6. www.tv.cntv.cn
7. www.travelchinaguide.com
8. www.chinavista.com
9. www.tourunion.com
10. www.chinahighlights.com
11. www.youku.com
12. www.omeida.com.cn
13. Wang Jun, Liu Lingyan, *Touring China*, China Travel & Tourism Press, 2000.
14. Chris Cooper, John Flecher, *Tourism Principles and Practice,* Addison Wesley Longman Limited, 1999.
15. Gwenda Syratt, *Manual of Travel Agency Practice*, Butterworth-Heinemann Ltd,1995.
16. Alan A. Lew (Editor), Lawrence Yu, *Tourism in China: Geographic, Political, and Economic Perspectives,* Westview Press, 1995.